PRAISE FOR
WE FOUGHT THE ROAD

"Despite isolation, brutal extremes of weather, plagues of mosquitoes, lack of proper equipment and systemic racism, the 93rd, and the other black regiments of the United States Army helped build the vital link to Alaska after the bombing of Pearl Harbor. With a few exceptions, the wartime contribution of the black regiments to the construction of this strategic military road has been overlooked, or worse, ignored. Finally, some light is thrown upon this hidden chapter of the Alcan story."

—Michael Gates, author of *From the Klondike to Berlin: The Yukon in World War I* Yukon Territory, Canada

"*We Fought the Road* is a major work of research on a subject that had been all but written out of history when my journalism department at University of Alaska Fairbanks staged a reunion for black builders of the Alaska Highway in 1992. Since that time, several interesting books and two documentaries have emerged, but none mingle the 'boots on the ground' experience of our beleaguered troops with a solid analysis on the strategic planning that drove them, which makes the McClures' approach unique."

—Lael Morgan, Professor Emeritus University of Alaska Fairbanks and Dept. of Communications, University of Texas, Arlington

"*We Fought the Road* is a wonderful story about the building of the historic Alaska Highway from the 'three cent love affair' letters that Christine's father, Lt. Tim Timberlake, wrote to her mother Helen. It is amazing how Christine and her husband Dennis McClure gathered her mother's collection with photos to write this book. They noticed that newspapers, magazine articles, film, and photos from 1943, all showcased white regiments and ignored black regiments. Although Christine's father was a product of his time as a white officer over his all black 93rd motor pool, he did not seem to be concerned about that."

—Jean Pollard, Chairperson, Alaska Highway Project

WE FOUGHT THE ROAD

Epicenter Press

Epicenter Press is a regional press publishing nonfiction books about the arts, history, environment, and diverse cultures and lifestyles of Alaska and the Pacific Northwest. For more information, visit www.EpicenterPress.com

Text © 2017 by Christine McClure and Dennis McClure

Cover photos courtesy of the Timberlake Collection
Back cover photo courtesy of Bureau of Public Roads 43-3765 National Archives

Cover and interior design: Aubrey Anderson
Editor: Lael Morgan and W.P. Garrett

ISBN: 978-1-935347-77-4

Library of Congress Control Number: 2017941683

Printed in Canada

10 9 8 7 6 5 4 3 2

This book is dedicated to Turner Grafton Timberlake and the men of the 93rd Engineers

Men, the road is through, and one might experience (although not enjoy very much) an auto trip from Dawson Creek to Fairbanks. But only those can really say "we have fought the road" who have actually worked with sweat and blood on its construction.

Captain Edward G. Carroll, "A Visitation to Whitehorse"
Chaplain 95th Engineer (GS) Regiment

WE FOUGHT THE ROAD

Christine McClure and Dennis McClure

Foreword by Russ Vanderlugt

Epicenter Press

CONTENTS

Contents

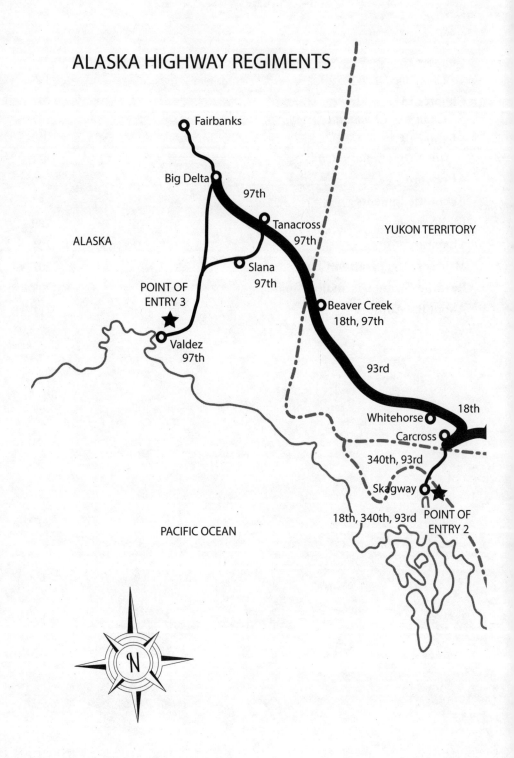

ALASKA HIGHWAY REGIMENTS

Fairbanks

Big Delta

97th

Tanacross
97th

ALASKA

Slana
97th

YUKON TERRITORY

POINT OF
ENTRY 3

Beaver Creek
18th, 97th

Valdez
97th

93rd

18th

Whitehorse

Carcross

340th, 93rd

PACIFIC OCEAN

Skagway

POINT OF
ENTRY 2

18th, 340th, 93rd

N

NORTHWEST TERRITORIES

Teslin
93rd
93rd

Watson Lake
340th

Contact Creek
35th, 340th

Fort Nelson
35th

BRITISH COLUMBIA

ALBERTA

Fort St. John
341st, 95th

35th, 341st, 95th

Dawson Creek

POINT OF
ENTRY 1

FOREWORD

BY RUSS VANDERLUGT

A rmy efforts to build a road to the Arctic remain one of the lesser-told stories of the Second World War. Colonel (Retired) Heath Twichell's *Northwest Epic* provides a sweeping macro perspective based in part on his father's letters and unpublished memoirs, which viewed the road's history from the "top-down" standpoint of a senior white officer commanding the all-black 95th Engineer Regiment. Inspired by Heath's work, Christine and Dennis McClure follow a similar but "bottom-up" methodology in *We Fought the Road*, a storyline based on love letters from Christine's father, Lieutenant "Tim" Timberlake, to her mother, "My Dearest Buzz." Though still a white perspective, Tim's experiences as a junior officer are more closely associated with those who worked with picks and shovels while building the Alaska-Canadian Highway. Indeed, due to the prevalence of racism in the Army at the time, the black regiments, armed with virtually no heavy equipment, were obligated to swing picks, wield shovels, haul dirt with wheelbarrows, and fell trees with axes and saws.

Did racism in the Army run deeper than in society during the early 1940s? President Roosevelt's paradoxical mandate involved segregation without discrimination. Understanding the Army could not change society, Chief of Staff George Marshall insisted that the Army contribute to the war effort by bypassing one of the Nation's most vexing social maladies—civil rights. Society was not ready to integrate. So how would the Army, generally understood as a reflection of society and still thoroughly racist, struggle with leading this momentous change?

The McClures assembled an impressive number of primary sources to tell the story from the troops' perspectives, exposing the reality of racism in the Far North as revealed by romance, Army rolls and records, and the intricate backgrounds and anecdotes of black soldiers themselves. A corporal in the 95th Regiment captured his experience of unequal treatment in a letter home, "that old southern principle of keeping Negroes as slaves is still being practiced." In addition to perspectives of black soldiers, the impacts on Native populations are also discussed (though a comprehensive Native perspective on the highway project and its effects on Native villages is still to be written). One of the unifying aspects that cuts across race in all sources is a true sense of pride and sense of wartime mission while accomplishing a feat similar in scale to that of the trans-continental railroad, though under Arctic conditions and the circumstances of world war. Troops were willing to do "anything to win the war" and had a sense that "my actions" were specifically contributing to the war's end. This attitude was commendable despite the challenge to morale when highway-building soldiers discovered their northern tour of duty would be extended into the Arctic winter. Working under these conditions was difficult for any soldier; for black soldiers, working with an added dose of discrimination went well beyond the call of duty.

The ability of *We Fought the Road* to draw readers into the construction of both the Alaska Highway and the incipient Civil Rights Movement in 1942 using perspectives of junior officers and soldiers represents a significant methodological contribution to literature and highlights an important cause: young people provide a crucible as agents of change for civil rights in our society. The battle against racism is most notably fought through the Army's young officers and soldiers on the front lines of civil rights in our society, specifically, while building the Alcan—an important landmark leading up to the Civil Rights Movement.

In 2013, the same year Christine and Dennis retraced their father's youthful military service along the Alaska Highway with *Northwest Epic* resting on their dash, I was serving on active duty along the Hudson River as an instructor in the History Department of the US Military Academy at West Point. I had the honor of hosting two seminars with Heath Twichell, my mentor and close friend, in the company of West Point cadets—of various ethnicity and gender—regarding their role and their predecessor's role leading social change. It was a fitting audience and a fitting location. Since before the Civil War, West Point has been central to the nation's racial debates and ideologies, and consistently yields one of the largest cohorts of future leaders. Though the Army in general has struggled to address civil rights alongside society, it was notably the first government entity to integrate. Both Heath and his father were graduates of the Academy and experienced the challenges of racial integration firsthand during their military careers at important moments in American History.

The first West Point history seminar focused on contributions and challenges of black regiments while constructing the Alcan; the second highlighted Heath's own experience as a young Lieutenant engaged in the Little Rock Crisis with equally compelling circumstances: should black troops be utilized to disperse a Civil Rights riot in 1957? These questions do not have easy answers then or now, but demand leaders with courage. Despite our struggle against racism and other forms of discrimination, I am encouraged that for every generation, young people represent our next step forward and our surest source of victory. The work of Heath Twichell's panoramic *Northwest Epic* and now the McClure's fitting "pick and shovel" companion, *We Fought the Road*, remind us of our shared history and pathway to ending discrimination.

—Major Russ Vanderlugt
Brooks Range, Alaska
May 2017

PREFACE

A NOTE FROM AUTHOR CHRISTINE MCCLURE

When my mother passed in 2009, we found among her effects boxes of photos and a collection of old letters from my father, Turner "Tim" Timberlake. Going through them was a revelation. We knew my father was involved in building the famous Alaska Highway during World War II, but mostly we knew a couple of funny stories—that was it. He wrote the letters while he was in the Yukon Territory. The young man writing to his girl was my father, but this wasn't the father I knew. This was a passionate young man, full of piss, vinegar and himself—the age of my oldest granddaughter and showing every one of the characteristics of that age.

I read the letters and then I dug into the photographs: grainy, black and white, images of the man who was—but also wasn't—my father, and images of a very different place and very different people. I read the letters again; between the lines, his passionate pride in what he was doing began to sink in. I read about the incredible construction project that created the first land route from the contiguous United States to the Territory of Alaska. Damn! This was a very big deal.

Another thing struck me as I looked at the old photographs. Most of the faces were black. I knew, vaguely, that Dad had served with black soldiers. I didn't understand that the United States Army was segregated during that era—that black soldiers served exclusively with other black soldiers and that their officers were white. There was something wrong about that, but my dad, who never struck me as racist, was part of it. How, exactly, did that work?

The three black regiments on the highway—the 93rd, the 95th and the 97th—were like ghosts. The 97th had landed at Valdez, Alaska, and faced some of the most difficult weather and terrain on the entire highway with no backing from white troops. The 95th had come up from Dawson Creek at the southern end of the highway, trailed two white regiments and endured especially virulent racism. My dad's 93rd regiment had built hundreds of miles of highway in the middle, through the Yukon Territory, apparently without much support.

Newspaper and magazine articles, film, photos from 1942—all showcased white regiments and ignored black ones. More recent material revealed a few details about the 95th and the 97th—but not the 93rd. My father's regiment was the faintest ghost of them all.

In 2013, at the end of June, armed with electronics, cameras and a worn copy of Heath Twichell's *Northwest Epic*, my husband and I piled into our truck camper. We drove north to find the highway and maybe some traces of my father's youth. The highway transformed our quest. Quiet, peaceful and utterly majestic as it rolled through the wilderness, it teemed with ghosts—and questions far more profound than any one man's experience.

At Sikanni Chief, British Columbia, in 1942, the black 95th Engineers Regiment triumphed over prejudice and discrimination to bridge the river in just three days—one of the great and enduring stories from the building of the road. In 2013, the remains of abandoned bridges, the sweep of the newest one, and the remains of a few old, hand-hewn timbers buried in the bank of the old road bed—all of this with the eternal river and the fierce blue sky and above all, the quiet—were a monument to how much these black men had given to a nation that couldn't bring itself to thank them.

Had the 93rd and the 97th made a similar statement about the vicious unfairness of racism—if only by their quiet endurance?

The highway landmarks came and went as we travelled west and north, Steamboat Mountain, Stone Mountain, Muncho Lake, and then we were over the Continental Divide, deep in the part of the highway that was the 93rd's turf—Rancheria River, Morley Bay and Teslin. In my heart that made it 'my' turf.

With Dad's photos, I had found a map—drawn in the field and copied by somebody in 1942. It represented the area where the 93rd worked, and we were about there. Train tracks into Carcross, a supply road from there through Tagish to Jakes Corner and on over the Teslin River to the village of Teslin—this was the precise ground on which the men of the 93rd had suffered and triumphed. Places on the map—Jacoby Lake, Boyd's Canyon, Pollock's Graveyard, Brooks Brook, Cassano Mountains—were named after men of the 93rd. Some of the names had survived on current road maps.

Dad's photos included several pictures of the bedraggled and muddy motor pool at Morley Bay with the mountain called "Three Aces" or "Dawson Peaks" in the background. The mud is gone and the trees have grown. Today it's a peaceful bit of forest.

We drove out of Teslin with the old map in hand and we found Dead Man's Creek and Brooks Brook, but no Boyd's Canyon. Big and Little Devil's swamps are still there, but the names aren't. We never could find Pollack's Graveyard, but it's there somewhere—and it contains a buried bulldozer. I'm sure of it.

The eight-month sojourn of the 93rd had left only traces.

On our last, somewhat melancholy visit to Carcross, we walked the beach and felt my father's presence. A product of his time, he had not concerned himself with the most important questions that now bedeviled me. The great accomplishment of building that road gave him pride, but he never seemed aware of its history beyond the boundaries of his individual experience. He worked with black soldiers in a racist environment but his letters offered no clues to what he had thought and felt about that—or even whether he had thought and felt about that.

There, on the beach in Carcross, we wanted so badly to take all of this back, not to the young man of 1942, but to my wise father who had lived the rest of a lifetime during the ferment of the 20th Century. We wanted to sit with him and ask for all the details of his experience and explain all the things we had learned. We wanted him to help fit it all together so it made sense.

But, that's not possible. We've made the attempt to do it by ourselves. We've written the book you hold in your hand using my father's story to lead readers, as it led us, into the larger and more important issues involved with the great road and the confrontation of racism imbedded in its construction. We hope it conveys some truth about what happened in the North Country in 1942.

CHAPTER 1

WHERE THEY CAME FROM

Turner "Tim" Timberlake could tell a humdinger of a story and he especially liked to make his listeners laugh. He got away with telling his best stories over and over and we never tired of hearing them.

His very best started with baseball. During Tim's teenage years, baseball was the most popular sport in America and to boys like Tim, its most popular player, Babe Ruth of the New York Yankees, was a bigger deal than the President.

In 1935, 18-year-old Tim played shortstop for a team that dominated a "whites only" league in southern Maryland. They were undefeated at the end of the season, but there was another undefeated team in the area—a team that played in the "blacks only" league. The situation demanded a playoff. Desperate to play in that game, Tim knew that his father, "Pop," descended from Confederate Army veterans and racist to his core, would never allow it. To hell with that. What Pop didn't know wouldn't hurt him.

On the appointed Saturday afternoon, a defiant Tim showed up to play, and play he did. A great game until, in the middle innings, a familiar figure strode onto the field. Pop marched grimly to the third base line, took his horrified and humiliated son by the left ear and marched him off the field.

The story ended a few years later in the Yukon Territory of Canada.

In November of 1942, First Lieutenant Tim Timberlake was a white officer in the all-black 93rd Engineer Regiment, and the 93rd was just standing down from its epic labor building Alaska Highway through largely unmapped wilderness. At Thanksgiving, the regiment was preparing their equipment for its next mission in the Aleutians.

After eight months of Vienna sausage, Spam and chili, the Regimental Motor Pool enjoyed a Thanksgiving dinner that included turkey, hauled on sleds over the river ice. Someone photographed Tim and his black mechanics at table, and a very white 1st Lt. Timberlake stood out—to say the least. A week or so later, back in Maryland, Pop Timberlake received a letter from his son. The envelope held one of those photos and on the back Tim had printed a note: "Dear Pop, Let's see you get me out of this one."

BY 1940, THE UNITED STATES Government was preparing for war and growing the Army rapidly. The controversial 1940 Selective Service Act applied to all young men in America. Significantly, though, when young black men showed up for registration or to enlist, they found closed doors. On October 10, 1940, a recruiting office in D.C. informed 569 black men that there was no quota under which "colored" men could be enrolled.

President Franklin D. Roosevelt, in the middle of a tough campaign for an unprecedented third term, couldn't afford to alienate the black community, but he also had to appease the southern whites who were a foundation of his political base. In a gesture he thought he could get away with, he promoted Colonel Benjamin O. Davis to Brigadier General—the first black man to attain that rank. He also appointed Judge William O. Hastie, Dean of Howard University Law School, as his civilian aide on "Negro" affairs, and he appointed Campbell C. Johnson, coordinator of the Reserve Officers' Training Corps program at Howard University, as an aide to the director of the Selective Service. Known informally as "The Black Cabinet," these three men had some impact on decisions made by the War Department—but not much.

The Selective Service Act mandated that ten percent of inductees would be black. Judge Hastie wrote a memo for President Roosevelt, outlining an approach for using blacks in the military. In October 1940, the military brass and Roosevelt approved an explicit policy for the use of black soldiers. They described it as "segregation without discrimination."

This ten percent would serve in every branch—combat and non-combat. Black reserve officers eligible for active duty would be assigned to black units. Once a black Officer Candidate School could be established, black soldiers would be eligible to earn commissions. Black soldiers would be allowed aviation training. It looked good on the face of it, but reality was very different.

Among the men charged with implementing the policies were some outright racists. Major General Henry "Hap" Arnold declared emphatically that there would never be "negras" in the Air Corps. In his view, the Air Corps was a club where "negras" would be out of place, and white enlisted personnel would never service an aircraft flown by a "negra" officer. Secretary of the Navy Frank Knox declaimed that while he was the secretary, there would never be a mixed Navy. If forced to implement such a thing, he would resign.

More damaging to black hopes for at least minimal fairness: even the most liberal leaders, focused on the war crisis, had little time or attention to spare for any other issue. FDR made it clear that he had little political capital to invest in civil rights. Army Chief of Staff George Marshall made the

War Department's attitude very clear: "The Army cannot accomplish such a solution and should not be charged with the undertaking. The settlement of vexing racial problems cannot be permitted to complicate the tremendous task of the War Department and thereby jeopardize discipline and morale."

Black leaders were, of course, furious. The black-owned newspaper, *The Pittsburgh Courier,* coined the "Double V" slogan. It called for two victories, one against fascism abroad and another against racism at home. However, in the face of embedded attitudes to race and of an increasingly overwhelming national emergency, all the righteous fury in the world was largely impotent.

According to *The Pittsburgh Courier,* two thousand black reserve officers were available to the Army in October 1940. Few of them made it to active duty except as chaplains or in the Medical Corps. On October 17, 1940, *The Pittsburgh Courier* reported the failed effort of Lt. Thomas Dale Davis of the New York National Guard to enlist in the Army Air Corps. On October 24, the same newspaper ran a story headlined, "No Negroes Being Trained by Army Air Corps, Says N.A.A.C.P." In November James H. Gray, who had enlisted in Detroit, Michigan and was accepted for duty with the Sixth U.S. Army Air Corps, showed up at the recruiting office. Shocked officials informed him, "…the order meant only white men and there had been some mistake."

Ultimately, as the threat of war progressed, black men did enlist and did get drafted into the Army—as enlisted men. For assignment of enlisted personnel, the Army used the Army General Classification Test. The test measured general knowledge but took no account of vocational skills. Troops, white and black with little formal education did poorly, typically scoring in the bottom categories: Class IV and Class V. White troops in those least desirable classes were processed while their black fellows were forced to wait. Worse, the high percentage of black troops scoring in classes IV and V reinforced racist attitudes, served as an excuse for shunting black troops into service units—Engineer and Quartermaster "General Service" regiments—and into jobs that required minimum training.

...

JUST BEFORE CHRISTMAS IN 1940, five white army officers arrived in the remote Kisatchie National Forest in southern Louisiana, to report for duty with the soon-to-be activated 93rd Engineer Battalion. They reported to the brand-new Camp Livingston, and had the devil's own time finding it. It didn't look much like an army post. It had only a few buildings and the dirt road entrance wasn't even marked.

Over the next few days, other officers joined them, along with a very few black non-commissioned officers (NCO) who had found a refuge from racism and the Depression in the segregated pre-war Army.

The white officers, about to create the 93rd at Camp Livingston, had education and training, but most of them had little experience. They weren't equipped to handle the thousand brand-new black soldiers the Army would soon send them. They badly needed experienced NCOs. In a segregated unit, enlisted NCOs had to be black. And the Army had precious few of those. Technical Sergeant Julius Tabb, Master Sergeant Herman Allen, Master Sergeant Alfred Sharp, all veterans of WWI, were worth their weight in gold.

Joseph M. Haskin, Jr., a black man who would serve in the Yukon Territory with Turner "Tim" Timberlake and the 93rd Engineers, enlisted in the Army in June 1941. Born in Louisiana in 1922, he was included in the 1930 census. The listing entry didn't include a father but it names his mother, Beulah, age 36, who was employed as a camp cook at a steam railroad. Haskin enlisted at Jacksonville Army Air Field in the Corps of Engineers and his enlistment record notes that he had some grammar school.

Many years later, in an interview with Lael Morgan, Haskin remembered, "Four of us went to the recruiting office and volunteered. If you volunteered, you could go to the camp you wanted. In 1941, we chose Camp Livingston. We greenhorns were assigned to the Engineers and thought we were going to be on locomotives. What a mistake we made."

Willie Lavalais served in Company B of the 93rd. Born in Marksville, Louisiana, Lavalais is listed in the 1930 census along with his parents, five brothers and two sisters. His father was a sharecropper. By the 1940 census, the family was living in Alexandria, Louisiana. His father was working in a mill and three grandchildren had been added to the household. Lavalais' draft card states that he worked for George Chatelain, a sharecropper. Lavalais enlisted in April 1941 at Jacksonville Army Air Field. His enlistment record notes that he completed grammar school. Private Lavalais spoke Cajun French and broken English, and he became famous in the Yukon for baking delectable biscuits and pies.

Born in Mississippi, Robert C. Mims of the 93rd Engineers was listed in the 1930 census along with his parents, three brothers and two sisters in Sunflower, Mississippi. The family worked on a cotton farm. The 1940 census found him working as a farmer in Jefferson, Mississippi. Private Mims enlisted in April 1941 at Camp Shelby, Mississippi. His enlistment record notes that he had completed the fifth grade.

Born in southern Louisiana in 1922, Anthony "Bobby Lee" Mouton's entire family spoke Creole French. His father disappeared when Anthony was eight-years-old and he quit school in the eighth grade to help support the family. Interviewed years later he said, "We were poor. Sometimes [my mother] didn't have enough to pay the one dollar monthly rent." The first coat he ever owned came courtesy of the Army, after he enlisted in June 1941 at Jacksonville Army Airfield. Anthony would serve with the 93rd in the Yukon and later in the Aleutians.

The 1940 census describes the household of Joseph Prejean—mother Aida, age 40; father Eulise, age 38; a niece, a nephew, two daughters and one son. Joseph was the nephew. Prejean's occupation was "tenant farmer." Interviewed years later, Joseph noted that he was illiterate in 1941—he'd learned a little bit of reading and writing from a buddy who was dating a teacher. He was making $1.50 a week, working in the fields, when he decided to join the Army in 1941. His landlord tried to convince him he was making a mistake. Prejean wound up at Camp Livingston and with the 93rd Engineers in the Yukon.

Born on August 5, 1920, Leonard Larkins shared a two-room house with 18 family members on the infamous Star Plantation in Assumption, Louisiana. The plantation offered a school that Larkins attended through the third grade. His father judged that sufficient, and Leonard joined the rest of his family in the sugar cane fields. Under the watchful eye of the "Man on the White Horse," he labored as a de facto slave "from can to can't" in the blistering Louisiana sun. Larkins escaped by enlisting and joined the 93rd Battalion at Camp Livingston in April 1941.

A few of the men who came to the 93rd had been luckier in life and had a bit more education or experience. They stood out and the desperate white officers of the 93rd elevated them quickly into the non-commissioned officer ranks.

When Samuel Hargroves enlisted August 13, 1941, in Richmond, Virginia, he left a job as a farm laborer in Henrico County. An orphan—his mother, Courtney, died when he was six and his father, Samuel Sr., died when he was 16—Samuel had managed more school than some of the other black men in the 93rd and would advance to Tech Sergeant 5.

Nolan Hamilton found his way to Camp Livingston and the 93rd and served in the Yukon Territory as a staff sergeant. His household in the 1940 census consisted of his mother, his grandmother, himself and a younger brother. Nolan was listed as being in his second year of college. He worked as a janitor. Hamilton enlisted at Jacksonville Army Air Field in June 1941.

John A. Bollin and Albert E. France, like Hamilton, came from relatively prosperous families. The 1940 census lists Bollin as living with his grandfather who worked as a hotel elevator operator in Richmond, Virginia. When he enlisted, he had graduated from high school. France's father worked as a track man for the railroad in Baltimore. France had made it through grammar school in 1941 and could read and write. France served in the Yukon with Company A of the 93rd. Both men quickly advanced to Sergeant.

Friends at Camp Livingston, LA.
Photo courtesy of Sherl Leverett, Hargroves Collection.

At Christmas 1940, when the officers of the future 93rd gathered in the woods at Camp Livingston, Tim Timberlake was reveling in his senior year at the University of Maryland. Tim had grown up in the Border South. Racism there was a casual racism of language and unthinking assumption and neglect—not the vicious racism of the heirs of the Confederacy who ruled the Deep South. In truth, Tim probably didn't think about race very much—unless it prevented him from playing baseball with players who happened to be black. In his path through the 1930s, he exemplified the hope the New Deal created for young white Americans. He worked hard to take advantage of opportunities and took justifiable pride in his accomplishments.

Pop Timberlake, Tim's dad, grew up in Winchester, Virginia. Hattie Grafton, his mom, grew up in Whiteford, Maryland. They met, and married in Baltimore in March 1917. Tim entered the world nine months later.

As a machinist, Pop enjoyed his share of prosperity in the 1920s. In 1926, he built his family a two-story house in Magnolia, Maryland. The market crash in 1929 tightened the Timberlake family's finances. The Depression sat hard on Pop's wages, but government contracts at Edgewood Arsenal made Pop's livelihood relatively secure.

Tim and his brother, George, attended Old Post Road High School, a one-room school. Tim joked in later years that he was elected senior class president by voting for himself, breaking a tie. After Tim's high school graduation in 1936, he found work with H.T. Campbell and Sons Road Construction Company and entered Jourdan Diesel School. He also earned a small scholarship and enrolled for night classes at Blue Ridge College in Baltimore. "Bonehead Math," he called the course in later years.

Pop had left high school after just one year and made his way in the world with his mechanical ingenuity and his talented hands. The house he built in Magnolia featured intricate systems of pulleys, weights and ropes to maneuver basement and pantry doors and the ladder to the attic. His shop behind the house bristled with the sophisticated tools of his trade and accounted for a large portion of the electricity consumed by the town of Magnolia. Tim loved and respected his father.

Hattie imbued Tim with loftier goals for his future. Tough, smart and ambitious, she had struggled through a year of college and played her own unique role in the Magnolia community. She served as secretary for both the Women's Democratic Club and the Harford County Council of Parent-Teacher Associations. She chaired the Committee for the Edgewood Library and the Joppa-Magnolia Civic Association. Hattie implanted ambition in her son. He hungered for the education that would let him make his way with his head instead of his hands—and let him live his life and make his career in the enormous and challenging world beyond Magnolia's boundaries.

He didn't know that elsewhere in the world, an FDR administrator named Morris L. Cooke was jump-starting his college future. Cooke was successfully lobbying Congress to pass measures that would provide electricity to rural areas. Those measures passed in 1935. The resulting Rural Electrification Program inspired Westinghouse, a prominent manufacturer of electrical equipment, to sponsor a Rural Electrification Contest for 4-H clubs, including the club in rural Maryland that was the center of Tim's social and intellectual life.

Tim wired his grandfather Grafton's 80-acre farm and submitted a report on the project as his contest entry, which won $50—a princely sum in 1936. Shortly after, he received a letter from Edward G. "Daddy Jenks" Jenkins, state leader for Boys 4-H, telling him he had been selected as an Eastern Region sectional winner. Then Daddy Jenks invited him to represent Maryland at the National 4-H contest in Chicago, where he won third place and a $200 college scholarship.

One of Daddy Jenks' most important responsibilities was working with officials at the University of Maryland in College Park, to identify talented young people in the state and make it possible for them to attend the university. More important than the $200 scholarship, Tim's contest entry had brought him to Jenkins' attention. The university invited Tim to enroll in its Engineering School in fall 1937. There were stipulations. He would be required to complete solid geometry, trigonometry and makeup English courses in addition to his normal class schedule. He was accepted and with additional scholarship money from the university and 4-H, campus jobs during the school year and summer work for H.T. Campbell and Sons, he was able to make it through.

On a brilliant fall day in 1937, twenty-year-old Tim, carrying a single suitcase, boarded the Penn Central, "the Pensy," and travelled to join about 3,800 fellow students on the campus at College Park. About a hundred of his alums would be joining him in the engineering school. For Tim that trip on the Pensy must have felt like travelling through a warp in space. Magnolia to College Park, Old Post Road High School to the University of Maryland—the difference between these two worlds must have literally taken his breath.

College students in the 1930s came overwhelmingly from America's middle class. Few of them had ever worked with their hands or worried very much about money. Transitioning from Magnolia to College Park certainly posed a social challenge—Tim took it in stride. A gregarious, homespun, gently self-deprecating raconteur with an infectious laugh, he found no problem making friends. He was handsome, with thick black hair and blue-green eyes that guaranteed his new circle of friends would include members of both sexes.

College students took themselves and their school very seriously. The University of Maryland's colors were black and gold. The school newspaper was the *Diamondback*. The yearbook was the *Terrapin*. In Tim's new world, these facts were important. The school mascot, *Testudo*, a large, sculptured turtle that sat on a pedestal in front of the Byrd Coliseum would have seemed silly in Magnolia. In College Park, it was an icon. It was rumored that rubbing his nose brought a student good luck. Tim's new society also had rules: "Rat Rules" for freshman required "frosh" to wear beanies, "rat caps" for boys and "rabbit caps" for girls, until the freshman-sophomore tug of war on Homecoming Day. The frosh assembled at the Coliseum prior to every home game to practice cheers. One doesn't have to wonder what Pop Timberlake would have thought.

Tim's university years transformed him—the first transformation of many in his life and perhaps the most important. He joined the staff of the *Diamondback* early on, serving initially in circulation and later as assistant sports editor. During his senior year, he became the sports editor and wrote a column called *Terrapin Talks*. He earned some of his college expenses as a stringer for the *Washington Post*.

At the beginning of his junior year, Tim proudly accepted a place in the

ROTC advanced course. The scholarship that came with it would help with expenses and the opportunity to earn a commission in the Army Reserve must have excited him. Events in the world, though only vaguely visible from College Park, endowed joining ROTC with ominous significance.

On April 4, 1941, the *Diamondback's Hall of Fame* column featured Tim Timberlake. The "Majestic Man of Magnolia" was honored for his sports articles, his grade point average and his appearance with Grantland Rice on the radio during the halftime of the Maryland-Florida contest. The feature noted that his hobby was stamp collecting, but he considered women to be his profession. His greatest ambition was to push Bob Considine off the sports pages.

On June 7, 1941, Tim graduated with honors from the University of Maryland with a degree in mechanical engineering. On June 24, he officially received his commission as a 2nd Lieutenant in the United States Army.

CHAPTER 2

INTO THE ARMY: THE FIRST STEP

Four months before Tim's graduation and commissioning, on February 10, 1941, the Army officially activated the 93rd Engineer Battalion at Camp Livingston. The brand-new military instillation was one of a constellation within a thirty-mile radius of Alexandria, Louisiana. The hurry-up construction that had commenced there in the fall of 1940, also included an expanded Camp Claiborne, a reactivated and expanded Camp Beauregard. Also constructed were a collection of air strips and facilities that would be named Esler Army Airfield, after the first pilot to die there, Lt. Wilmer Esler. The Army intended many of these facilities, especially camps Livingston and Claiborne, for housing and training black soldiers.

The Army brought prosperity to Alexandria. The town paved its streets—in white neighborhoods—and bought air conditioned buses. A new telephone company, on Murray Street, installed new dial telephones in many homes. According to Truman Gibson in his book *Knocking Down Barriers*, in less than a year, the Army brought to the area "tens of thousands of soldiers, as many as twenty thousand of them being black." By the end of 1941, Alexandria's population had tripled and the number of blacks had swelled proportionately. When it came to the new black residents, prosperity be damned, Jim Crow would craft Alexandria's version of "southern hospitality."

In that city, patterns of black soldier and white community interaction emerged quickly. Black soldiers were still "niggers" and the white community would go out of its way to make sure they remembered "their place." Black soldiers could come to the black sections of town, but they were not allowed in white sections. They were expected to cross the street when a white person approached to avoid passing too close.

Many of Jim Crow's rules were unwritten and black soldiers from the North often didn't know them. Even if they were inclined to accept their place—and they weren't—they had little idea of what was expected. Violations of the rules were common. Black soldiers were arrested, verbally attacked, beaten and some were shot, for slight infractions. Black residents in the towns ignored the violence and pulled closed their curtains or shades, fearful of retaliation. Bus drivers carried guns under their seats.

If racism permeated Alexandria, it also permeated the Army.

> The black soldier lived in a segregated area of camp because of army regulations. He could not eat at certain specified locations or enjoy recreation at others because of army regulations. He could live for a year in a segregated camp, less than a mile from his best friend in the same camp and not see that friend because of regulations affecting his off-duty hours. Under pain of disciplinary action, he had to swallow daily insults.
>
> And what rankled most was not having to risk his life for a country that disowned him in many ways, but having to see that classification by race took precedence over the state of war between Germany and the United States of America.
>
> (Motley 1987, 29)

In the southern Louisiana camps, blacks were quartered in the least desirable areas. At Camp Claiborne, the blacks' camp was referred to as "Swampland." It was full of snakes, rats and ankle-deep mud. Perhaps most important, white southern officers commanded the young black men.

In the brotherhood of Army officers, southern traditions ran deep and southern attitudes dominated. The War Department determined that specifically southern officers had the greatest understanding of black character and the most experience at dealing with "negroes." They explicitly tried to staff black regiments with officers from the south. A white officer at Camp Claiborne commented "he had nothing against 'nigras' but he had never seen or met a 'nigra' qualified to be an officer."

Perhaps worst of all, white military police patrolled the black sections of towns like Alexandria, equipped with pistols and swinging batons, prepared to enforce not only the Army's rules, but also Jim Crow's. White MPs made no secret of their belief that the Army didn't need black soldiers. If there were going to be black soldiers, then the MPs would, by God, keep them in line—even if that meant killing a few as examples.

In June 1941, a staff sergeant from the 93rd—Joe White—was in a "Grog Shop" in Alexandria. MPs arrested the non-commissioned office (NCO), a 24-year veteran, beat him severely, and charged him with disorderly drunken behavior. *The Pittsburgh Courier* reported that words were exchanged; the

MPs overpowered Joe and hauled him off to jail. Sergeant Mixon, a white MP from Texas, continued the beating that had started at the Grog Shop. Fellow inmates witnessed that Joe was "laid out" and overheard Mixon's telling comment: "I'm from Texas and I've been looking for a chance to whip a 'nigger' for a long time." A civilian who was in the process of paying his fine and being released overheard more of Mixon's monologue. Mixon was "glad to knock his damned head off. When you damned niggers get that uniform on, you forget how to talk to a white man, but you are one damned nigger. I am going to teach you how to talk to a white man. Shut up! If I hear you say anything else, I'll kill you. That damned nigger sergeant will come and get you out and you better not tell Sergeant Bess who hit you."

Staff Sergeant White suffered multiple head lacerations but he survived the beating.

Through winter and spring 1941, the 93rd continued to assemble and organize itself at Camp Livingston. The empty tent frames in long rows next to the Regimental area gradually grew canvas skins. Each tent offered a wooden floor, four-foot-tall wooden sidewalls, a screen door and a natural gas space heater along with iron cots, mattresses and pillows for five men. Captain George T. Derby commanded the unit-in-progress until February 22, when Lt. Colonel John F. Zajicek arrived. The first real commander, Zajicek was a 29-year veteran from Pittsburgh who had seen action in World War I. For all his experience, though, he had never served with or commanded black troops, and his Polish ethnic background bequeathed little understanding of African-American culture.

On March 3, a medical detachment arrived and at intervals, a few inductees, temporarily assigned to the H&S (Headquarters and Services) Company. Assignments, for the sixty enlisted cadre in place, changed constantly as the nucleus of the battalion grew and took shape. Ultimately, a formal command structure would form in April, as the trickle of new recruits grew to a flood. Wednesday morning, April 16, the first significant installment of several hundred new recruits arrived. They ranged in age from 17 to twenty and most of them were from New Orleans, the rice and cane fields of the Bayou. They also came from the corn and cotton fields of northwestern Mississippi. Each man carried a Form 22 with his name, serial number, age, birth place, religion, recent vaccinations, educational attainment, and AGCT score.

Leonard Larkins came to Company A of the 93rd Battalion that April, fresh from Star Plantation. Like most of the young recruits, he had survived to young manhood by knowing exactly what "the man" expected of him and doing it. At Camp Livingston, he had no idea what the Army expected of him and walked through those early days in constant terror. Larkins served for four years in a racist army, labored and suffered conditions and cold in the

Yukon and the Aleutians, but he remembered his introduction to the Army at Camp Livingston as the most difficult time of all.

In later years, 1st Lt. Robert Boyd remembered "young, frightened boys, who had not the first idea how to march in formation and had been in the Army only a few days. They had been shoved around, fed haphazardly, vaccinated at the reception area." Boyd greeted them and introduced his two lieutenants. Watching their blank, nonresponsive faces, he realized they didn't understand anything he was saying. "What the hell was a company commander to say to these new recruits? So I backed up and started again. I am the 'head boss' and I have the total and final authority and say so on any and everything that happens in this company and to you." He thought that did the trick.

At this stage, still only a battalion, the 93rd consisted of four line companies—each with about two hundred men. Reviewing stacks of Form 22s sobered the new company commanders. Among their assigned troops, they found precisely zero high-scoring Class I's or II's and very few Class III's. Many of their new soldiers could neither read nor write and several from the Bayou only spoke Cajun French. A company required squad leaders and assistant squad leaders, mechanics, supply clerks, cooks, drivers. Class IV and V troops would have a hard time filling those roles. The officers, studying the depressing forms, began to devise strategies. Most of them revolved around distributing the few educated troops evenly among the companies, using them not only to perform necessary tasks but to provide simple training for their fellows.

Staff Sergeant Nolan Hamilton taught many of his fellow troops the rudiments of reading and writing. He wrote many of their letters home. To receive an army paycheck, the recipient had to sign for it. Lieutenant Boyd taught 27 men in his company how to do that. Tech Sergeant George Kennedy organized and directed a choir and managed to find a bugler. Private Arthur Lewis Knight, Jr. was an expert in demolition—a major training asset for an Engineering Company. It turned out that Pvt. Willie Lavalais was one hell of a Cajun chef.

Company commanders were creative. Boyd procured a four-by-eight-foot sheet of plywood, cut it in half and hung the halves on a wall in the Orderly Room. Each half sheet contained a chart listing the names of his troops. Next to each name his clerk would hang a colored circle that communicated that soldier's status—red for AWOL (Absent Without Leave), blue for Hospital, green for Detached Service, etc.

The new recruits came straight to the 93rd from civilian life to start with "basic training." During the first two weeks, they learned to love calisthenics and close order drill. They learned discipline and military courtesy. They stood their first guard duty. After two weeks, attention shifted to technical training—rifle or pistol marksmanship, bridge and culvert construction, explosives and demolition, scouting, patrolling and camouflage.

A news article in *The Pittsburgh Courier* reported on the troops of the 93rd's grenade training. It turned out that the art of throwing a grenade wasn't at all like that of throwing a baseball. Unlike a baseball, a grenade was set to explode in a matter of seconds. Throw it too soon and the intended victim might just throw it back. Throw it too late and it might blow up in your hand. In any case, once the grenade left the recruit's hand, he was trained to "duck and cover." Slowly but surely, in fits and starts, the 93rd jelled into an Engineer Battalion. In August 1941, the Army's gigantic Louisiana-Texas Maneuvers gave the 93rd Engineers their first chance to operate as a battalion in the field.

General George C. Marshall, Army Chief of Staff, conceived the maneuvers to address the critical problem that every peacetime army faces when it transitions to war. Peace makes an army rigid and bureaucratic— wedded to outdated tactics and equipment. Officers who advance in peacetime often trade on very different virtues than those required of a war leader. The largest war game ever, the Louisiana-Texas Maneuvers would involve over 400,000 troops, 19 divisions, divided into two armies—Blue vs. Red. They would conduct their mock conflict over 3,400 square miles of southern Louisiana. Marshall fervently hoped that the exercise would reveal the weaknesses in organization, tactics, equipment and personnel before the battlefields of Europe revealed them the hard way. The mistakes would be made in Louisiana, not in Europe, he hoped.

The exercise would not come cheap. Congress gave the Army $21 million (more than $344 million in today's dollars) to spend on it. It would also be dangerous. According to *The Corpus Christi Caller-Times*, the Army estimated it might suffer as many as "236 deaths and 70,000 casualties." The 93rd played its part in the great exercise. Three weeks before the official start, the battalion moved into a field in a pasture near Kinder, Louisiana, and covered it with two-man pup tents. Troops started by building "turnouts," large wide spaces adjacent to the highways that would allow maneuvering room for tanks and artillery moving from the roads into fields and pastures and back again. They inserted double-hinged gates into already-standing fences. They reinforced or rebuilt bridges to accommodate the weight of war machinery. They built "hardstands"—paved areas to support the weight of water purification stations. It may have been an exercise, but the 93rd were no longer simply training—they were building.

In addition to building roads and bridges, the 93rd laid logs to simulate mine fields along the flank of the Third Army. Lieutenant Boyd recalled that while the mines were being placed, Colonels George S. Patton and Dwight Eisenhower walked by. Patton doubted that his tanks could be stopped by a mere minefield; Eisenhower countered that the log mines should be at least as effective as the field artillery's cannons made of stovepipe.

The 93rd built prisoner of war camps and demolished the bridges on the Third Army's east flank. The work of its motor echelon and its demolition work impressed the brass enough that the battalion received a commendation. Lieutenant Boyd's company had been augmented by the addition of a demolitions specialist—Lt. Harry Traback, who was fresh from Officer Candidate School and knew his business.

With the maneuvers done, the men of the 93rd remained in the field to clean up. They rebuilt fences, graded tank-rutted fields smooth, and rebuilt small bridges that hadn't survived the battle. They were still there when their first and only black officer reported for duty. First Lieutenant Finis H. Austin, an African American from Virginia, would serve the battalion and later the regiment as chaplain.

Throughout fall 1941, the battalion worked on various road and railroad projects at Camp Livingston and Camp Claiborne. In mid-November, Colonel Zajicek fell ill and was replaced by Captain Arthur M. Jacoby as Battalion Commander.

...

ON AUGUST 15, 1941, 2ND Lt. Timberlake, brass "butter bar" and leather boots perfectly shined, reported for duty at Camp Lee, Virginia. The Army had commissioned Tim as a Quartermaster officer, so the first order of business was getting him trained, and the Quartermaster Officers training school was in the process of moving to Camp Lee. In late 1940, the Army had hastily begun transforming "a peaceful game refuge ... into a sprawling military installation" at Camp Lee, turning it into the "Quartermaster Replacement Center for white and colored troops." Every 13 weeks, 10,400 men, mostly from states east of the Mississippi River, cycled through the center, emerging trained, classified and assigned to various organizations throughout the Army. When Tim landed at Camp Lee, he landed next to an equally fresh "shavetail" named Theodore "Ted" Laputka, from Pennsylvania, by way of Boston University. Both men were assigned to Company D of the 1307 Service Unit. Tim and Ted quickly became friends and through a chain of coincidental Army decisions, would serve together and remain close friends through a series of transfers that landed them both in the Yukon in 1942.

Young Tim had always had an eye for the ladies, and at the university and in 4-H at least some of them had an eye for him too. They saw an athletic body, a shock of dark hair, blue-green eyes—and more important, they saw a broad grin. The lad from Magnolia had brought a bit of rural Maryland charm with him to College Park—wry, self-deprecating humor, an ability to tease without offending. Tim liked everybody and they liked him back.

For the past two years, Tim had kept company with Roberta "Bobbie" Ritchie. Pretty and available, part of his social circle at the university and especially in 4-H, Bobbie had become his regular date almost by default.

At Camp Lee, out of the cocoon of the university, Tim's weak emotional connection to Bobbie got weaker. His new buddy, Ted, had a girlfriend, Audrey "Mac" McNiff, who was going to Jackson College in Boston. The relationship between Ted and Mac went far beyond social convenience and familiarity. It's possible that Tim found that inspirational.

Tim found his thoughts turning to Helen May Bryan, a young lady he had worked and socialized with in 4-H. To the lad from Magnolia, Helen May had class. Slender, graceful with brown, medium-length hair, long legs and a pretty, oval face, Helen May could smile with winsome innocence. She could also infuse a smile with subtle challenge.

Tim loved sports. Helen was an athlete. She had played basketball and softball, both rather well, through her years at Bethesda-Chevy Chase High School. She took 4-H as seriously as he did and had advanced through its leadership ranks as fast and as far as he had. Her competitiveness and competence charmed Tim as much as her ladylike innocence. Helen embodied the world Tim had transitioned to when he left Magnolia for College Park. At Camp Lee, Tim found her lissome body and that winsome smile in his thoughts—a lot.

Socially, Helen would be a bit of a stretch, of course. Helen lived with her parents, sister and three brothers in the town of Somerset in Montgomery County, a prestigious address (today, Somerset is known as "Chevy Chase"). Her father, George W. Bryan, had come up from very humble beginnings to become the publisher, treasurer and vice president of the magazine that would later be known as *U.S. News and World Report*. He had not accomplished that by being shy and retiring. The young man who would court his oldest daughter didn't impress him a bit—blue-green eyes and thick dark hair be damned.

Undaunted, on his third day at Camp Lee, Tim wrote Helen the first of a series of letters that would span the war years—the "three cent love affair" Tim would later call it—referencing the cost of a postage stamp in 1941.

> Monday August 18, 1941
>
> Dear Helen,
>
> I'll bet you'll die when you receive this letter, but really something tells me I should have done it long ago....

…What I am writing about is something I've been wanting to do and never have, even though I have promised to a couple of times. I want a couple, not one, dates over the Labor Day Holiday….

…But first write a letter in your spare time, if any, and, well, just, I don't know, give me a break. Bye, Turner.

P.S. Please Helen, I really want a date with you something terrible. I promise, cross my heart, to keep it and everything. Bye Tim.

Helen's half of this letter exchange hasn't survived, but we know she responded—in green ink on very fancy paper—and she accepted the date. She was curious about Roberta Ritchie. Hadn't he already arranged to be in Cumberland, Maryland, with Roberta and her family?

This put young Tim on something of a spot. His next letter was all but incoherent as he tried to explain Roberta away without looking like a cad, nail down his date with Helen who was clearly his new love interest, and make some exceedingly complex social arrangements—all at the same time.

Friday August 22, 1941

Dear Helen,

Thanks for the letter. Oh, yes about the Cumberland trip falling through. No it hasn't, I just haven't considered it much. I don't know Helen, but Roberta just don't want to give me a break. I have been wondering about her for a long time and I finally think there isn't any use.

I don't want you to think I am after you as a second bit (for Gosh sakes no) it's just the fact that for a period of a couple of years you always impressed me as being a swell gal for any fellow and by golly I sure would like to be considered as one of the fellows….

I know you think I am cracked, but by golly I bet if a guy could have a gal like you sorta' steady like it sure would be grand.

No kidding everytime I looked or talked to you during All Star Weekend [4-H] or the time you came over during school I have often wondered and thought how swell gal you were.

…This is the longest letter I have ever written in my life and I just read it over and it sure sounds screwy but really if you can believe what I said. I just want some gal that is mine than a gal to a guy (oh not a wife), a gal that means something to you.

Yeah I know I ran around at school with some gals, but it wasn't the way I like to, just for what you can get. You know what I mean.

Well, Bye, Helen and I am hoping when I can see you. Tim.

Three days later, he wrote again. Letters from Roberta had further complicated both the love triangle and the social arrangements. Clearly Tim was digging himself ever further into a hole and his confusing incoherence hadn't improved things a bit.

Monday August 25, 1941

Dear Helen,

Kinda' looks like I made a mistake and I really want to mend things. Sunday I rode to Norfolk to the old boarding house and there were two or three letters from Bobbie that explained about the Cumberland trip.

Well "old top" try and be ready to go up for the weekend on this Saturday and I'll call for you about 10:30 in the morning, that is Saturday morning and you and I will go to Lonaconing, Md, get Bobbie and Bill Schumaker and have a wonderful time and on the way up I'll explain a couple of things.

I have written Bobbie and she'll contact Bill, so for gosh sakes I hope you can go … Love, Tim

P.S. If anything happens I'll send a wire.

As a social director, Tim made a hell of an engineer. His arrangements for the weekend left everybody confused and unhappy. Bill Schumaker thought Helen was his date. Bobbie thought Tim was hers. The foursome spent the uncomfortable weekend at the Ritchie family home in Cumberland, Maryland. Helen remembered this messed-up first date for years and never allowed Tim to forget it.

In the wake of the disaster, on September 2, Tim pushed the reset button.

He explained to Helen that she was the girl he had in mind.

> September 2, 1941
>
> Dear Helen,
>
> ...First of all I believe I would be better off to forget Bobbie, in fact, I have made up my mind to do just that. I would like to start all over again at 505 Cumberland, if the lady there is interested at all. Tim.

A few days later he was back at Helen's home in Somerset, and the evening of September 7, 1941 was clearly pivotal for the three-cent love affair. Back in the Army in the early morning hours of September 8, Tim couldn't wait to write her. And in the margin of this letter, Helen penciled "big night."

> Monday September 8, 1941
>
> Dearest Helen,
>
> Arrived here at 10 to 3 from your house. Honest after Sunday nite I feel like I found a pot of gold or something. I whistled all the way from your house to Camp Lee and that darn moon almost drove me crazy.
>
> When I got in bed Monday morning, all I could think of was that hour or so parked in front of your home. I didn't even get sleepy today. I have met a gal that I'd believe and stick to, to the last ditch.
>
> ...Love and tons of it, Timber

Clearly neither Tim nor Helen had much attention to spare for the ominous war clouds gathering that summer, but the outside world did succeed in getting Tim's attention when he drove to Portsmouth Navy Yard to see the *HMS Illustrious*. He reported to Helen, in his letter of September 15, that it had been under attack for nine hours back in January and nearly a third of its crew had been killed. The *Illustrious* was at a repair facility in Norfolk, but the extensive damage she had suffered was still very evident—and impressive.

> September 15, 1941
>
> Dearest Helen,
>
> ...It's entire stern was blown off and had 3 direct hits on 16 inch gun turrets ... Boy but those guys looked

like they had a taste of it.

Thanxs Helen for candy and cake. Gosh I love you, Timber.

In the end, though, the parts of the outside world that succeeded in getting his attention included Maryland's football team and the pennant race between the New York Yankees and the Brooklyn Dodgers as readily as the war.

His letters continued to focus on the Dodgers in the World Series, the Redskins' football prospects and the upcoming Louis-Nova bout.

September 30, 1941

Dearest Helen,

...Heck I think Louis will flatten Nova before the tenth round, but it will be a good fight. Louis is black but he sure is a great fighter.

And, of course, he continues to focus on Helen. On the weekend of October 4, the happy soldier made it back to "505"—Helen's address in Somerset.

October 6, 1941

Dear Helen:

Arrived at Lee just a little after one and I didn't go over sixty once and boy was it a beautiful trip. That moon was shining all the way and little Timber was singing, "I Got 505 On My Mind".

Helen if this thing gets any better (which it will) I'll sure be one guy in a million. Gosh every time I hug you I just love you about ten times more. Bye and Gosh I Love You, Timber

Not until October 8, when he wrote to tell her that the Army had shot down their plans for Homecoming Weekend at Maryland and gave her a new address did some sense of the more ominous outside world creep in. He had finally entered the Quartermaster School and that brought to mind the reality of his future deployment—and what that might mean to the three-cent love affair.

Wednesday October 8, 1941

Dearest Helen,

Gosh, but I hope we are doing the right thing in getting into this thing so deep .... My only hope is that nothing will ever happen that will make either of us feel terrible .... We just must be careful and make sure it's the right thing and I know it is. Bye Dear, Timber

Quartermaster school kept him busy. He didn't write again until October 19. This letter was about the Army's rapid growth, a war bill pending in Congress and the attack on the *USS Kearny*. Allied shipping losses in the North Atlantic had increased dramatically that fall. Both sides understood that the British, alone on their island, could not survive without supplies from the United States and Canada. During September, the Allies lost 84 ships and 285,900 tons of cargo. Merchant ships travelled in convoys, escorted by ships of the U.S. Navy. When the *USS Greer* was attacked in September, the act of "German Aggression" allowed FDR to order his ships to "shoot on sight."

Even though the United States hadn't entered the war, the Navy was, effectively, in it. On October 16, a German submarine attacked a convoy escorted by the *USS Kearny*—torpedoed three merchant ships and then hunkered down to endure the *Kearny's* depth charges. At mid-watch on the 17th, the *Kearny* took a torpedo on the starboard side. The crew succeeded in confining flooding to the forward fire room and power from the aft fire room allowed them to escape. The *Kearny* arrived in Iceland on October 19 having suffered 33 casualties—11 men killed and 22 injured.

October 19, 1941

Dearest Helen,

...I wish I knew who was guessing on this right time to do the right thing, Uncle Sam or Hitler. Seems funny with this big war bill in congress and with new men being pressed in the service until right now one out of every male citizen is in one of the armed services, that a ship gets blown up. Bye, Timber.

On October 29, he revealed a bit of apprehension and a clearer sense that all the events in the news might have a very personal impact on his life. He described his efforts to influence his assignment after school—he suspected his assignment might be in Iceland and he was trying to head that off. "We must be careful and don't do or plan anything until at least the first of the year." He refers to a Roosevelt speech about the *USS Kearny*. "We're going to get in the war yet."

A bit further from the leading edge of events than Tim, Helen was still sending letters and cakes, but she was upset that he hadn't written more. Tim, still in Quartermaster School and very busy. He knew that wherever he was going, it would be a long way away and it would be for a long time. Helen wanted more commitment before that happened. Tim was confused and hesitant. He wrote on November 14, "I honestly believe that you are too nice and too good a girl for me." A few lines on, he explains, "I would say different, but I don't want to ruin two lives."

On the November 16, he made his decision even more explicit. He planned, for her sake, to end their relationship. He was coming up on Thanksgiving weekend so she could visit Magnolia and his family and they could talk about their future. The Thanksgiving visit must have reassured him. It was clear in his letters through the end of November that the three-cent love affair was back on track.

Helen May Bryan—the photo Tim carried throughout.
Photo courtesy of the Timberlake Collection.

CHAPTER 3

LAND ROUTE TO ALASKA

The seeds that ultimately grew into the Alaska Highway Project had been planted back in the 19th Century. F.H. Harriman, railroad builder, had envisioned a railroad linking Alaska and Canada. Donald MacDonald, a Fairbanks engineer in 1928, proposed and mapped a highway from Alaska through Canada to the United States. In the early 1930s, General Billy Mitchell, a controversial and outspoken critic of America's lack of military preparedness, had argued that, "Alaska is the most central place in the world of aircraft ... for whoever holds Alaska will hold the world."

Later, in the 1930s, as the Roosevelt administration turned its attention to looming military threats, the seeds began to germinate. Looking at the map and assessing the military threat, Army and Navy planners were worried. The military of the United States faced the very real possibility of a two-front war—a strategic nightmare. As Mitchell had predicted, an important subset of the issues they confronted involved the distant territory of Alaska. The remote chain of about 150 islands, known as the Aleutians, extends from southern Alaska in a broad arc that ends pointing directly at Japan. One of the islands, Attu, was only 650 miles from the Japanese military base at Paramushiro, in the Kurile Islands. The chain pointed toward Japan, but also back toward the United States.

The strategic importance of Alaska posed two enormous problems for the United States. First, the outpost had 15,000 miles of undefended coastline. Second, no transport route, other than the sea, existed between Alaska and the contiguous United States. At the end of the 1930s, the Army had no way to transport defenders to that coastline or to supply them once they were in place other than with Navy ships. When war came to the Pacific, the Navy's resources would be stretched to the breaking point.

In summer 1938, Congress proposed and the President approved and appointed an International Highway Commission. A short time later, the Canadian government appointed a similar group. The two commissions reviewed data collected by their predecessors, arranged for new ground and aerial reconnaissance surveys, and then met—first in Victoria in July 1939 and then in Ottawa in January 1940. Significantly, the Japanese government strongly protested the construction of a road to Alaska.

There were few American soldiers stationed in Alaska, most of them at Chilkoot Barracks in Haines. On June 27, 1940, a small supplemental force of 780 officers and men arrived at Fort Richardson in Anchorage. In July 1940, when the War Department dispatched Colonel Simon B. Buckner to take command at Fort Richardson, Alaska defense existed in name only. By the middle of 1941, Buckner, now a Brigadier General, had increased the size of his command to six thousand men—better, but far from enough. Getting more men in position raised the far more difficult problem of how to transport and supply them.

The Navy did its best to provide sea transport, but that service was tasked not only with transporting men and material but also with defending the sea lanes should war come to the Pacific. The Navy was desperately short of resources.

In 1941, Canada stepped up and began building the Northwest Staging Route—a string of airfields across its territory toward Alaska—Grand Prairie, Alberta; Fort Saint John and Fort Nelson, British Columbia; Watson Lake and Whitehorse, Yukon. The area spanned by the Northwest Staging Route is unique in the world, rugged, remote, austere, breathtakingly beautiful and viciously inhospitable. Nature is a dictator, not a "mother" in the North Country.

Canadian efforts to build the Northwest Staging Route provided a first look at what massive construction in the North Country would be like—to anyone paying attention. Men from Tomlinson Construction Company arrived at the Northern Alberta Railroad terminus in Dawson Creek, Alberta, Canada, in early spring 1941. As anticipated, they ran head-on into the gargantuan problem of getting supplies and equipment to the airfield sites.

Getting freight to Fort Nelson meant, first, bringing it to Dawson Creek via Edmonton. From there, the old trail north wound through heavily wooded mountains and across the Sikanni Chief River. Years after the fact, Gerri Young interviewed Dean Hoy, who was with the contractors and recorded his memories of how the equipment was moved.

Tomlinson put together a convoy of ten gigantic sleighs—five for freight and five for crew—to be towed five at a time by a D7 Caterpillar tractor. D8 Cats would growl ahead along the old trail, gouging a path through the timber. The D7 would tow five sleighs up to the advancing trailhead and then go back for five more. Progress through the frozen landscape was slow and incredibly difficult—but steady—until they reached Sikanni Hill, a steep drop to the banks of the Sikanni Chief River. That last mile to the river took three agonizing days.

Then, there was the river itself. It was still frozen, so a D7 and its cargo could make its way across. The ice turned out to be rotten, and fifty feet from the west bank, a tractor plunged through the ice to the bottom. The crew spent three days rigging a makeshift tripod of logs and cables to lift the tractor and get it to land where it could be dried out under a makeshift canopy and returned to service.

The contractors worked 12-hour shifts for 40 cents an hour, sleeping in a bunkhouse on a crew sleigh that usually rested on a steep mountainside, chained to a tree. The never-ending cold, ice, mud and struggle against some of the most unforgiving terrain in North America devastated morale. They spent four months getting their cargo from Dawson Creek to Fort Nelson.

For the Watson Lake airstrip, contractors shipped supplies to Wrangell, Alaska, pushed the boats up the Stikine River to Telegraph Creek, disassembled and hauled them 75 miles, on a sleigh road, to Dease Lake. At Dease Lake, they reassembled the boats and towed them up the Liard River to Lower Post. From there, they followed an existing 25-mile portage road to the solitary cabin of Frank Watson, a prospector and trapper, whose name graced the lake that bounded the airstrip.

A legacy of the famous Klondike Gold Rush made transport to Whitehorse, the most northern location in the chain, comparatively easy, as the pioneering White Pass and Yukon Railroad connected Whitehorse to the port at Skagway.

For all the heroic effort, the Northwest Staging Route was only marginally better than nothing as a means of transport to Alaska. An airplane's ability to move numbers of men and large quantities of supplies was extremely limited. Excepting a very few uniquely qualified "bush pilots," pilots found the North Country an implacably hostile and dangerous place to ply their trade. Early in January 1942, 25 P-40 (fighter) aircraft and 13 B-26 (bomber) aircraft took off from Great Falls, Montana, headed, via the Staging Route, for Fairbanks. One month later, 13 P-40s and eight B-26s had arrived. Five P-40s were still en route. A total of 17 aircraft crashed.

...

ON SATURDAY, DECEMBER 6, 1941, military officials in Alaska, Ottawa and Washington, D.C. were worrying about preparations for war. The 93rd Engineer Battalion was at Camp Claiborne, assisting the 711th Engineers with construction of the Camp Polk-Camp Claiborne Railroad. Lieutenant Timberlake was working on his future and the three-cent love affair.

The next morning, December 7, the Japanese changed everything— forever.

On a pleasant, sunny Sunday morning in Hawaii, twisting and turning Japanese attack planes decimated the United States Pacific Fleet and spearheaded a coordinated assault across the Pacific. In an "all-in" roll of the dice, the Japanese armed forces aimed to overwhelm all their enemies at once, establishing dominance in the Pacific and securing the natural resources that would allow them to maintain it.

In Washington, D.C., awareness that war was imminent was not the same thing as being prepared. The President and the War Department had been dealing with a steadily rising level of tension, adjusting their defenses and preparing at a steadily increasing pace. Now events overwhelmed them. The first days of war reduced them to a frantic effort to find out exactly what was happening and where. A blizzard of confused and contradictory orders billowed out of the War Department.

Events galvanized the military. At every level, from private to general, from seaman to admiral, America's soldiers and sailors responded with patriotism and impotent fury while their civilian brothers flooded the recruiting offices anxious to join them.

In the thick fog of confusion at Camp Lee, frantically busy, Tim had no time for the vague anxieties about the future that had permeated his interactions with Helen. The "fat was in the fire." Vague anxieties gave way to immediate fears and concerns, and the time had come to deal with them.

> Tuesday December 9, 1941
>
> Dearest Helen,
>
> I am sorry I haven't written but we have been very busy and you know why ... We have been issued and equipped with gas mask, helmet, blanket roll, rifle, rifle belt and pistol. All leaves and weekend passes have been revoked. All officers have to stay on camp and leave only with special permission...
>
> I never in my life was so glad that you and I only talked of our future and didn't do any acting to mess up two lives would be terrible.
>
> So keep a stiff upper lip and I'll let you know if anything happens-maybe you could sorta' write mother a letter. As to when I'll be up I don't know but the first chance I get I'll see you. Bye, Tim.

In southern Louisiana, the same confusion reigned in the life of the 93rd Engineers. Commanders at all levels organized and reorganized troop units while transfers and new recruits flooded in. Companies and battalions released experienced troops to serve as a nucleus for new companies and battalions.

Many of the black troops felt the same patriotic fervor that white troops felt after Pearl Harbor, but their feelings were mixed and confused. Others felt they had no obligation to fight for a country that oppressed them. The number of men going AWOL increased significantly.

In nearby Alexandria, Louisiana, after pay day on January 10, 1942, black soldiers on weekend passes wound up in "Little Harlem," the Lee Street district, doing what soldiers on a pass do—drinking and looking for women. Armed white MPs showed up and arrested a black soldier. The arrest ignited two hours of rioting. According to *The Pittsburgh Courier*, five black soldiers were shot in a "street clash" between five hundred blacks and sixty white military police.

At Camp Lee, the three-cent love affair took a sad turn.

> January 8, 1942
>
> Dearest Helen,
>
> As yet we have no news of what is going on. There seems to be no news … There are 15 officers going on foreign duty but no one seems to know who they are. You just keep your fingers crossed and hope for the best…
>
> This will be my last letter from here, I guess, but I'll wire as soon as I know where I am again…
>
> …If I do go on foreign duty, I want you above all people to just forget me for awhile, maybe it might be a long time and then again it might not be. Just the same, for your own good you'll just have to forget, cause it isn't fair to you…
>
> I told Mom the last time I was home that I would never meet another gal like you, but I can't and won't do anything that will wear on you forever until I know what the score is. It's only good common horse sense.
>
> Look what a mess Ted will be in when the 44th goes out and they are set to leave now. His folks or Audrey's either one didn't approve of the marriage anyway. [Ted and Audrey had responded to Pearl Harbor by eloping].

So please Helen remember that I love you, will marry you if nothing happens when this mess is over, but right now I don't want you to feel attached to me in any way. Do as you please, remembering that someday, maybe, I'll be back. But if by chance another guy comes along better grab him while you can, cause Uncle Sam is getting them right and left...

It takes all kinds of guts to tell you what I have, it takes more guts to do it, but Helen love is a funny thing and marriage is something that's never undone even if the hubby is dead or alive.

Nite and love, Timber

Four days later, on January 12, Tim sent the promised wire. He'd been ordered to Camp Livingston, Louisiana. He drove his car, dropping off another shavetail on the way, at Camp Shelby, Mississippi, stayed one night at his uncle's house in Mobile, Alabama, then moved on to Alexandria. He passed through one week after the Lee Street Riots, but there's no evidence that he knew anything about that.

January 19, 1942

Dearest Helen,

When I get my regular address I'll write an air mail letter at once, or better yet drop a wire. It's going to be funny now, all kinds of experiences and stuff, maybe foreign duty and all, but I like it. The social life is going to be halted, however and if I ever see a woman again I'll bite her to see if it's real.

Please, Helen, don't pass up any dates or any parties cause of me. Please!! It is a mighty hard thing to do but have a good time, you must. It's only fair to you

Gosh I got to start to make new friends over again and won't that be a mess. New faces and stuff. That's all I have been doing since coming in this army...

Love, Timber

Tuesday January 20, 1942

Dearest Helen,

Well here I am 1568 miles from home and 1458 miles from you.

The address is 107th QMC Regiment, Camp Livingston, LA.

Guess you are plenty down in the dumps, honey, but remember it was great while it lasted-we are sure to leave here anytime...

Love, More Love and Mosted Love, Timber.

In January 1942, the Japanese war machine rumbled through the Pacific, striking with horrific effectiveness wherever it chose. In Washington, D.C., senior officials' strategic worries about Alaska turned into panic. The Navy had suffered grievous losses and a flood of new commitments stretched its resources to the breaking point. Clearly, the Navy couldn't guard the sea lanes leading to Alaska and the Aleutians and at the same time ferry supplies to land-based defenders there.

The issue of a land route to Alaska made it to the top of the national agenda when Secretary of the Interior Harold Ickes raised it on January 16 in a meeting of FDR's cabinet. Discussion moved around the table. What had come of the efforts of the International Highway Commission? Had a route been chosen? The President directed the Secretaries of War and the Interior to find out.

On February 2, 1942 Secretary of War Stimson met with Ickes and the Secretary of the Navy, in his office, to follow up on the President's instructions. Stimson's notes from the February 2 meeting have survived. Efforts on the ground in Canada and Alaska had to be under way before the spring thaw made it impossible to move in men and equipment. The Corps of Engineers was to survey routes and available equipment and had one week to furnish that information.

A note by the Assistant Chief of the Corps of Engineers, Brigadier General C.L. Sturdevant, makes clear the impact of the meeting at the next lower level of command:

On Monday, February 2, 1942, the writer was called to the War Department and told that a decision had been reached to undertake the construction of a highway to Alaska on a route connecting a series of airfields from Fort St. John, British Columbia, to Big Delta on the Richardson highway in Alaska; that the Chief of Engineers would carry out the project: and that a plan for surveys and construction must be submitted within the next few days. Such a plan was submitted on February 4th and a formal directive to proceed with the project was received on February 14th.

(C.L. Sturdevant, "Memorandum, 4 February 1942," to Asst. Chief of Staff, War Plans Division, War Department General Staff: Outline of a plan for construction of supply road to Alaska. Archived at U.S. Army Corps of Engineers Office of History, Humphreys Engineer Center, Fort Belvoir, Virginia)

Sturdevant submitted the required plan on February 4, an unbelievable two days after he received the order. Four routes had been proposed by the Commission, but the engineers chose a fifth. The road would follow the Northwest Staging Route, linking the airfields and joining the proposed route "C" for the last 500 miles to Big Delta and the Richardson Highway.

The Corps assumed that four white engineer regiments would build the road. The 18th Engineers would be in Whitehorse, Yukon on April 1, prepared to build the highway north from there. The 340th Engineers would be in Whitehorse by May 1, prepared to build southward. The 35th Engineers would be in place to make a winter march north to Fort Nelson before the spring thaw, ready to build north from there. The 341st Engineers would be in Fort Saint John by May 1, ready to build north to Fort Nelson.

Even as the plan was being submitted and considered, efforts to implement it were already under way. Much of the road would pass through Canadian territory, and that should have meant extensive negotiations with the Canadian government to work out a detailed agreement. Things weren't working that way. The State Department was working with Canada, to be sure, but the Corps was headed to British Columbia and Yukon come hell or high water. Canadians had been in the war for two years and they weren't about to stand in the way.

Verbal approval for a route survey came through on February 13 through Pierrepont Moffat, American Minister to Canada. Further permissions to proceed with construction would be worked out through the Joint Board of Defense. FDR had given verbal approval to proceed—two days earlier, on February 11. The next day, on February 12, General Sturdevant had dispatched Colonel (soon to be General) William Hoge to conduct reconnaissance on the ground in Canada and figure out the logistics of building the road.

On the 14th, the War Department directed the Chief of Engineers to begin construction of the highway at once. By the time the Joint Board met in New York on February 25 and the Canadian Government gave its formal permission on February 26, the survey was already happening and the construction engineer regiments were on the way.

On March 3, FDR's formal letter approving the project and allocating $10 million (more than $150 million today) to pay for it arrived at the War Department. On the same day, two formal orders from General Sturdevant arrived at Fort Belvoir. One order appointed Colonel Hoge Commander of a Provisional Engineer Brigade. The other approved his travel north. By then, Hoge had already completed the recon mission and the plan FDR approved was under way—and changing on the fly.

As word of the Corps' impending invasion of the North Country spread, the business and political leaders of the Alaska International Highway Commission reacted with shock and anger. Clearly the Corps intended to plunge ahead, choosing its own route; ignoring years of studies and reconciliations; oblivious to the very existence of the Alaska International Highway Commission.

In a letter dated February 24, Thomas Riggs, Acting Chairman of the Commission, indignantly informed Secretary of War, Henry L. Stimson, that the commission had tried for two years to meet with the Corps of Engineers to discuss the proposed highway. Now, without consultation, the Corps plans to build the highway paralleling the string of airfields constructed by the Canadian government—a serious mistake!

The time for bureaucratic study and negotiation had passed and the Corps was in "lead, follow, or get out of the way" mode. In the rush to the road, the War Department simply ignored the objections of Riggs and his allies.

• • •

ARRIVING IN JANUARY AT CAMP Livingston, Tim assumed that the Army had finally assigned him to a position where he could apply his education and training. The Army, even in the best of times, spends little effort matching junior officer assignments to junior officer qualifications. Now, in the first weeks of war, it spent no effort at all on that. The Army was throwing names at a shifting mosaic of organizational slots. Qualifications and real assignments would be assessed and made as they went—by frantic commanders on the ground, not by personnel experts in the War Department.

Tim, of course, knew nothing of this. Still, at Camp Livingston in January, he began to realize that the Army didn't really know what to do with him. By February 4, he was "no longer adjutant for the Division Motor Maintenance Officer, for there isn't any." His new assignment, to a "light maintenance organization" initially pleased him, but it proved frustrating. He considered a transfer to the Air Corps, but finally applied for a transfer to the Corps of Engineers.

To make matters worse, gregarious Tim found himself living alone in a one-man tent. The training center at Camp Lee had been relatively small, well appointed—hospital, church, post exchange, classrooms—surrounded by the towns and amenities of Petersburg and Hopewell, Virginia. By comparison, Camp Livingston, designed as an infantry replacement training center, sprawled through a huge swath of raw, fetid, semi-tropical swamp.

The Army had deposited his buddy Ted Laputka and Ted's new wife, Mac (Audrey), at nearby Camp Claiborne, which helped assuage Tim's loneliness, but spending time with them amplified his indecision about his future with Helen. Ted had married Mac right after Pearl Harbor—a serious error in judgment in Tim's opinion. He envied their life together, but it struck him as dreadfully precarious.

The war that raged "out there" would reach him—soon—and the graceful girl in faraway Somerset seemed a distant dream. It would be a long time—maybe forever—before he saw her again. Could he, in good conscience, let Helen commit to him? He was terribly afraid he couldn't.

> February 4, 1942
>
> Dearest Helen,
>
> …It sure is lonesome here. Say did you get the photo ok. It's not so hot but you can't make a Gable out of a monkey anyway. I hope you like it. How about putting it on your dresser next to your own, for right now I have yours and mine both alongside each other in my office.
>
> Did Mom say much to you about you and I? I wrote her a letter and told her to explain that maybe we should throw in the towel for the good of both of us.
>
> I often wonder when I'll be home and to see you and that really hurts when you are way down here and you way up there, in fact I am so damn sick of these three cent affairs, it drives me nuts, you can't get leave. Love, Nite and say hello to all, Timber

February 8, 1942

Dearest Helen,

…Helen don't lose your head over this thing—kinda' forget me … please, please, please just go as if I never existed. Write and stuff and you wait and see—if the good Lord wants us together we'll be together—and he does I know. Say Hello to the folks, Bye, Nite, Love, Timber

February 11, 1942

Dearest Buzz [Helen],

…So mother introduced you as the better half, gettin' a little ahead of the story. Sometimes I wonder if we should talk like I have just done and like we do often when we are out together. Gosh knows we may never get married … Nite, Love, Bye Timber

February 17, 1942

Dearest Buzz,

Thanks for the box and stuff Helen—it sure was great—even sent matches with the smokes—what a gal.

The big news first—yesterday received a letter from Mom and guess what! George [Tim's brother] is married. Gosh knows it knocked me for a loop. That gal sure must have worked on him—why I don't even know her last name. Hope they did the right thing, but sounds to me as if it might be a bit foolish … Love, Nite Timber

Photo Tim sent to Helen from Camp Livingston, LA.
Photo courtesy of the Timberlake Collection.

CHAPTER 4

LEAD, FOLLOW, OR
GET OUT OF THE WAY

The "very highest authority" ordered the Corps of Engineers to build a land route to Alaska and do it immediately. The Corps leaped into action. The Corps built things fast under difficult circumstances. It existed for that purpose. Asked for a plan, General Sturdevant had submitted one in two days, knowing, as he did so that it was at best an outline of a plan. Even as he wrote it, he set the bureaucratic machinery of the Corps in motion.

He had already made his most important choice—his commander on the ground would be Colonel William Hoge. From 1935 through 1937, Hoge, a West Pointer with an advanced engineering degree from MIT, had commanded the 14th Engineers in the construction of the Bataan Highway through the Philippine jungles, reporting directly to Sturdevant.

The two men met on February 12, 1942, to consider their most urgent task—turning Sturdevant's outline into a real plan. Because they were both Army Engineers, they understood one thing that civilian engineers would have considered absurd—they did not have the luxury of time to complete the plan before they started to implement it.

A week later, Colonel Hoge's boots were on the ground in Edmonton. With him were Fred Capes, a construction engineer from the Public Roads Administration; Lt. Colonel Edward Mueller of the Quartermaster Corps; and Lt. Colonel Robert Ingalls, Commander of the 35th Engineering Regiment. Twenty-four hours later, they met Homer Keith, the Canadian assigned to liaise with them in Dawson Creek, British Columbia.

Leaving Mueller in Dawson Creek to deal with the logistics of supply, Hoge and his contingent climbed into Keith's car and headed north over the frozen winter road to Fort Nelson. Crossing the thick ice of the 1,800-foot-wide Peace River and then the 300-foot-wide Sikanni Chief River, Hoge got his first look at the challenge his troops would face. He most urgently needed to locate the men who knew what he needed to know about the North Country, and Keith led him to Knox McCusker. An experienced guide, McCuster had invested years in finding and improving trails through the wilderness and happily educated the American. Most important, McCusker warned Hoge that the winter trail he had just travelled—from Fort Saint John to Fort Nelson, would disappear in the March thaw—a huge potential problem.

In a 1968 interview, Hoge remembered the trip:

> Arriving in Dawson Creek, we were met by Homer Keith. He offered to drive us over the road in his car to Ft. Nelson.
>
> I left Mueller behind there to study the feasibility of making contracts with various people to furnish trucks to haul enough oil, gas and rations to Fort Nelson to support a regiment for six months. He found this entirely feasible because we offered to pay them $65 a barrel to haul gas in there.
>
> I also ran into Knox McCusker who was stationed at Horse Track, the stopping point on the road near the Sikanni Chief River. He was keeping an eye on the last of the supplies cached there awaiting transportation to the Fort Nelson Airport and bringing some of his maps up to date.
>
> I took him back to Ft. St. John. We spent most of one night going over his maps and talking about the country and the obstacles we might face. One of the things we hadn't realized was the winter road would become useless in the summer time as it traversed frozen muskeg. He suggested taking it further west along the foothills.
>
> The result of the trip was that I ordered an engineering regiment moved into Fort Nelson over the winter road before the spring breakup and have it work towards Watson Lake.
>
> (Schmidt 1991, 41)

Hoge, already desperately behind schedule, sounded the charge. He ordered Ingalls to return to his regiment, the 35th Engineers at Fort Ord, California, and move them immediately to Dawson Creek, British Columbia, by rail and then push them on north to Fort Nelson before the thaw.

His first troops on the way, Hoge continued his recon through Canada, assessing the breathtaking scale of the problems he and his men faced. He didn't even have maps of the rugged country and the vast distances, in and over which his men would have to work.

"There were no plans ... except we had to go to these points where airfields were to be built," he later recalled. "Somebody had made a partial air survey of this route .... The airplane maps were about the best we had .... I think a lot of them came out of the *National Geographic*." Army Headquarters back in Washington, D.C. clearly had no idea what the regiments were getting into.

The pioneer road standards and specifications that would govern his construction weren't very demanding: "Clearing, thirty-two feet wide minimum; grade, ten percent maximum; curves, fifty-foot radius minimum; surfacing, twelve feet minimum; shoulders, three foot minimum; ditch depth, two feet; crown, one inch per foot maximum; bridges, single-lane H-15 minimum loading." In the thick timber, permafrost, muskeg and rugged mountains of the North, these road standards verged on impossible.

The only way Hoge could see the country and plan his effort was from the air. "I had a bush pilot who was a civilian ... a crackerjack. He's the one that showed me the route to follow." The bush pilot, Les Cook, flew Hoge everywhere. Hoge's experience flying in Army transport planes hadn't prepared him for the experience up north. "The first time I was up there, I had to ride on oil barrels. He [Les Cook] was delivering oil to one of these construction outfits ... on the way back he would take me by different routes and showed me a pass over the mountains."

After World War I, many pilots, trained by the military but no longer needed, wanted to keep flying. The planes they flew, also surplus, were available and cheap. Perhaps inevitably, some of these pilots made their way north.

Not just pilots, but bush pilots, these men had to be masters of the ground as well as of the air. A pilot suffering mechanical problems and needing to ground his plane had few options. Usually, he found a remote lake. He rarely enjoyed the luxury of communicating his plight to anybody who might be able to help him. He must be capable of repairing his own aircraft and if that proved impossible, of surviving in the rugged wilderness and navigating his way out of it on foot.

On the ground, gigantic mosquitoes and merciless black flies tormented a bush pilot in the summer. In winter, they were gone, but then he had to deal with the bitter cold that had driven them away. Once the engine, keeping the oil warm and fluid, shut down, temperatures—dramatically below zero—quickly rendered engine oil unusable. The pilot had to quickly drain the oil before it congealed in his engine. Before he could restart and fly away, he had to somehow warm the oil and return it to the engine. Creative bush pilots devised alternatives to draining the oil; they used devices like a plumber's fire pot—a pressurized gasoline stove—to keep the oil liquid in the engine. The fiery explosions caused by this practice could be dramatic.

Of all the skills a pilot needed in order to be a bush pilot, navigation was the most important and the most difficult. There was no radar in the North Country and radios worked sporadically, if at all, because of the vast distances and because of magnetic and atmospheric interference. Worst of all, even compasses were of relatively little use so far north. Bush pilots flew by dead reckoning over terrain they had memorized through long experience. If cloud cover made it impossible to see the ground, they "pruned the treetops," scouring what they could see for a familiar mountain, lake, or stream.

It wasn't a trade for the faint of heart.

Of the men who plied this trade, Les Cook came to mean the most to the Corps of Engineers in the Yukon and Alaska. Hoge remembered flying with Cook during poor weather. "We suddenly came up to a blank wall. I don't think we were 200–300 feet from it when it suddenly loomed up. We turned quickly enough, but all the way back, if you could get your foot out of the door, you could touch the top of the trees. Those were hair-raising experiences."

...

IN THE "LAND OF THE midnight sun" Hoge's troops could work in shifts 24/7, but the working season was very short. Fifteen hundred miles, "that would be a hell of a long way ... so we had to find some way of breaking it [the Highway] into segments." Hoge decided to build the highway in two main sectors, divided by the natural barrier of the mountains at Watson Lake, Yukon Territory. Headquarters for the Northern Sector would be at Whitehorse, Yukon Territory. Headquarters for the Southern Sector would be at Fort Saint John, British Columbia. Lieutenant Colonel A.C. Welling, Executive Officer of the Southern Sector, arrived at Dawson Creek on March 15.

Hoge further divided the route into five three hundred-mile segments (*see map on pages 8 - 9*). Troops and equipment would come in at three main ports of entry—Dawson Creek, Skagway and Valdez—and then move to designated starting points, along the path. Some regiments would work from each end toward the center while others worked from the center toward the ends.

The first troops, a Quartermaster detachment of five officers and 125 men, arrived at Dawson Creek at 1:20 a.m. on March 9. The troops detrained into a temperature of 35 degrees below zero, a biting wind and six inches of drifting snow. The ice crystals forming on eyebrows and mustaches were but the first of many nasty surprises to come.

Right behind the Quartermasters came the first troops of the 35th. The five officers and 160 enlisted men of Company B completed their five-day, two thousand-mile journey to Dawson Creek in the very early morning of March 10. Even as they disembarked from the train, the remainder of the 35th was boarding trains back at Fort Ord. Company B's officers set up a temporary headquarters in a local hotel. In the cold, the enlisted men erected tents—much easier said than done.

Cold stiffened the soldiers' hands and fingers as they tried to pound tent pegs into the frozen ground. Some found trees or other external structures to anchor their tent ropes. They fumbled to unfold cots and blanket them with down sleeping bags, stuffing duffle bags and trunks on the floor beneath the cots.

"Volunteers" dug latrine ditches into the frozen ground—downhill from the camp and, hopefully, downwind. Miserable soldiers discovered that if a man didn't do his business quickly, his urine would freeze almost before it hit the ground.

For Company B, the first miserable encampment lasted only one night. The following morning, they traveled 36 miles, crossed the 1,800 feet of the frozen Peace River; climbed the steep bank on the north side, at about midnight on March 11, then traversed ten miles of deeply rutted wagon road to Fort Saint John. The very next morning, Company Commander Mike Miletich and twenty of his men piled into their trucks and moved on. On the afternoon of March 20, they stumbled out of their vehicles—exhausted, hungry and above all, cold—into Fort Nelson,

While Company B moved north, four locomotives, each pulling 35 Pullman, coach and flatbed cars, transported the rest of the 35th to Dawson Creek. The last of them arrived in late afternoon on March 16. These men would move through Dawson Creek, on to the Peace River and out to Fort Saint John and Fort Nelson just as quickly as Company B had. Also on March 16, the 35th was in country, strung out the length of the trail to Fort Nelson, coping with miserable conditions and moving as fast as humanly possible.

As the 35th moved through, Hoge flew into Fort Saint John to observe and direct the movement. Setting up temporary headquarters in a log cabin, he initially directed Ingalls to divide the regiment, send half immediately to Fort Nelson and keep the other half at Fort Saint John. As the movement progressed, though, it became evident that the gift of frozen rivers wouldn't last much longer. He threw everybody onto the trail, determined to take advantage while he could.

The troops welcomed the short periods of warmth offered by early spring—at first. Unfortunately, warmth softened the ice, and soft ice created problems that trumped comfort. The ice undulated and heaved under the weight of the twenty-three-ton tractor and large, dangerous cracks appeared.

Lieutenant Colonel Welling sent troops to collect sawdust, wherever they could find it, and spread it over the frozen Peace River, hoping to blanket and insulate the precious ice. Planks over the sawdust kept the tracks and wheels from scattering it. Colonel Ingalls ordered soldiers and equipment to cross the river only during colder night-time hours. The ice held, but it wavered menacingly as men and machines worked their way across.

Tractors and trucks, piloted by shivering operators, led the companies of the 35th up the primitive trail, with troops bundled in frozen parkas, faces frosted and noses blanched white.

Hoge took a huge risk in deciding to move the entire regiment. Troops struggled to move themselves and their equipment up the road. Once in Fort Nelson and beyond, though, a thousand men would require a staggering amount of "stuff" to survive and make a road. They absolutely had to get that "stuff" across the winter trail before it disappeared.

Back in February, while Hoge had been picking the brain of Knox McCusker, his Quartermaster, Lt. Colonel E. A. Mueller, had been at Dawson Creek planning the looming issue of supplying oil, gas and rations to the troops who would soon be making their way to Fort Nelson. Like Hoge, Mueller looked for experts in place. "Find a man named Spinney," the locals told him.

When McCusker had pushed the winter trail through in the first place, it was his friend E.J. Spinney who solved the problems of transporting equipment and supplies for the effort—establishing "service stations" every seventy miles along the route. Taking a leaf from Spinney's book, Ingalls and Mueller divided the 300 miles between Dawson Creek and Fort Nelson into three one hundred-mile sections and set up what amounted to a gigantic "conveyor belt."

Each section had an emergency base camp with an officer in charge and a roving tow truck. Stockpiles of fuel, oil, tents with cots, sleeping bags, stoves, and a 24-hour chow line completed each camp.

Troops "walked" an unbroken line of bulldozers, graders and loaded 2½-ton trucks down the steep and crooked hill to the frozen Peace River. Once across the heaving ice and up the steep bank on the north side, the line negotiated the arduous 250 miles to Fort Nelson. At each base camp, relatively rested and fed troops replaced exhausted ones and the belt kept moving. From Fort Nelson, the troops returned to Dawson Creek to reload and repeat the trip.

Private Chester Russell, of Company A, remembers hauling an Osgood Shovel. On its own, the shovel was very clumsy and moved slowly so it was loaded on to a trailer pulled by a D8 bulldozer. They were going down the hill to the riverbank when the weight of the shovel and the trailer pushed the dozer down the hill and both slid out of control. "The whole rig jack-knifed and the trailer turned over, spilling the Osgood shovel onto its side..."

Periodically, warming temperatures turned the road surface into thick, sticky mud, drastically slowing the belt and threatening to bring it to a halt. Then the temperature would plummet, the ice and the road surface would harden, and the movement would return to speed.

Ingall's "conveyor belt" got the job done, but the men who moved up the line with it in that early spring of 1942 found the experience excruciating. In a memo to Hoge, Lt. Col. Welling describes dozer operators along the route next to their parked equipment "crying violently, so great was the cold." Upon arrival at their destination, soldiers who had made the trip in the back of cargo trucks could hardly climb out or walk. Finally, in a tent and near a fire, their "blood warmed and thinned," and they would become dizzy and fall asleep.

The soldiers of the 35th and all the attached units pulled it off. They and their equipment made it to Fort Nelson before the thaw. That being said, they were far from ready to make a road. As hard as the trip had been on the men, it had been even harder on their equipment.

The Army flew in mechanics from Union Tractor Company from Edmonton to help get the heavy equipment back in shape. One of their number, Harry Garriott, found himself shocked and "staggered by the immensity and scope of the project."

Vehicles with flat tires and no spares sat everywhere. Many had broken axles. The mechanics did a quick triage then sacrificed the totally unserviceable vehicles, cannibalizing parts for the rest.

Lt. Col. Heath Twitchell wrote home:

> "Now we are safely encamped on top of a hill ...
> overlooking the [Muskwa] river, in a clearing carved out
> of the woods. I traveled over 3,000 miles in two weeks,
> with only a few hours' sleep each night ... a mountain
> of supplies and gasoline, every ton of which represents
> a struggle to get here. We are housed in pyramidal tents
> heated by a new type of army stove. We have eighty
> tons of fresh meat in an ice house ... a field bakery ...
> powdered milk and eggs ... dehydrated potatoes ... We
> are going to live the life of Riley until our supplies run
> out sometime this summer."

(Twitchell 1992, 86-87)

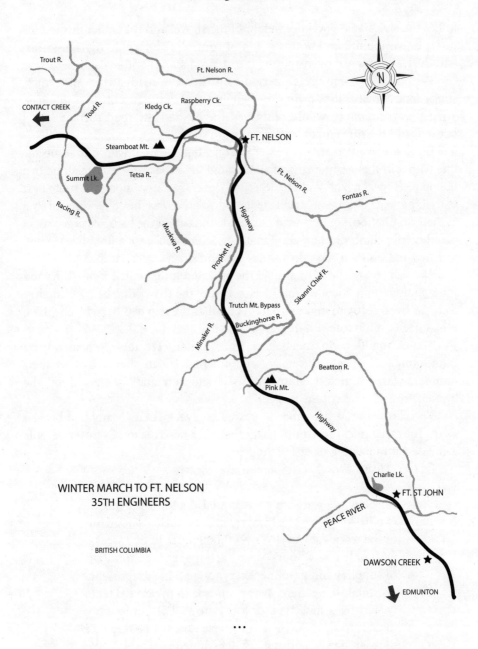

WINTER MARCH TO FT. NELSON
35TH ENGINEERS

• • •

THROUGH MARCH, PROBLEMS HAD PILED in front of Hoge's juggernaut like snow in front of a plow blade—bigger problems than just getting the 35th in place. Sturdevant's preliminary plan had called for four regiments. Colonel Hoge's survey of the route made it very clear that four regiments could not possibly push the road through in the required time.

Washington, D.C. responded. The Army would create a new regiment by expanding the black 93rd Engineer Battalion into the 93rd Engineering General Service Regiment. In addition, the Army would send the black 97th Engineers to Alaska. Ultimately, the black 95th Engineers would join the 35th and the 341st in the Southern Sector. The commands cascading down the chain of command rolled over the color bar as easily as they had rolled over the Alaska International Highway Commission.

On March 27, Hoge became a Brigadier General, commanding a Provisional Brigade. His 35th Engineer Regiment was, of course, already in place. The 341st, forming at Fort Ord, California would follow the 35th into the Southern Sector to turn the winter trail into a permanent trail before the 35th's supplies ran out. From Florida, the black 97th Engineer Regiment would head for Valdez, Alaska, to build the northernmost portion of the highway. The white 18th Engineer Regiment would come up to Whitehorse from Vancouver Barracks to build north from there toward Alaska. The white 340th and the black 93rd Engineer Regiments would come to Yukon to build the road between Whitehorse and the Southern Sector. A few weeks later, the black 95th Engineer Regiment would come up from North Carolina to assist the 35th and the 341st.

General Buckner's feelings about using "colored" troops in the North Country were well known, so a somewhat awkward letter from General Sturdevant to his friend "Buck" broke the news on April 2. The black regiments were already on their way.

> Dear Buck:
>
> ...This sixth regiment is the 97th (General Service - colored).
>
> I have heard that you object to having colored troops in Alaska and we have attempted to avoid sending them. However, we have been forced to use two colored regiments and it seems unwise for diplomatic reasons to use them both in Canada since the Canadians also prefer whites.
>
> I hope, therefore, that you will not protest this action since I believe it would only cause delay with no different result because the urgency of the project prevents reduction of the force and all remaining white regiments are assigned to task forces. We are now organizing two of the white regiments especially for this job. We cannot organize two others due to limitations of

time, cantonment space, and output of training centers.

It is planned to have the colored regiments return to warmer stations South of latitude 49 next fall. They will be hard at work in two reliefs on a 20-hour schedule in out-of-the-way places and I cannot see how they can cause any great trouble...

(Morgan, Collection of interviews and notes, 1991 - 1992)

Buckner's response makes clear that priorities had changed. It also makes clear just how thoroughly racist his Army truly was.

Dear Sturdy:

...I appreciate your consideration of my views concerning negro troops in Alaska. The thing which I have opposed principally has been their establishment as port troops for the unloading of transports at our docks.

The very high wages offered to unskilled labor here would attract a large number of them and cause them to remain and settle after the war, with the natural result that they would interbreed with the Indians and Eskimos and produce an astonishingly objectionable race of mongrels which would be a problem here from now on.

We have enough racial problems here and elsewhere already.

I have no objections whatever to your employing them on the roads if they are kept far enough away from the settlements and kept busy and then sent home as soon as possible. I hope, however, that none of them will be placed at the ports of entry, since here is where our principal problem will arise.

(Morgan, Collection of interviews and notes, 1991 - 1992)

...

THROUGH MARCH, IN SOUTHERN LOUISIANA, the 93rd worked on range roads, constructed bridges and did general construction work at Camp Livingston and Camp Claiborne. Officers and men worked in blissful ignorance of the Alaska Highway Project. Tim Timberlake, at Camp Livingston, struggled to make sense of his life and keep his spirits up.

February 26, 1942

Dearest Helen,

Went over and saw Ted Sunday and yesterday he came over for supper…

During the night here I have been fixing up my scrap book … Remember when your photo was taken for the Balto [Baltimore] News Post at Club Week …? Well I have the clipping … I remember the day (like it was yesterday) that picture was taken. You said "now, Timber, save me a copy of the paper." Every time I think of you, I can year you saying "Now Timber".

Gosh, wonder when I'll get home … Love Timber

March 24, 1942

Dearest Helen,

We have been right busy. I haven't been feeling very well. Just can't seem to get into the writing mood.

You asked me some questions. First about coming here, to be real frank about the situation, I really don't know whether it's wise or not. We might just up and pull out of here anytime. Second, it cost to darn much money.

I am still waiting to hear from the Engrs Corp here, it seems that my request has to go to the Third Corps Area that is in Baltimore. It has been approved by the Army Headquarters here and the Engrs Staff, too, and I sure hope it goes by the 3rd CA, if it doesn't I'll be dam if I know what I'll do.

Haven't been doing much, no place to go, no body to see, just sit in my tent and wish I was over there where the Japs could have a shot at me. Can't do much around here but a little drinking now and then. Love, Turner

April 2, 1942

Dearest Helen,

...I don't know when I'll ever get any vacation. I sure would like to get home before the blitz comes, just for a few days.

Mother gets plenty lonesome now. She said it sure is wonderful how you fit into our family. Guess better keep you in it.

Say about the QMC pin. Wait 'till I see how this engineering situation works out ... Love to swell gal at 505, Turner

The day after Tim wrote those words, he received orders over the signature of Brigadier General Alfred M. Gruenther of Third Army Headquarters to report forthwith for duty with the 93rd Engineers. On that same day, command ordered the 93rd back to Camp Livingston. General Hoge's project had finally grabbed the 93rd—and Lt. Timberlake.

Three days later, on April 6, the army enlarged and reorganized the 93rd into a General Service Regiment—two battalions plus an H&S Company. The very next day, the Army ordered the brand-new regiment to prepare for immediate overseas assignment.

Samuel Hargroves of the 93rd had managed to get a furlough and travelled home to Virginia, and on April 7, married his sweetheart, Mayola Pleasants. The 93rd cancelled Samuel's furlough, and Mayola's honeymoon lasted all of three hours.

...

WITH HUNDREDS OF NEW SOLDIERS reporting in, the regiment struggled for five days to assimilate them, even as they loaded equipment on flat cars, chained it down and sent it on ahead. Then, on April 12, 1942 the soldiers, including Lt. Timberlake, boarded a troop train, the Rock Island Railroad, and headed northward to parts unknown.

Tuesday April 14, 1942

Dearest Helen,

Enroute to Somewhere

Well we are off. I guess for one of the greatest things

that will ever happen in my life. It will be packed full of thrills, all kinds of sorrow and stuff, but the adventure will be worth a million bucks ...

Boarding the Rock Island Railroad at Camp Livingston, LA.
Photo courtesy of the Timberlake Collection.

CHAPTER 5

BOTTLENECK

In April, Hoge and the Corps grappled with the biggest challenge of the project—organizing and assembling thousands of men and tons of equipment and moving them into the remote wilderness, where they proposed to put them to work. To make matters worse, only two of Hoge's regiments—the 35th and the 18th—had existed long enough to be fully organized and experienced.

Army regiments are teams of over a thousand men, each of whom, from the Commander to the lowliest enlisted man, knows his place and responsibility in the team effort. The material and equipment required for this team to perform its mission is specified in very detail. Every item, from bulldozers to rolls of toilet paper, are somebody's assigned responsibility.

A regiment that has been around for a while works like the proverbial well-oiled machine. Given an urgent mission, the team can respond quickly, getting people and equipment from point A to point B and arriving at point B ready to accomplish its mission. A new regiment? Not so much.

Back in March, General Hoge had launched one of his experienced regiments, the 35th north out of Dawson Creek. At the end of March, he launched the other, the 18th, into the Yukon, ordering Colonel Earl G. Paules to move his from its Vancouver Barracks in Seattle to Whitehorse, Canada. Paules sent his advance Company A north aboard the *SS Aleutian*.

The gateway to Yukon Territory starts at the end of the Inland Passage—the port of Skagway, Alaska. On April 2, when the *SS Aleutian* docked at Skagway Harbor, snow-covered mountains towered over the little city and cold winds funneled through the narrow valley of the Skagway River. The soldiers of Company A billeted overnight in City Hall, wrapped in sleeping bags. Early the next morning, breath steaming into the frigid air, they walked to the train depot and boarded the White Pass and Yukon Railroad for Whitehorse.

With rotary plows clearing deep snow from the tracks ahead, the forward engine climbed three thousand feet in the twenty miles to the Canadian Border.

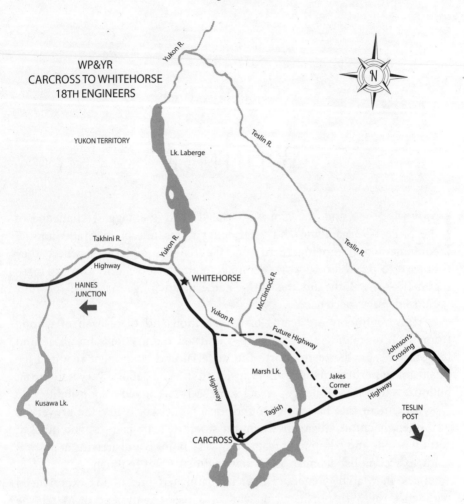

From the border, the train rumbled and rocked between high snow drifts for another ninety miles to the red-painted depot in Whitehorse. The rest of the companies of the 18th, along with support units that would be attached to Hoge's headquarters in Whitehorse—topographic engineers and pontoon engineers who would serve all of Hoge's regiments—followed close behind Company A. Colonel Paules and his regiment moved directly from the Whitehorse depot to a frigid plateau overlooking the little city.

From Whitehorse, Hoge directed the 1,500-mile project from a ramshackle office with a home-made desk, using empty packing crates as file cabinets. The 18th spent April trying to get out of Whitehorse and by May was on the road. Hard on its heels, the U.S. Public Roads Administration brought in thousands of civilians to build a new city and upgrade and expand Hoge's headquarters.

Harbor at Skagway, AK, in 1942.
Photo courtesy of the Signal Corps, CS 163102.

...

ON APRIL 3, AS THE 18th moved through frigid Skagway, the warmth of early spring bathed southern Louisiana. Ordered to transform their battalion into a brand-new 93rd Engineer Regiment, senior officers knew something big loomed, but they had no idea what. With a regiment to staff, they scrambled to secure junior officers wherever they could find them and among others, they grabbed Tim. He didn't know it yet but his boots were headed for the Skagway pier and his butt for a bench on the WP&YR.

Captain Arthur M. Jacoby, leading the 93rd through the first stages of movement and reorganization, ordered 1st Lt. Frank Holtzapple and his Company A to head out as the advance for the regiment's move—setting up support and accommodation for the rest of the regiment coming behind.

On April 7, at 8:45 a.m., Company A left Camp Livingston, Louisiana, in a miserable rain, on the *Missouri Pacific RR*. On April 12, five days and 3,400 miles later, it arrived at Prince Rupert, British Columbia. At 5:30 p.m. that same day, it embarked on *SS Princess Louise* up the long inland passage to Skagway, Alaska. On April 15, the men disembarked in Skagway and marched a half a mile to billets in town. Five days later, they marched to an airfield one mile north of town and pitched a temporary camp.

Even as Company A climbed off its train in Prince Rupert on April 12, the rest of the 93rd boarded five trains on the Rock Island Railroad bound for Camp Murray in Washington state. Tim boarded with them. He'd been part of the regiment for just eight days. Neither he nor anybody else had any idea what his role in the regiment would be. Tim didn't care. The Rock Island train was a hell of a lot better than his lonely Livingston tent and Tim could feel that he was finally done marking time.

Reporting to Helen, he was excited and full of himself again—as a young man off to adventure ought to be. His feelings were much clearer than his prose in his letter from the train on April 14.

> Tuesday April 14, 1942
>
> Dearest Helen,
>
> …We are now in Iowa, somewhere … hey, wait a minute I am informed by some of the officers that we just entered Minn. We will arrive at our port [Camp Murray] on the 16th. A total trip of about 3470 miles. Just in the U.S.
>
> Boy Helen you talk about funny feelings when we got on the train. I really had them. We all marched from our Regimental area on Sunday [April 12th] about 3 pm. Here's what I wrote mother about it.
>
> It seemed that everything that I ever did bad in my life kept coming into my brain, sorta haunting me, and then I wondered if the good Lord would excuse me for all those things and then let me come home someday safe and sound.
>
> It kinda' made me want to holler out and say to George [his brother] and Leebay [his sister] that if they think they didn't have a fine home and a fine Mother and Dad, well just pack up some day with a 150 lbs. of stuff to your name, a loaded pistol and hop on a train that is going gosh only knows where to meet a boat that is going gosh only knows where.
>
> I LLLLOOOOVVVEEEE YOU, Turner.

On April 15, he reported their progress through the northern tier of states—Minnesota, North Dakota, Montana, Idaho and Washington. The snow-covered peaks of the Rockies got his attention, but in general, he thought the northern tier of states "dead and poor." He missed his home and his girl: "Looks like I won't see you for a long time."

Recalling his trip on the Rock Island, Anthony Mouton of Company E of the 93rd remembered a one hour stop in a small Arkansas town. White soldiers had climbed down from their trains, and a patriotic white woman moved along the tracks, passing out doughnuts. Officers on Mouton's train hurriedly ordered the men to stay aboard—out of sight and without doughnuts.

On the train carrying Company B of the 93rd officers had ordered shades lowered so people along the tracks couldn't see into the cars. When private Eddie Waters, who hadn't gotten the word, innocently raised a shade, a young white officer rushed over, slapped him and shouted, "You will not pull shades up. We don't want them to see you niggers."

Captain Boyd, commander of Company C, recalled in his memoir, *Me and Company C,* detraining with the rest of the regiment at Camp Murray, Washington, early on the morning of April 16. They breakfasted in a mess hall, for the first time in days, and then went to assigned barracks for hot showers, a change of uniform and some sleep

The next morning, Company C and part of Company D left the rest of the regiment behind temporarily, climbed back aboard the train and headed on to Prince Rupert. From there, it was slated to move on to Skagway on the *USS Prince George*. Tim and some other junior officers still unassigned and for the moment, just along for the ride, went with them.

Their train rolled through Seattle, Vancouver and north and east toward Jasper National Park. On their stop to transfer onto the Canadian National Railroad, the troops stretched, grabbed their duffle bags and marched off the train. The sight of black troops startled local Canadians. "I don't think many of them had ever seen black boys (sic) before," Boyd recalled. The young local girls were mesmerized by the muscular soldiers and, of course, the soldiers loved the attention.

Tim recounted their progress from Camp Murray in his letter of April 18.

> Dearest Helen,
>
> The country here is sure beautiful. Deer running wild, even saw a bear of some kind. Looking out of the window now I see a high peak just touching the clouds, snow hanging to it as a tree. I rode about 60 miles in the locomotive, up in the cab in a seat right next to the Engineer, it was really a thrill, when you go around so darn many curves. Mae West hasn't anything on these mountains. I love you, Tim.

At 2:00 a.m. on Monday, April 20, the train brought them to Prince Rupert, the harbor giving access to the inland passage to Skagway, Alaska. In pitch-black darkness and pouring rain, the only things the tired soldiers could see as they climbed off the train were strings of blue lights running along the ground. Stumbling over tracks and switches in the large switching yard, they were guided by a beam of light shining through the crack of a massive dockside warehouse door. They emerged from the warehouse, confused but thrilled at their luck, to board the luxury liner, *USS Prince George*

The ship was, indeed, a luxury liner and the crew didn't propose to change that because their passengers were black soldiers. Troops took their first shipboard meal at tables draped with white linen, set with real china, silver, cut glass and were served by uniformed waiters. After nine days on troop trains, eating G.I. rations, they gorged on fresh fruit, oatmeal, scrambled eggs, fried potatoes, bacon and sausage with hot rolls, butter and jam, coffee and milk. This was the Army they *wished* they had joined!

After dinner, as the ship moved up the inland passage past massive glaciers and steep mountains, most of the soldiers enjoyed the equal luxury of their berths. The warm glow of morning, though, woke them to an incredible vista. They had sailed past Ketchikan and Juneau and up the ninety-mile fjord known as the Lynn Canal to anchor at mid-morning in Skagway Harbor. At 10:30 a.m., on Tuesday, April 21, the detachment assembled with duffle bags on the dock.

Tim tells about his arrival to Helen in his letter of the 24th. The change in his mood and his feelings about the three-cent love affair is vivid.

> April 24th
>
> Dearest Helen,
>
> Well we are here. Can't tell you much. Censorship and etc. … The situation isn't so bad, but if only I would have hugged you once more …. When I get back I am going to quit this darn foolin' around and its going to be Mr. and Mrs. Trouble with me is I don't know a wonderful gal when I see her. Do I?
>
> Love, mtns of it, Tim.

Back at Camp Murray, Washington, Captain Jacoby relinquished command of the regiment to the man who would lead it through the Yukon, 54-year old Colonel Frank M.S. Johnson. Promoted to Major, Jacoby became the regiment's Executive Officer.

Second Lieutenant Mortimer Squires had been yanked, like Tim, into the 93rd as they left Camp Livingston. He remembered Colonel Johnson as "rather portly and too old." To young Lt. Squires, the new commander "looked as if he was ready to retire…"

The rest of the 93rd followed Company C into Skagway, sailing in two groups. First Lieutenant Homer Pierce headed out first with his E Company and the balance of D Company on the *USS Princess Louise*. On April 21,

Colonel Johnson and the rest of his regiment boarded the *USS Columbia*. Both groups ran into a traffic jam of crisis proportions because, even as the 93rd completed its transcontinental move and landed in tiny Skagway, Colonel Russell Lyons was rushing his brand-new 340th Engineer Regiment up from Vancouver Barracks, aiming at the same spot on the map.

Lyons' First Battalion, half of his regiment, left by train for Seattle on April 18. His Second Battalion left on April 23. Both immediately moved from train to ship and headed north.

On April 22, when the *USS Mihiel*, carrying the First Battalion of the 340th, docked in Skagway, Boyd, Tim and the other officers of the 93rd assumed she carried the rest of their regiment. Lieutenant Homer Pierce and Company E of the 93rd didn't arrive until the next day when the *USS Princess Louise* wedged itself into the little harbor.

Company E morning reports reflect the confusion of the situation. On the April 23, the men set up tents in the bivouac area on the airfield. Then, on the 24th and 25th they were moved to a public building in Skagway. On the 24th, while the men of the First Battalion of the 340th were setting up at the airfield and others were looking for a place to sleep, *USS Columbia* found parking space in the harbor and delivered Colonel Johnson and the rest of the 93rd.

The *USS Prince George*, the ship that had provided Company C's (and Tim's) luxurious ride to Skagway, had sailed back to Seattle to provide a similar ride for the Second Battalion of the 340th. She wedged into Skagway Harbor on April 25. Skagway strained at the seams, hosting two full regiments.

One of the regiments was black.

Skagway nestled at the end of Lynn Canal.
Photo courtesy of the Signal Corps, SC 76274.

...

CARL MULVIHILL WAS SIX YEARS old and lived in Skagway in 1942. He fondly recalled riding to school in Army jeeps. He also recalled that some black troops were quartered across the alley from his house and he remembers his consternation when they ignored his waves and smiles. He learned later that the men were under orders not to talk or visit with their white neighbors. His memory offers a glimpse of how the town and the army felt about black soldiers.

It had fallen to the 93rd to introduce race to the North Country equation. In an interview many years later, Sgt. Albert France, a black non-commissioned officer in Company A recalled bitterly, "One thing I remember quite well is that segregation existed even though we were a part of the United States Army." Joseph Prejean from Company A wrote in a letter, "I prefer to file my memory of Alcan on top of the 'trash can' of history." Clarence L. Thomas of Company B simply never talked about his highway experience.

The black soldiers duly noted that segregation already existed in Skagway. Native Tlingits lived in two poor neighborhoods on the outskirts of town and didn't mingle with the white folks—but that didn't help the black soldiers.

The events that shaped a black soldier's reality weren't big and dramatic. They were, rather, thousands of small, mostly unrecorded indignities and yes, brutalities that they suffered on a daily basis.

Sergeant John Bollin of F Company was 22 when he landed in Skagway. He had known segregation in Louisiana and at Camp Livingston. "We didn't exist before the war and we don't exist now in a war." It was the same in Skagway.

Private Paul Francis recalled being marched to the movie theatre in Skagway. For the first time in his life, he wasn't relegated to the balcony. That, of course, was because the black soldiers were the only patrons. The Army wasn't allowing mingling of blacks and whites. Still, for Francis, "It was a special time alone."

The Army's rules for black soldiers in the 93rd were the same in Skagway as they were in Louisiana. The Army embraced outright discrimination and made it policy. White residents of Skagway didn't know quite what to make of that. They reacted to the blacks with curiosity—cautious curiosity.

On one occasion, residents, checking the credibility of some white officer, asked a group of black soldiers if they had tails. An exasperated soldier dropped his pants and asked, "Do you see it?"

The fact that the soldiers of the 93rd were black is strangely absent from Boyd's account, from the official record and from Tim's letters. The white officers took their segregated regiment for granted. That their regiment consisted of black soldiers was almost, if not quite, a guilty secret. In 1942, Tim's friend, Mortimer Squires, was a 2nd Lieutenant in the 93rd. Interviewed about it in 2013, the 94-year-old veteran lowered his voice to a whisper. "You do know these men were black?"

In his letter of May 2, Tim routinely mentions that his "orderly" just delivered a letter from Somerset. On the face of it, in 1942, the Army didn't routinely assign orderlies to any officer, let alone junior officers. But Mortimer Squires remembered that all officers, including junior officers of the 93rd, had enlisted orderlies. An orderly cooked his officer's meals, shined his shoes, did his laundry, kept his stove burning during cold weather and made sure the officer received his mail.

Lieutenant Donald J. Schmitt, Company D, with his commanding officer, Sam Lowry shared a tent and an orderly, Charlie Knowles. Knowles prepared breakfast and his respectful "Your breakfast is served, sirs," gave each day a good start. In cold weather, Knowles had the tent warm when the officers got up.

Captain Boyd of Company C affectionately remembered his orderly, Private First Class Leroy Anding.

> Leroy's duties included taking care of all my gear, airing my bedding, washing my clothes, taking care of the officer's lantern and latrine, acting as waiter for the officers, washing our dishes, keeping our tent policed and my wash pan clean.
>
> His duties also included keeping the fire going, keeping a five gallon can of water warmed on the stove, scraping mud off my boots and anything else that needed doing. Each officer was allowed a foot locker.
>
> I jumped Leroy about my underwear, because they were getting raggedy looking. I discovered that I had worn only two pair all that time. Leroy washed them every time I change and put them back on top, in the footlocker.
>
> I don't know how I would have gotten along without Leroy. He was most helpful and loyal.
>
> (Boyd 1992, 87)

It is surprisingly difficult to determine whether other regiments provided orderlies for all of their officers. Probably not. Twichell and Ingalls, the most senior officers in the white 35th, assigned Pfc. Francis F. Beckman who was a manservant in civilian life to take care of their tent. When he took command of the black 95th, Twichell inherited the services of Corporal Little, "my driver, bodyguard, and general handyman." The 93rd, as a matter of course, assigned orderlies to every single officer—black orderlies. It's hard to escape the conclusion that their color rendered this practice acceptable—but no one complained. Even the black soldiers appear to have taken orderlies as just one more part of military life.

The soldiers weren't just victims, of course. Their ranks included sinners as well as saints. At the end of April, a private in Company C slipped away, walked up the mountain and knocked at the door of a cabin in the woods to ask for a drink of water. When the trapper's wife invited him in, he assaulted her. She vigorously resisted his attentions, but he was younger and stronger .... The soldier was examined by the Regimental Surgeon, tried by a General Court Marshall and sentenced to 40 years' confinement.

Put two thousand soldiers in one place and the crime rate will go up. Skagway's longtime marshal, Louis Rapuzzi, took to carrying a pistol after the soldiers arrived. A unique tension simmered in the black 93rd. Tim wrote about it in his May 2 letter.

> May 2, 1942
>
> Dearest Helen,
>
> The situation grows more tense here every day. The burden on the officers is really great. Even now, so soon, I have had one scare big enough to last me for 100 years.
>
> Already we have had a rape case, near murder and robbing. Boy we officers go here and there with a loaded pistol. Morale is a hard thing to handle … Love, Tim

The reference to the "burden on the officers," jars a modern ear—insensitive and totally lacking in empathy. Tim, like most of the young white officers, took racism for granted; thought little about it. The racism implicit in the Army system was a given in Tim's world. The Army had put a few young white men in charge of one thousand young black men and the young black men seethed with anger at the injustices they endured. Living among black troops made the officers nervous and fearful.

...

PERCHED PRECARIOUSLY ON A BIT of land between the jutting crags of the mountains and a harbor with one pier, the tiny city of Skagway is divided into rectangular blocks, 100 by 150 yards. Drive a car across the east-west streets and then up and down the north-south streets and you travel just 13 miles. The four longest streets run north to south and are less than a mile long.

At the beginning of 1942, Skagway was home to approximately 450 souls. The great gold rush at the end of the 19th Century created Skagway. A boomtown of mythic proportions sprouted at the boundary between the towering mountains of the coastal range and the water of the Lynn Canal. When the gold rush ended, as suddenly as it had begun, the thousands disappeared. The saloons and brothels emptied and the little city almost, but not quite, disappeared. The detritus of the boom remained—empty buildings, some of them only shacks, scattered across the little bit of flat land at the edge of the fjord. The gold rush left Skagway with a harbor, a narrow gauge railway to the Yukon interior, an enduring place in the legend of the rush—and a few people who, for a variety of individual reasons, chose to remain.

For old-timers, the sudden arrival of the Corps in 1942 brought memories of gold rush days to vivid life. Swarms of soldiers lived in pup tents in a swelling canvas city on the airfield. Their trucks, jeeps and endlessly pounding boots packed the dirt streets hard. Foot traffic on the streets of Skagway—people walking shoulder to shoulder—resembled the exits from a great stadium after a football game.

For their part, the arriving soldiers were largely disappointed. Tim told Helen, in his April 27 letter, "The place was a real ghost town if there ever was one. May have been something in '99, but not now."

As equipment and supplies began to arrive in Skagway, they quickly overwhelmed the tiny harbor. Worse, the harbor's twenty-foot tides made the process of unloading the vessels complicated. Barges had to time their arrival for high tide. As the water level fell, the port battalion troops hurried their crawler cranes in to unload them before the tide came back up. Behind the crawler cranes, trucks sped back and forth, moving cargo to higher ground.

In the end, the engineers dug a long, deep barge slip, piling the dirt and rocks they removed into a fill alongside. Barges could remain afloat in the slip and cranes could work from the fill whatever the status of the tide.

Material safely above the water line in Skagway, of course, still had a long way to go to reach the highway and its builders. The WP&YR provided the next link in the transportation chain. In April, trains crossed the pass ten to 15 times a day—a huge increase from anything the tiny railroad had ever experienced. In May, that number increased to 34 daily trains.

Eight to ten heavily loaded railroad cars, pulled by three to five locomotives and pushed by one, would roar laboriously up the three thousand-foot climb to White Pass—negotiating four percent grades and 22-degree curves. What goes up must, of course, come down. Emptied of cargo in Carcross or

Whitehorse, each train had to return to Skagway over the same difficult route. Soldiers called the WP&YR "The Wait Patiently and You Can Ride."

As the number of trains increased, the old narrow gauge track became increasingly difficult to maintain. Herb Wheeler, retired president of the WP&YR railroad, was bitter and frustrated with the Army's lack of care for his valuable railroad. The Army brought in locomotives and rolling stock, but it couldn't do anything about the track and hauled much heavier loads than the equipment and roadbed could stand.

The Army adapted, eventually learning to run smaller trains. One engine and a pusher would pull small trains up the mountain to White Pass where crews assembled them into a longer train that a single engine could pull on to Whitehorse.

Colonel Johnson had the 93rd Regiment and most of its soldiers set up on the level grassy airstrip, adjacent to, if not mingled with, the white soldiers of the 340th Regiment. The regiment's home featured mess tents with stoves up and cooking, a hospital tent open for patients and perhaps most important, latrines dug and open for business. The hospital tent offered the services of a dentist and a physician. In an interview, many years later, former Lieutenant Squires recalled that Major Jacob Altman, their physician, had served before the war as physician to the famous Rockettes at Radio City Music Hall in New York.

Regimental transportation equipment, jeeps and trucks, landed on the dock, but there was no sign of their essential heavy equipment—bulldozers. Pallets with 270 pyramidal tents and gasoline-operated heating and cooking stoves appeared, then 1,200 canvas cots, 1,200 wool comforters, 1,200 cotton comforters and twice the number of wool blankets.

To the west, the swollen Skagway River roared. Winds churned the water of the Lynn Canal into whitecaps. Nighttime brought below-zero temperatures. Fully clothed, wrapped with comforters and wool blankets and snuggled in sleeping bags, soldiers still slept shivering. No matter. Up in Whitehorse, General Hoge, the commander of the Alaska Highway Project, had no intention of leaving the 93rd settled in Skagway.

Colonel Johnson, commander of the 93rd, knew his time in Skagway was short, but with a camp set up and his still-forming regiment all in one place, seized the opportunity to attack his organization problem head on. He summoned his officers and the top three grades of NCOs to the new schoolhouse and outlined for them—for the first time—the mission of the Corps in the North Country and the specific mission of the 93rd.

Col. Johnson first explained the Japanese threat to the Aleutians and Alaska and the Army's conviction that a land supply route to Alaska would be vital to their defense. The path of the urgently needed highway covered 1,500 miles from Dawson Creek to the southeast to Delta Junction to the northwest.

Other regiments, he explained, were starting at each end, working toward the center. The 93rd would build 300 miles of road in that center—in the Yukon.

He proposed to operate the 93rd like a train. Company A would cut the initial trail. Company B would follow, doing rough grading. Company C, in turn, would do intermediate grading, and Company D would do final grading. Companies E and F would lay gravel—E Company over short distances as required and F Company over longer distances to complete the road.

When Johnson took command, his senior officers and staff were in place. He had had at least a few days to get acquainted. It would be up to him to match junior officers and NCOs to their jobs, and he knew but few of them. He proposed to begin remedying that right away. For each officer, an Army Form 66 provided a sense of his background and experience—education, previous assignments. Talking briefly to all of them, Johnson and his staff laid the groundwork for the process of assigning these men to the myriad leadership slots the regiment required. The process would go on well into the summer as talents and weaknesses revealed themselves and leaders were assigned and reassigned.

Of significance for Tim, Capt. Boyd remembers that he [Col. Johnson] was disappointed at the lack of engineering experience and the small number of officers who had actually studied engineering."

Tim checked in with Helen on Monday, April 27. Obviously pressed for time and inhibited by the censors, he reported that "they are still at their landing point [Skagway] and probably won't establish their base camp [Carcross] for another three weeks."

CHAPTER 6

REORGANIZATION, TRAGEDY AND HOGE'S PLAN

On April 5, the 35th Engineers camped at Fort Nelson. Getting there had exhausted them and beat up their equipment, but they had come to make a road. And make a road they would, through the heart of the Canadian Rockies to meet the 340th at Watson Lake—as soon as their commanders and surveyors found them a route.

While commanders in the Southern Sector struggled through April to find that route, General Hoge struggled with everything else. Nearing the end of the month, he had six regiments on the ground and one more on the way. Supply, equipment and transportation problems were just getting started. Worse, communication between Fort Nelson and Whitehorse was poor to non-existent, and the weather and Southern Air's unpredictable schedules made travelling back and forth extremely difficult.

This was a problem for General Sturdevant, back in Washington, D.C. On April 24, General Sturdevant wrote to Hoge. "It is believed that the two headquarters are too far apart for proper supervision by one officer." Sturdevant divided authority for the highway between two sectors. The Whitehorse or Northern Sector would belong to Hoge. He would command four regiments. Colonel "Patsy" O'Connor would take command of three regiments in the Southern Sector.

A new actor on the Corps' North Country stage, O'Connor was 57-years-old. A graduate of both the University of Michigan and West Point, he certainly had the intellectual qualifications. He transferred from Fort Belvoir where he had commanded training for Army Engineers; he had experience. He assumed command of the Southern Sector at Fort Saint John on May 1.

Most of the difficult problems that would plague the highway project emerged in April. They snowballed in May and the Corps' hell-bent advance into the wilderness threatened to dissolve in chaos and confusion.

In Valdez, Alaska, far to the north, spring hadn't yet sprung when the black soldiers of the 97th Engineer Regiment, unwelcome in Valdez, negotiated the primitive Richardson Highway from the harbor to a campsite 13 miles north of town under decidedly wintry conditions.

The 97th and its commander, Colonel Stephen Whipple, faced two especially daunting problems. The regiment's heavy equipment lagged somewhere behind—the troops had nothing to work with—and General Hoge expected the 97th to start building road at Slana, Alaska, a hell of a long way inland from Valdez.

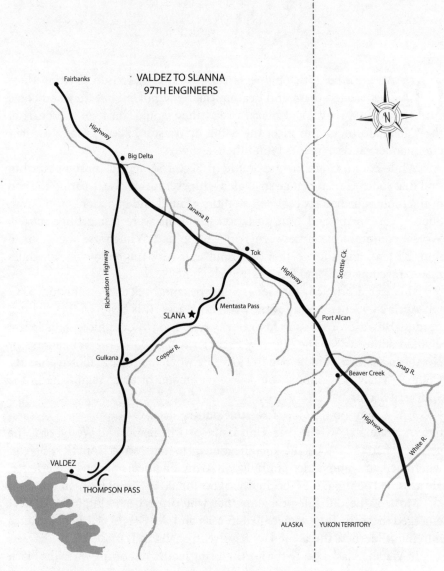

To make matters worse, the first leg of the trip would take them on the Richardson Highway over Thompson Pass, but an avalanche had plugged the road. In May, while Whipple grappled with the problem of getting his regiment to Slana, his troops labored in the pass, helping the Alaska Road Commission unplug it.

Racism, of course, raised its ugly head, complicating Whipple's efforts. The 97th answered to General Hoge who later recalled his harshness with self-satisfaction.

> I remember up there when we got that regiment …
> in at Valdez. Those Niggers just looked at all that snow-
> it was all white … and they got worried about whether
> they were going to get out of there … I told them …. The
> only way you're going to get home—back to Alabama
> or Georgia—is to work down south.
>
> Head down south and keep working.
>
> (G. W. Hoge 1974)

Worse, located in Alaska, the 97th fell in General Buckner's jurisdiction too; to Whipple's intense frustration, Buckner refused to allow the men of the 97th to unload equipment and supplies as they came into Valdez. He insisted that a "white handling detachment" perform this task. Equipment and supplies for Whipple's regiment would come in at Valdez, but trucks would deliver the material to the Regimental encampment at Gulkana. Whipple's men could take it from there to their trailhead.

Far to the southeast, in British Columbia, the soldiers of the 35th were sick. At Fort Ord, the Corps had hurriedly vaccinated everybody in the regiment to protect them from Yellow Fever. The vaccinations produced an outbreak of serum hepatitis. To compound the problem, the 35th, isolated in Fort Nelson at the end of the thawed, 250-mile winter trail from Fort Saint John, began to run low on food.

The 341st Engineers tasked to upgrade the 250-mile supply road and make it useable had arrived in Dawson Creek on April 31, but the 341st had been together less than two months. General O'Conner needed a supply road to Fort Nelson—yesterday! The Corps had brought the 341st to Canada to provide that road and for better or for worse, the under-equipped and inexperienced regiment had to move out.

Colonel Albert Lane, Commander of the 341st Engineers, decided to bypass the 12 miles of sucking mud out of Fort Saint John by moving his Second Battalion to the upper end of Charlie Lake, using the lake to transport its equipment. The 74th Pontoon Company built Lane a broad, flat raft, equipped with several 22-horsepower outboard motors riding on three pontoons. On May 14, loaded with a radio car, a small angle dozer, two officers and 15 enlisted men, the ungainly craft motored out onto the placid lake and headed north. Quite suddenly a storm came up and churned the quiet mill pond into raging surf. Two hours out, just a couple of miles from their destination, the violent combination of wind and waves capsized the raft and pitched its passengers and cargo into the icy water.

A survivor, Corporal Robert Wooldridge, described the accident in a letter to his sister from his hospital bed.

> At 8 o'clock, I was ordered by Lieut. Nelson to take my radio car down to a lake and load it on a pontoon float ... there was a Caterpillar and gas cans [on the pontoon] ... it was only eight inches out of the water supported by three flat pontoons ... we had to go against the waves all the way ... as we rounded the last bend in the lake ... the wind was the strongest and we started shipping water faster ... we put all hand pumps to use.
>
> The Major [Turvey], a Lieutenant [Hargis] and myself were inside the car keeping warm ... trouble started and the Major got out ... he ordered us to head into shore.
>
> As the pontoon under the Caterpillar started turning broadside of the waves, I could see it would sink ... we got out of the car. I just put my feet on the raft when the whole thing went over and over. The command car was tipping towards me so I jumped and swam as fast as I could to keep from being pinned under it .... The Lieutenant couldn't swim and was yelling "please save me".
>
> A mile upstream was a little cabin and the trapper eating his breakfast had seen us bobbing in the water ... so he hopped into his row boat and came after us ... he rowed so hard the oar cracked ... he made three trips and I was in the second.
>
> (Wooldridge 1942, 30-31)

Not much happened to disturb Gus Hedin's routine. On the morning of May 14, though, the tough old Swedish trapper watched the progress of the raft through the window over his breakfast table with mounting concern. When the raft disappeared, leaving "some black things bobbing around," he grabbed his small skiff and rowed to the rescue.

Notified by a racing messenger, Lane hurriedly gathered some men and found a pontoon boat. With long poles, they pushed themselves along the shore to Gus' cabin. In broken English, the old trapper explained how he rescued the five, but lost Lt. Hargis. On his second trip, two men hung on the side of his boat. One could not hang on any longer and dropped off. He said that the other men yelled out "That is our Lt. Hargis. Save him if you can. He is the best ever." Gus went out again but could not find him.

Lane and Gus rowed Gus' skiff out to where the accident had occurred and Bill Leonard, Lane's Executive Officer, came up to meet them in a single pontoon boat. "We searched the vicinity and the nearby shores, but were unable to find any more of the men," he said

Working with grappling equipment, a crew from the 341st found two more bodies. Wallace Lytle remembered, "We was out searching for the bodies. It's not a happy thought, but we just, we just went on. That's, that's the way it was."

Dynamite brought more bodies to the surface—ghastly, frozen stiff by the icy water. They recovered 11 corpses, but Lt. Hargis remained unaccounted for until June 9.

On the very day of his death in Charlie Lake, the regiment had received a telegram for Lt. Hargis from his wife. Their baby boy had choked to death and she implored her husband to come home for the funeral. It fell to Colonel Lane to tell her that her husband had drowned. "I will never forget that night."

On the May 15, unsatisfied with the regiment's progress, the new Southern Sector commander, Patsy O'Connor, bypassed Lane: he ordered a survey party to make a final survey of the completed road. The tragedy absorbed Lane's time and attention that day, and he didn't know about O'Connor's changes. When he made time to visit the construction site that afternoon, he found O'Connor's surveyors obstructing progress, and he ordered them out of the way.

Two days after the tragedy, a livid O'Connor stormed into Lane's office tent and ordered Lane to stand down and stop countermanding his orders. An equally livid Lane, still grappling with the tragedy, made clear that he thought O'Connor's actions inexcusable. The impasse didn't last long, and O'Connor ultimately apologized. In a matter of three days at mid-month, the intense pressure to build road, brought to bear on inexperienced commanders, had not only killed 12 men, but also inspired breathtaking incompetence and just plain bad behavior at the most senior level of command.

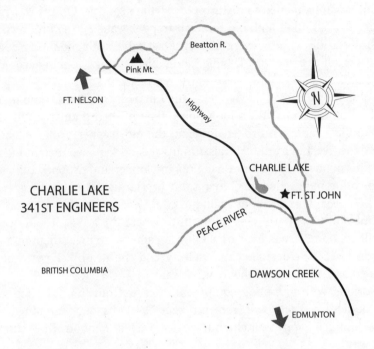

In a sad denouement, Lane, eating breakfast at "Ma" Hunter's restaurant a few days after the accident, overheard Rene Dhenin, a local surveyor and guide, talking with his friends about the drowning. Had they asked, virtually any local resident could have shown the soldiers a route around the 12 miles of mud—and around the lake.

In May, two problems—getting equipment to the North Country, and then getting the equipment and the men who would use it through a seemingly endless wilderness to the work site—emerged as potential "deal killers" everywhere along the road, threatening to end the project before it even got started. The Corps of Engineers officially allotted the road-building regiment twenty D8 diesel bulldozers, 24 D4 gas bulldozers, six pulled road graders, three patrol graders, six rooter plows and six 12-yard carrying scrapers. To support and supplement these, each regiment was assigned 93 half-ton dump trucks, a six-ton prime mover truck, seven 4-ton cargo trucks, nine 2 ½-ton cargo trucks, 25 jeeps, ten command cars, one sedan, 12 three-quarter-yard pickup trucks, a truck crane and two half-yard shovels. Smaller equipment included portable electric generating units, a half-yard concrete mixer, a 315-foot portable compressor, eight small portable compressors, six plows, 24 gas-driven saws, two portable electric welding machines and several drop pile hammers.

The 35th had brought its equipment and all but destroyed it getting into position. The other regiments were waiting for theirs and organized to get into position. Those few troops they managed to put to work attacked the road with axes, shovels, picks and wheelbarrows. Heavy equipment jammed the docks in Seattle and the jam was getting worse by the day. Hoge wouldn't be building the highway until he broke that jam, and at mid-month he flew to Seattle to see what he could do.

The demands imposed by the war had overloaded the system of ocean transport. Military commanders and civilian managers all over the world required resources—men, supplies and equipment—that had to be found or manufactured and then moved over the oceans. Demand for ships and harbor facilities vastly exceeded supply and everybody's requirement had an urgent priority.

The highway, in fact, was deemed a project, not a campaign. Other men's requirements trumped Hoge's. At Seattle's harbor, he found large-scale confusion and disorder. Luckily, he also found E.W. Elliott, a private contractor who had managed to acquire tugs and freighters and had shipped equipment north for the U. S. Public Roads Administration. Elliott agreed to do the same for Hoge. Elliott's talents proved equal to the challenge. He assembled a collection of freighters, tugs, barges, scows and several pleasure yachts and talked the Navy into assigning a gunboat named *Charleston* and several converted fishing boats to protect his ragtag convoys. By hook or by crook, he began to move Hoge's equipment.

As May progressed, a trickle of equipment began to arrive in Skagway, Carcross, and Whitehorse. Now problem two, getting the men and the equipment into the Interior, loomed. Hoge had assigned the 340th to build two hundred miles of road southeast from Nisutlin Bay over the Continental Divide to Lower Post where they would meet the 35th coming northwest. Morley Bay offered an initial base camp. Nisutlin Bay at Teslin Post offered a starting point far in the Interior, east of Carcross and southeast of Whitehorse. Hoge proposed to send the regiment via the WP&YR from Skagway to Whitehorse and from Whitehorse via the Yukon and Teslin rivers to Nisutlin Bay. He knew that ice would choke the rivers at least until the end of the month. More, given the shortage of water craft, moving the entire regiment over this route would be slow going. The regiment wouldn't be building road until the middle of June! By mid-June he would only wish it had started that soon.

So Hoge divided the 340th regiment—one battalion would go via Whitehorse and the rivers, but the other would leave the WP&YR at Carcross —and march overland to Teslin River where the men could board boats for a relatively short trip to Morley Bay.

RIVER ROUTE TO MORLEY BAY
340TH ENGINEERS

YUKON RIVER

TESLIN RIVER

Lk. Laberge

WHITEHORSE

YUKON R.

McClintock R.

Future Highway

JOHNSON'S CROSSING

TESLIN RIVER

Highway

Dead Man's Creek

Nisutlin R.

Marsh Lk.

Jakes Corner

Highway

Lone Tree Ck.

NITSUTLIN BAY

Highway

Tagish

Ten Mile Ck.

TESLIN

Hays Ck.

CARCROSS

Teslin Lk.

Regt Dump

Strawberry Ck.

MORLEY BAY

Morley R.

YUKON TERRITORY

BRITISH COLUMBIA

WATSON LAKE

Marching from Carcross to Teslin River, though, would require a road—seventy miles of road—so Hoge ordered Colonel Johnson and the 93rd to move out immediately from Skagway to Carcross to build one.

If they needed to get the men of First Battalion of the 340th to Teslin River, why not let them build their own supply road as they went? The 93rd could come behind them and improve the road to pioneer road standards. That's how the two regiments worked together later in the summer.

Racism played a part in Hoge's decision-making. The Army forbade black soldiers to fraternize with civilians or even to talk to locals. Since Skagway offered no black post exchange, saloon, or theater, they got limited use of white facilities—but only as a group, under escort.

No matter how he played it, a lot of Hoge's troops would be in Skagway for a while, and Hoge needed those to be white troops. Col. Johnson accepted the loan of two bulldozers from the 18th Engineers and aimed his regiment at WP&YR. The race problem left Skagway with Johnson's troops.

Over half the men of the 340th—five companies—stuck in Skagway, occupied themselves with community projects. Some improved the Dyea Road using shovels, picks, wheelbarrows and a few trucks. Others improved sidewalks, streets and the general appearance of Skagway. William Gilman of *The Fairbanks Daily News-Miner* described the scene: "They were swarming around like bees … tearing down eyesore buildings, sidewalks, stringing power lines." Colonel Lyons even assigned some soldiers to help the ladies of Skagway prepare and plant their spring gardens. "It'll help keep the boys in shape." Scraping at the thawing ground, soldiers planted seeds and bulbs. Young men on a great wartime adventure—helping the ladies of Skagway tend their flowers.

By May 1, the whole 93rd Regiment was on its way to Carcross. A railcar held sixty men and each train hauled four to five cars. Moving the regiment required several trains and each took seven to ten hours to make the trip. Sergeant John Bollin, Company F, remembered his trip over the pass. "To see a mountain close up, and to go up it, it's a thrill of a life time. And you get to wherever you think the top is, and there's more snow up there than you've ever seen."

The trains out of Skagway headed directly up into the coastal range, negotiating a 250-foot tunnel and two precarious bridges over the Skagway River in the first few miles. A 215-foot cantilever bridge arched high above Dead Horse Gulch—the highest railroad bridge in the world in 1942.

Dozens of slow, winding, cliff-hanging miles beyond the tunnel and bridges, six feet or more of snow covered the roadbed. Locomotives equipped with rotary plows had thrown up towering cliffs of snow along the tracks. Bennett, British Columbia—one church, a few dilapidated cabins and a depot—perched just beyond the summit at the tip of Lake Bennett. The lake, long and slender, wandered away eastward into the crags at the top of the Coastal Range, its waters, azure in summer, dark under the ice.

93rd encampment at Carcross, YT, Caribou Mountain in background.
Photo courtesy of the Timberlake collection.

After lunch at Bennett, the train clung to the side of the cliffs as it roared and rocked along the lakeshore for forty miles to where Carcross nestled into the backdrop of Caribou and Nares mountains. Rattling over a rusted swivel bridge across the watery narrows, the train groaned and clanked to a stop at the Carcross Depot.

Most of the 93rd marched to the airfield and began to set up its encampment. However, Colonel Johnson most urgently needed a route out of Carcross toward Teslin Post. The 29th Topo sent men down the old wagon road from Whitehorse (today's Klondike Highway), to help find it. They hired famous local hunting and fishing guide, Johnny Johns, to help. Famously, the road to Teslin Post wound and twisted through the woods, ostensibly to follow the easiest, fastest route. Local lore has it that the real reason had nothing to do with ease of route and everything to do with access to Johnny's favorite fishing and hunting locations.

Carcross was quaint; mostly comprised of Matthew Watson's general store, a small post office and the Caribou Hotel and Bar. The depot bordered the narrows at the end of Lake Bennett. The dry-docked sternwheeler, *Tutshi*, was the most impressive structure. A few small, wood framed houses and log cabins were scattered along the lakeshore. Tiny St. Saviour's Anglican Church stood behind the depot where mountain slopes dwarfed its steeple.

Mortimer Squires remembered Carcross as "just a spot on the road." The little town existed to serve the tourists and hunters who stayed at the Caribou Hotel, the oldest operating hotel in the territory. Its citizens eked out a meagre living serving the outsiders, working for the railroad or the hotel. Matthew Watson's store offered groceries and other staples.

Carcross townspeople knew that there was a war. They even installed black-out curtains on their windows—just in case. Even so, the sudden influx of soldiers came as a shock. At first, the soldiers simply moved through to Whitehorse, but in May, they began to pour off the train and set up camp.

Ten-year-old Millie Jones had spent her life in Carcross—Mom cooked at the hotel, Dad and Grandpa worked for the railroad. Interviewed in 2013, Millie remembered the arrival of the 93rd vividly. Bursting with excitement, she ran to the depot with her schoolmates to see the "black white men," noting that some carried musical instruments.

That the black soldiers never came into the hotel or even to the front door mystified Millie. They did come to the back door to request drinking water, and Millie's mother supplemented that refreshment with fresh baked bread.

Decades after the fact, Millie remembered, most of all, the black soldiers' music. One day, a soldier noticed a piano in the hotel and mentioned that he could play. He couldn't go in, but the piano could be rolled out and the soldier banged out a tune unlike any she'd ever heard. Seventy years after the fact, Millie's face shone at this memory from her girlhood. Asked, somewhat hesitantly, whether she remembered the name of the tune, she flashed a broad grin and, without hesitation, said, "Pistol Packing Mama." The music became a regular event. The soldiers brought their own instruments—guitars and harmonicas—to supplement the piano.

A striking feature of the photograph that hangs in the depot at Carcross today, a large group of black soldiers in front of the depot in 1942, is the number of musical instruments they carried. Mortimer Squires, who served as Regimental Motor Officer in 1942, remembered the soldiers spontaneously breaking into song—sometimes forming into quartets or breaking out a guitar or harmonica. To little Millie's delight and to some of her elders' consternation, by May 6 the 93rd Engineers had occupied Carcross.

Colonel Johnson put his men in camp a mile outside the village near the Northern Airways airstrip at the base of Caribou and Nares mountains. The canvas city featured long rows of 16-foot pyramidal tents, with enough room between the rows for a jeep to pass. Enlisted men bunked five to a tent, officers two. Similar tents, equipped with makeshift tables, chairs, boxes of files and typewriters, housed offices such as the Motor Pool, Payroll and Command.

A field hospital and dispensary sprouted among the tents at the airfield. From there, doctors and aide men would travel up and down the line inspecting camps and holding sick calls; dentists would travel with them, pulling and filling teeth.

Along with the physical needs of its soldiers, the Corps provided for their spiritual needs. Each regiment included a chaplain; if a segregated regiment included a black officer, he typically occupied the chaplain's slot. Lieutenant Finis Hugo Austin, the chaplain and the only black officer in the 93rd, ministered to the regiment. More important he mediated between the white officers and the black men—helping bridge the cultural divide that separated them. Austin, age 35, had grown up in Virginia and earned a B.A. from Virginia Seminary College and an M.A. from Oberlin College in Ohio. Black men with credentials like Austin's confused American society in general, so it's no surprise that they confused the Army. Secretary of War Stimson, expressed a typical attitude: "...leadership was not embedded in the negro race yet." It followed that allowing black officers to lead men would inevitably lead to "disaster followed by confusion."

A prominent member of Roosevelt's "Black Cabinet," Judge Hastie explained that, regardless of a black officer's education, training, or experience, the Army viewed him as "past the stage of youthful daring and initiative, short on education and self-confidence, poorly selected and inadequately trained for the job." The result was that the "...black officer had to agree with the white man and try not to make decisions on his own and to employ whatever devices would protect him from the unjust, illogical and irrational hostility of the white Army."

Only fragments of information about Chaplain Austin's service in the 93rd survive, but they suggest that he played a more assertive role than Judge Hastie might have expected. Former Lt. Squires remembered that "the whites had to be careful about what they said around the blacks and you especially had to be careful what you said around the Chaplain." Squires struggled to describe a man who had nothing in common with his fellow officers, but had even less in common with the black troops of his ministry. Austin helped the officer cadre maintain order among the black troops. At the same time, he represented the interests of his fellow blacks in officer country. Totally isolated and surely terribly lonely, Austin's courage and indomitable will are beyond question.

Military planes flew constantly in and out of the small airfield. A Quartermaster unit with one officer and 11 enlisted men moved into the tent city in May and took up duty at the depot, unloading supplies and equipment. Army trucks met 25 to thirty trains a day at the depot, hauling supplies to the companies as they moved into the woods. The trucks couldn't keep up and the quartermasters piled supplies along the tracks northwest of the depot.

Two men worked inside the depot—Bill Dickson, the telegraph operator and little Millie Jones grandfather, the station agent. Dickson monitored the constantly chattering telegraph. Grandpa unfortunately worked himself nearly to death, suffered a stroke and had to retire.

Soldiers dancing and making music at Carcross Depot.
Photo courtesy of Ted Parker, Parker Family Collection.

...

To the north, the 18th Regiment had spent May building road toward Alaska. The Public Roads Administration (PRA) men and the thousands of supporting units attached to Hoge's headquarters who poured in behind them swelled the little town of Whitehorse into a city.

Arguably the most esteemed building in town—certainly the one with the longest line out front—was the liquor store. Liquor sales were limited to one bottle of whiskey and 12 bottles of beer a month per person. Bootleg whiskey sold for $30.00 a pint and up to $110.00 for a quart.

Mortimer Squires remembered that on the whole "Whitehorse was a firetrap. The higher ups banned smoking." He remembered sleeping at the Whitehorse Inn on one of his many trips to Whitehorse: "I could smell smoke and Captain Dickson on the top bunk said, 'that's me.' He never stopped smoking."

The 93rd's occupation of Carcross connected two young second lieutenants—Mortimer Squires and Tim Timberlake. Many years later, Squires vividly remembered being appointed Regimental Transportation Officer and being intimidated by the difficulty of moving the regiment's heavy equipment from Skagway into the field. He asked Colonel Johnson for help. "They sent me Timber," said Squires.

On Wednesday May 8, Tim reported to Helen.

> May 8, 1942
>
> Dearest Helen,
>
> Well honey, it looks like you are going to have a 1st Lt. in your clan. I have been recommended and it has gone thru.
>
> We have been busy as a bee here. Moving inland and starting on our road construction. I am Assistant Operations Officer that is, I have to actually get out on the job and boss.
>
> We plan our own route, do our own surveying. It sure is some country.
>
> This is the greatest country I have ever seen. These mtns here, have the Rockies beat all to heck and the northern lites shine every nite. Lots of wild animals. We ate moose meat and talk about mink. We are only a mile from a big mink farm.
>
> We haven't received all of our equipment, yet. Some is still on its way here. Lots of things we need we haven't received.
>
> The situation here has changed considerably since moving the men further inland. We are now at Carcross ... Since we left Skagway we are sending parties further inland each day...
>
> Love, Tim.

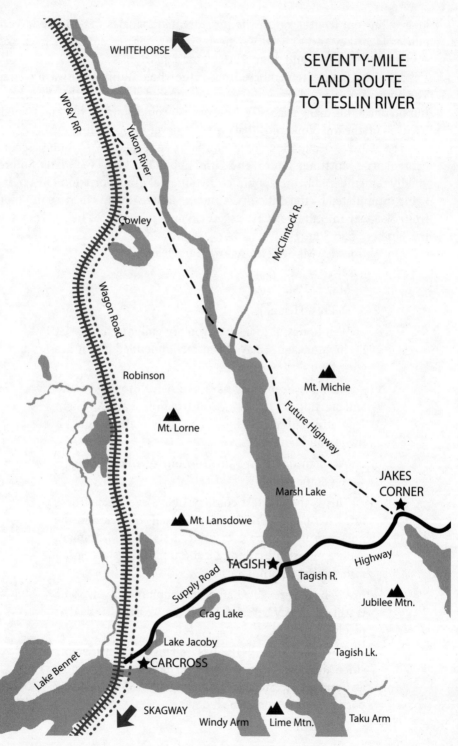

WHITEHORSE

SEVENTY-MILE
LAND ROUTE
TO TESLIN RIVER

WP&Y RR

Yukon River

Cowley

Wagon Road

McClintock R.

Robinson

Mt. Michie

Mt. Lorne

Future Highway

Marsh Lake

JAKES
CORNER

Mt. Lansdowe

Highway

TAGISH

Tagish R.

Supply Road

Jubilee Mtn.

Crag Lake

Lake Jacoby

Tagish Lk.

CARCROSS

Lake Bennet

SKAGWAY

Windy Arm

Lime Mtn.

Taku Arm

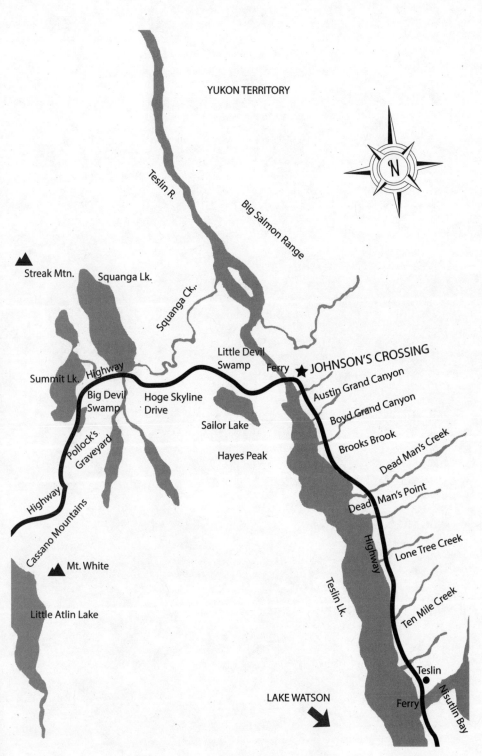

YUKON TERRITORY

Streak Mtn.

Squanga Lk.

Teslin R.

Big Salmon Range

Squanga Ck.

Little Devil Swamp

Ferry ★ JOHNSON'S CROSSING

Austin Grand Canyon

Summit Lk. Highway

Big Devil Swamp

Hoge Skyline Drive

Boyd Grand Canyon

Sailor Lake

Brooks Brook

Dead Man's Creek

Hayes Peak

Pollock's Graveyard

Dead Man's Point

Highway

Cassano Mountains

Lone Tree Creek

Mt. White

Teslin Lk.

Highway

Ten Mile Creek

Little Atlin Lake

Teslin

LAKE WATSON

Ferry

Nisutlin Bay

CHAPTER 7

INTO THE WOODS

On the wintry early morning of May 6, companies A, B and C of the 93rd began moving their men out of Carcross toward Crag Lake, about eight miles away. The 93rd's heavy equipment had yet to arrive, so the men lugged hand tools—saws, axes, picks, shovels, rakes. They also borrowed two D8 Caterpillar bulldozers.

Officially, the Corps doubted the ability of black soldiers to operate complicated earth moving equipment. *The Corps of Engineers History of Troops and Equipment* stated flatly, "Negroes lacked the sense of responsibility necessary for the care of equipment ... and were slow to absorb instruction." The Army expected little but got a lot.

Events on that frigid morning outside of Carcross serve as a case in point. The Corps needed a road in a hurry. The 93rd had two bulldozers with which to build it. The men available to run them were black.

In fact, many of the soldiers had worked on the levies of Mississippi and Louisiana long before they enlisted in the Army. Many more had worked on roads, railroads, bridges and culverts at camps Livingston and Claiborne, operating gas-powered Allis Chalmer dozers. They transitioned easily to the larger diesel D8.

That May morning, a thoroughly competent black operator shifted into the lowest of six forward gears, raised his blade high and moved his mechanical goliath to the first large tree, nestling the blade high against the trunk. Opening the throttle and letting the clutch in, he looked up, watching for falling branches. The D8's engine roared and the steel tracks ground heavily into virgin Yukon soil. The tree resisted, bent, finally cracked and then fell, crashing to the ground.

The 93rd Engineer Regiment was building road. The dozers cleared a right of way along the single-lane, barely passable Tagish wagon road. The bulldozers laid down trees, pushed dirt and brush to the side. Other troops with hand tools scrambled over the right of way, shoveling dirt, raking the right of way clear, sawing up logs.

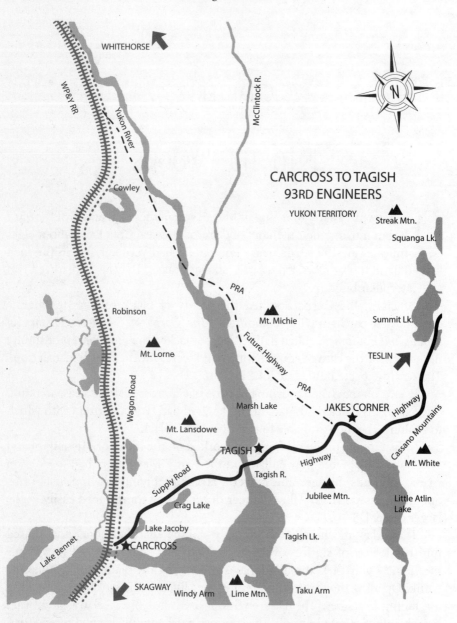

CARCROSS TO TAGISH
93RD ENGINEERS

Anthony Mouton, a twenty-year-old Louisiana native who served with H&S Company, had grown up listening to plantation workers sing as they plowed and planted the earth. Now, in 1942, he heard his fellows sing the same way on the road—gospel hymns and jazz tunes—their chunking picks and hammering axes establishing the rhythm.

"We eventually had to move out of that base camp [Carcross] and go to our stretch of the highway that we were supposed to work on," Sergeant John Bollin remembered. "And to see nothing but trees, trees and more trees, and then be told that you're going to put a road through that was a big deal for us."

In every company in the Army, first sergeants prepared morning reports—a day-by-day record of activity in the company. Most morning reports for 1942 have vanished, but some remain in the Army's archives. First sergeants weren't writers. Their morning reports were terse and fragmentary descriptions of companies working on the road.

Johnson had a confused welter of men and equipment piled onto the first few miles of road from Carcross toward Tagish, 23 miles away. Companies A, B, and C were at Crag Lake. Back near Carcross, the rest of his men were working very hard and accomplishing relatively little.

The 93rd brought race issues to Carcross, as it had to Skagway. Worried Royal Canadian Mounted Police officers queried Colonel Johnson about his plans. He assured them that only about 130 soldiers and a few officers would stay in Carcross. Not only did Johnson and his men confront a morass of operational confusion and nervous locals in May, they also discovered the unpleasant realities of the Far North.

Some problems yielded to simple solutions. Arriving at Crag Lake, Captain Boyd ordered his mess sergeant to cut a hole through the ice to access water. An hour later, the kitchen supervisor presented his commander with a hole through six feet of ice that ended in frozen mud. In the end, they chipped the ice and put it into mess cans to melt.

Muskeg—a soft, swampy mixture of dirt and decaying vegetation—froze to solid ground in winter but turned to bog from spring to fall. A thick layer of vegetation covered and insulated the muskeg, so while normal spring thaw turned it to mud a few feet down, the quagmire had a frozen bottom. When a company first ventured out on solid ground to clear away insulating vegetation, its trucks and equipment moved without difficulty. Then, as warming days passed, that same equipment would sink inexorably into muck, seeking an endlessly retreating bottom.

The engineers called their solution "corduroy." They cut trees into thirty-foot logs and laid them perpendicular to the path of the road, covering them with gravel and dirt to create a fairly smooth roadbed. If the corduroy sank too deep, they installed another layer—and another. The fill in some places reached depths of six or more feet.

The Far North also offered mosquitoes. From mid-April to mid-May, warming temperatures and thawing ground brought them out of the ground in endless swarms. They came early in 1942. The nasty little creatures liked the soldiers' food as much as they liked the soldiers. They could cover the contents of a mess kit in seconds. They speckled pancake batter like some strange seasoning. Rumor had mosquito netting on the way—but it wasn't there in May. Mosquitoes flew into your mouth when you spoke. No matter how tightly you zippered and tucked your sleeping bag, they found a way in— and bit and bit and bit. Repellants worked, but had to be applied every half hour. Men broke out in hives and experienced "moments of mild hysteria." They just wanted to lie down on their cots and cry. Sergeant Albert France of Company A remembered May in the North Country this way: "The mosquitoes droned like airplanes and the muskeg swallowed tractors."

The six line companies of the regiment—each with about two hundred men—functioned as independent units in the field. To organize and coordinate their road-building efforts, the Corps grouped them into two battalions. Company commanders reported to battalion commanders who, in turn, reported to Colonel Johnson. The Headquarters and the H&S Company, whose commander reported directly to Colonel Johnson, provided an array of support—including in the Motor Pool, where Tim Timberlake would settle in to work. In early May, with the line companies beginning to move out into the field, Tim and the H&S remained in Carcross, getting organized.

At mid-month, Tim checked in with Helen. The Army's rules about what he could say clearly changed significantly, and he gave Helen much more information than his previous, self-censored letters.

> May 15, 1942
>
> Dearest Helen,
>
> Got three letters from little Buzz today and say it only takes four to five days for an air mail to get here, so that isn't so bad...
>
> Last Saturday nite I went hunting ... We left the camp about midnight...
>
> We had a swell time, climbed up one of the mtns and I got some swell pictures, didn't see any bear but plenty of tracks and stuff...
>
> ...Our present location is about 65 miles east of Skagway, Alaska, the name of the place is Carcross, which is in Yukon Territory. Skagway is right on the coast of Alaska where that long piece comes down into British Columbia.
>
> Gosh do we have a job here the government or rather Uncle Sam is changing the method of property responsibility and accountability and we are busy

setting up our books under the new system. We have been working every nite on the dam thing and still we need more work to be done.

He added to the letter on May 16:

> ...I was just figuring it up and I believe I am some 4450 miles from Washington...
>
> There is a rumor that we may return in the latter part of November, we are not equipped to stay here all winter when the temperature drops to about 65 below as an average, that honey is dam cold.
>
> Sure be glad when that 1st Lt. comes thru I'll be getting' it in the last week this month or the first one in June....
>
> I don't know whether I would plan much yet for awhile for you and me for the situation here seems all mixed up. First they say we are going to return after this job is done and then they say we are sure to get into combat, which I think isn't all a pipe dream, to tell the truth I think we will never see the US for one hell of a long time, they are building RR's in other countries and such as that and that will keep us busy. Nite and love, Turner.

In the field, company bivouacs moved every three to four days, following the work., Tents, designed to be pegged were often just tied to trees, scattered informally. Army field manual descriptions—tents clustered just so, pyramids arranged in neat lines—rarely applied, but latrines were an exception. Troops located and prepared these critical facilities—12 feet long, 18 inches wide and six feet deep—with care. Officers were not forced to share their latrine with enlisted men—and whites weren't forced to share with blacks. For the 93rd, this amounted to double coverage.

Company bivouacs didn't always offer showers—but they sometimes did. Lieutenant Mortimer Squires of H&S Company described the field showers: "They had built a shower for our people and the officers. It had three heads. It was very cold water." Asked how often they used the facility, he responded, "When we had to."

The H&S Company travelled with generators. Line company generators powered equipment, not bivouacs. Company bivouacs made do with lanterns.

Boyd placed one in the orderly room, five to the mess tent, one to the supply tent and one to the officer's tent. This left two for spares. The lanterns used cloth mantles—always in short supply. Captain Boyd's father shipped him about a dozen every month.

A company kitchen came equipped with four white gas ranges and a 55-gallon galvanized dishwasher. The dishwasher used a submersible heater which, given enough time, heated the water enough to clean a mess kit.

Joseph Prejean, who worked in A Company's kitchen, remembered having to start a white gas burner by throwing gas on it. The mess section supplied the company with water from streams and lakes, purifying it with chlorine tablets. Squires remembered containers labeled "White" and "Black."

From the company bivouac, the company mess followed road builders with portable kitchens on log sleds towed by a bulldozer. Few of the men remembered their food with pleasure. Occasionally, though, opportunity knocked. When his orderly spotted a grazing moose near the bivouac one morning, Captain Boyd shot it. Tech Sgt. Willie D. Davis had been a butcher in civilian life and he rendered 1,200 pounds of moose into steaks that fed the company for a long time.

Soldiers get paid, even in the wilderness, and this responsibility fell on the Company Commander. Privates received $21.00 to $28.00 per month, Private First Class $32.00 per month, corporals $42.00, sergeants $56.00, staff sergeants $76.00, tech sergeants $110.00 and a first sergeant $150.00 per month. The company commander picked up and distributed cash pay for the whole company.

Trucks carried each soldier's sleeping bag and two full barracks bags from one bivouac to the next. Many soldiers also had "private boxes." Besides clothes and toiletries and incidentals, men kept family photos, letters and other personal treasures. In their tents, they slept in sleeping bags on canvas cots without mattresses or pillows. Each tent had a stove—essential in cold weather. Since the heat thawed the floor into slimy mud, soldiers festooned their tents with strings, ropes and rigging from which hung clothing, rifles, photos—anything the soldier did not want on the ground. Less valuable gear they jammed under the cots. Boots got the most precious storage spot in the tent—tucked into sleeping bags to keep warm.

Initially, the Army supplied kerosene heaters, but a chronic shortage of kerosene inspired creativity. Captain Boyd's men threw away the base of their heater, but kept the top with its fittings for stovepipe. From an empty 55-gallon fuel drum, they fashioned a replacement for the bottom half and burned wood in the converted drum. This solution to the fuel problem quickly spread throughout the regiment. Boyd created a permanent three-man firewood detail, rotating the duty weekly between his platoons. The detail wielded crosscut saws, axes and machetes to make stove wood out of the detritus of the road, stacking it next to or inside each tent. Incidentally, the firewood detail supplied other services to the bivouac—the soldiers felt free to air their stale bedding, knowing that, in the event of rain, the firewood detail would stuff it back into their tents.

To vent smoke from the stoves, the soldiers penetrated the canvas with stovepipe, installing a spark arrester on top of the chimney. Live coals, though, escaped the arrester all too easily, smoldering on flammable canvas and eventually igniting it. Company B lost over half its tents in one spark fire. The most important guard duty on the highway was the fire guard mounted at every bivouac.

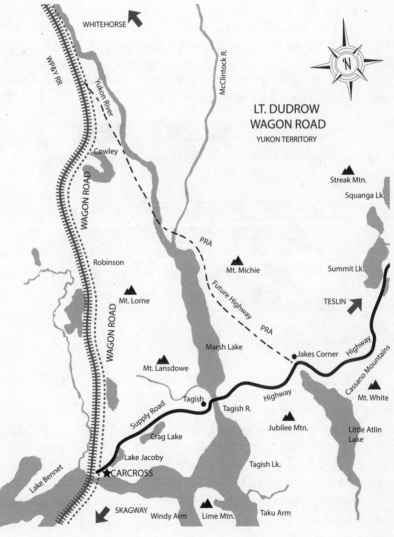

As the lead companies of the 93rd approached the Tagish River, the old fifty-mile wagon road that tenuously connected Carcross to headquarters in Whitehorse, suddenly became important. General Hoge would dispatch the 73rd Pontoon Company to bridge the river; the only route for their equipment would be down that road to Carcross and then out on the new road to the river. General Hoge ordered Johnson to get the old wagon road repaired and passable.

Working with hand tools, hauling their supplies and equipment in a 1 ½ ton truck, Lt. Walter Dudrow and his Third Platoon set out from Carcross toward Whitehorse. Within a mile, they came to a tiny desert—642 acres. Intermittent gusts of wind sent small cyclones of sand skittering across the surface. Beyond the desert lay the Stikine Bill Robinson's Roadhouse. In 1942, one-time miner and current postmaster Charlie McConnell and his wife lived there. To deliver the mail, Charlie had long since swapped his dog sled for a 1924 Ford touring car. Dudrow remembered an "alert, active old gentleman."

The platoon's cook, a cheerful Cajun named Willie Lavalais who spoke broken English, turned out excellent pies and biscuits. Dudrow called his men by their rank—except for Lavalais, who became "Willie."

Bulldozer blazing a trail out of Carcross, YT.
Photo courtesy of the Timberlake Collection

...

ON MAY 16, COMPANY A, in the lead, bivouacked at Crag Lake and worked east from there. Vehicles chewed into the mud and the mud fought back. Cursing, muddy soldiers scrambled to winch the trucks and dozers free only to have to do it again in a few minutes. They made progress. On the 25th, Company A's bivouac moved four and a half miles closer to Tagish.

The company commander had at his side the single, most valuable, asset a junior officer can have—a thoroughly experienced and competent first sergeant whose army service went back to World War I. Ashel Honesty knew exactly how to do the job and brooked no nonsense. A callow but confident young lieutenant might walk by the grizzled black sergeant and into the commander's office tent without an appointment. He did so at his peril. He wouldn't do it twice.

Company B labored right behind Company A at Crag Lake, working past a forest fire. A common menace, the dense growth made it easy for fire to climb to the dry tree tops, moving quickly and almost impossible to extinguish.

A day behind Company B, Company C laid corduroy road and built culverts while the 73rd Pontoon Company struggled to move its pontoon ferry and associated equipment over the rough road. It reached Tagish with the lead companies and immediately set about floating the ferry that would serve for crossing the 1,275-foot wide Tagish River until it could be bridged. The craft—a fourteen by forty foot platform, securely fastened to the top of five four-by-24-foot pontoons, equipped with three twenty-horsepower outboard motors—could carry one D8, or two large trucks, or four weapons carriers.

Bulldozer boards Tagish River scow.
Photo courtesy of the Signal Corps.

On May 28, Company A reached Tagish, 22.7 miles from Carcross, at 7:00 p.m. It spent the 29th and 30th crossing the river. Company C crossed on the 30th. Company B crossed on June 1.

From Tagish, the road would continue—ten miles east to Jakes Corner, ten more miles to Big Devil's Swamp and Summit Lake, six more miles to Johns River, six more to Squanga Lake and finally eight miles to the Teslin River—a total of forty or more tough miles. The Engineers would build a one-lane "truck trail," just sufficient to allow the 340th to pass through. They could improve it later.

On Sunday, May 17, Tim Timberlake got a day off.

> May 17, 1942
>
> Dearest Helen,
>
> It is Sunday and today we went up to the Carcross Hotel and ate ham and eggs, even had bread and butter and honey let me tell you it was swell. [Millie Jones' mother's food.]
>
> This afternoon we also had a thrill, there happens to be a branch of the Canadian Airmail Service and they have one airplane or crate that flies mail up to the Yukon towns and into British Columbia, well for five bucks a piece, four of the officers, including myself, took a little ride, for about 20 minutes over these mountains.
>
> These mountains are sure something from here and the lakes are really the berries, these glacier mountains and ice are sure something, canyons way down for at least a mile, and then a peak way up for at least 5,000 feet, we were flying right up one of these canyons one with mountains on both sides.
>
> The darn ship isn't any too hot and the landing field is about as big as our back yard, when the lakes open up [thaw] they put pontoons on the ship and land on them in the lake. The ship was not equipped with chutes or nothing and it was plenty bumpy and hard on your ears.

In the next paragraph his thoughts took an amazing turn. Clearly the three-cent love affair had progressed to a whole new level.

> Well honey it won't be long 'till I am going to be making almost as twice as much money as I am making now …. If we were married I would get $18.00 more for you and $60 for board …. Looks like we could be well on our way to a start with that setup…

He wrote several paragraphs, detailing a plan for their future … and then got cold feet.

> I really don't know, its all my dam foolishness

anyway. I never figured that we would get like this and I kept on playing around figuring hell nothing will ever happen, something will turn up and the first thing you know Helen will be on her way to someone else.

I knew darn good and well that you did love me and was willing to take me for the better or the worst, but darn it I didn't see to want to do anything about it for some reason I don't know …. It's just one hell of a mess, maybe the best thing for you to do is to look where the grass is greener and act as if I never existed. I don't know, why hell at this rate I'll be 29 or more years old before I can start living and your best years are behind you then…

Think it over Helen and be real frank with yourself and see just how you do add two and two … Love Turner

It's impossible to know what happened during the six days between May 17 and May 23, but Helen had clearly been visiting Tim's mom, who had written to her son. Tim struggled to be responsible and adult in the face of his longing for the dream girl back in Maryland. His mother, the strongest adult influence in his life, would have been the one person in the world who could have convinced him to go for the dream.

May 23, 1942

Dearest Helen,

Got two letters from 505. Mother gave me a hint for a swell idea and by golly I am going to do it, so guess?? … Mother surely enjoys having you up, and the way the letters sound you are having a wonderful time.

…Gosh honey I sure hope you don't get tired of waitin', it may be a long time but please wait and I'll do my damdest not to make you sorry. If only this mess gets over with, so we can be together and do things together, have a home and a family.

Our possible danger of any invasion seems to increase as we hear war news.

But I think we are safe. Bye, Love Tim

...

As THE 93RD DISPERSED INTO the wilderness, communications became increasingly difficult. The Army had attached the 843rd Signal Corps Battalion to the Alaska Highway project, and a portion of that battalion came up to Skagway on May 18 to join the 93rd. Corporal Bob Rapuzzi, communications specialist in the 843rd, had grown up in Skagway. He and his partner, Tom Whitsett, followed the engineers in a large Dodge command car, equipped with a radio and whip antennae. Radio signals reached only about 25 miles—and that depended heavily on the vagaries of weather and terrain, so they kept the Dodge moving through the mud and ruts and around brush and fallen trees. Rapuzzi and Whitsett ate in the company mess, but they carried their own tents and equipment. Given that they were white, it is significant that they chose to sleep in tents next to their vehicles instead of in the company personnel tents.

With half of his regiment across the river at Tagish and moving east, Johnson prepared to move his H&S Company to join them. On May 29, three officers of the H&S Company left Carcross with 67 enlisted men to scout a bivouac at Tagish for the remainder of the company.

Company D remained at Jacoby Lake through May. Company E was strung out over the seven miles between Carcross and Crag Lake. Company F worked in the same vicinity. Colonel Johnson, waiting for his three lead companies to get out of the way, had a hard time finding gainful employment for the other three.

At the end of May, the 93rd, had completed the first two miles of the road to Tagish and was working on the remaining twenty miles. Captain Cassano, Johnny Johns and the 29th Topo Engineers had laid out the road all the way to the Teslin River.

Colonel Lyons and his 340th waited impatiently in Skagway. Its heavy equipment, when it arrived, was to travel to Whitehorse on the WP&YR, to be transferred to boats and then carried via the Yukon River, the Teslin River and Teslin Lake to Morley Bay—just a few miles from Nisutlin Bay. As soon as the ice cleared from that route, Lyons planned to deploy Company F of the 340th along with it, positioning platoons at Skagway, Whitehorse, and Morley Bay to load and unload the equipment. At the same time, as space became available on the trains to Whitehorse and the boats to Morley Bay, he would cram in the platoons of his Company D. He needed to get at least one company started on his road. The rest of his regiment would continue in Skagway, waiting while the 93rd built them an overland path to the Teslin River.

The ice cleared from the water route on May 22 and Companies D and F moved out. Leonard Cox of Company D remembered his 240-mile trip from Whitehorse to Morley Bay on the *SS Nisutlin*—five days hanging out on the boat, enjoying the ride and the scenery. "The crew," Cox remembered, "treated us like kings." The boat's boilers generated steam from wood so they made repeated stops at, Native-run wood camps along the way.

The swollen Teslin River fought the boat's progress upstream. When the way narrowed to as little as one hundred feet, movement against the surging current became impossible. When that occurred, the boat would maneuver close to the bank, then crewmen would jump to shore, pull a rope or cable up and tie it to a tree. An on-board winch would drag the boat a few feet and then the crew would drop anchor. A man on shore would tie a rope to a tree just a little further along and the winch would move them a few more feet. The crew repeated this process endlessly, moving the boat upstream a few feet at a time until the river widened. Their passengers had it "pretty soft." They relaxed, played cards, and enjoyed meals served on tables covered with white tablecloths.

The steamboat reached Morley Bay in the early morning of May 31. On June 1, the troops unloaded the boat and the barges it had towed, and the boat returned to Whitehorse. As of that day, the 340th had yet to build even a mile of road.

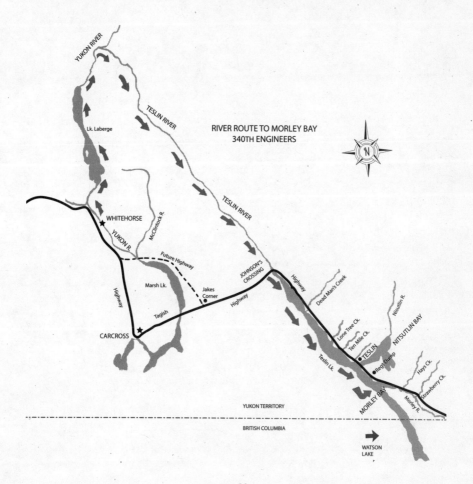

CHAPTER 8

THE JAPANESE ATTACK

For the engineers of the 93rd and 340th, working frantically to get the 340th to the Teslin River, May, rolled into June. Day by day they soldiered on, forcing their road through the wilderness. They didn't forget that they soldiered in an Army at war.

In Alaska, the Yukon Territory, and British Columbia, soldiers shared scraps of information, gleaned from letters or an occasional out-of-date newspaper or magazine and talked incessantly about the war. Hard news came slowly. Rumors circulated at the speed of light. Tim ended his letter of May 23, "Our possible danger of any invasion seems to increase as we hear war news. But I think we're safe."

So far, the Japanese had succeeded beyond even their own expectations. Their planners grappled with the problem of regrouping and exploiting their advantages. In early June, they targeted the island of Midway, two thousand miles south of the Aleutians. Their strategy for the conquest of Midway involved the Aleutians and the American air and naval base at Dutch Harbor.

In late May, the Japanese dispatched two naval forces to assault the Aleutians. First, a carrier group centered on the brand-new carrier *Junyo* and the somewhat older *Ryujo* would attack Dutch Harbor. With two heavy cruisers, three destroyers and an oiler surrounding them, they steamed through the night of June 2 in cold rain and icy fog, hiding from American spotter planes at the edge of a storm—less than 170 miles from their target. Second, three cruisers, nine destroyers, three transports and a screen of submarines steamed somewhere west of the Carrier Group, carrying the 2,500 Japanese soldiers who proposed to occupy Adak, Kiska, and Attu.

The success of the Japanese plans at Midway and in the Aleutians ultimately depended on surprising the Americans, but that didn't happen. On May 15, a team of crypto analysts at Pearl Harbor had broken the Japanese naval code and American intelligence knew at least the outline of the Japanese plan.

Admiral Nimitz, overall naval commander in the Pacific, convinced that the decisive action would be at Midway, committed most of his resources there. To defend the Aleutians, he dispatched Rear Admiral Robert Theobald north with a token force of nine ships and instructions that amounted to "do your best with what you can scare up." American folklore offers a hoary bit of advice about the wisdom of bringing a knife to a gunfight that is applicable to Theobald's mission. The Japanese were bringing carriers to the fight; Theobald was not.

Theobald, tasked with defending the 1,100-mile long Aleutian Chain, deployed his few ships in an arc facing south and west toward the oncoming Japanese force. He knew the futility of trying to cover so many miles with so few vessels, and he knew the Japanese would almost certainly slip through.

On May 28, Theobald forced Brigadier General William O. Butler to move his precious 11th Air Force from Elmendorf Field in Anchorage to two unfinished airfields closer to the coming action. Fort Randall lay 267 miles east of Dutch Harbor on the Alaska Peninsula at Cold Bay. Fort Glenn was on the island of Umnak, 90 miles west of Dutch Harbor.

At 2:43 on the morning of June 3, the two Japanese carriers steamed out of the storm into the clear and launched thirty-five warplanes—bombers and fighters. The planes from the *Junyo* lost their bearings, couldn't find Dutch Harbor, and had to turn back. The fifteen planes from the *Ryujo* made it through.

At 5:40 a.m. the seaplane tender *USS Gillis,* moored at Dutch Harbor, picked up the attacking planes on radar and signaled the base. Air raid sirens howled. The six ships in the harbor started their engines and went to battle stations. The base telegraphed an alert to Cold Bay and Umnak. The pilots on Umnak didn't receive the message, but P-40s (fighters) instantly scrambled from Cold Bay. Unfortunately, they scrambled 267 miles from Dutch Harbor and would take too long to get there.

Ten minutes later, the fifteen planes from the *Ryujo* caught a break. The eye of the storm passed over Dutch Harbor, clearing the rain and fog just as they descended into the attack. They had a clear view of the base and harbor, which they hammered for the next twenty minutes.

American batteries saw them as well and launched puffs of flak into the sky. Machine gun tracers arced up from the ground, seeking the range. Two lumbering PBYs, seaplanes moored in the harbor, managed to get into the air. The first went down immediately, but the second managed to down the only Japanese casualty of the raid before escaping up a mountain draw where the zeros couldn't follow. In the end, the Japanese bombed and strafed with relative impunity. Flak and machine gun bullets found only empty sky, and the racing P-40s from Cold Bay came late to the fight. When they finished dropping their payloads into the churning smoke and flame boiling up from the ground, the Japanese pilots climbed to form up and fly away, convinced that they had heavily damaged their target.

Luck had been with the Americans on the ground. Knowing little about the layout of the base, the Japanese pilots had engaged targets at random; and as smoke and flame obscured their view, the targets became more random. They killed fifty Americans—most of them in a smashed Army barracks. They destroyed a tank farm and its fuel dump, but, as the fires died down and the smoke cleared, vital facilities emerged largely unscathed. Getting from the carriers to their target and back, the Japanese had struggled with the awful Aleutian weather—even lost planes and taken casualties—but the American defenders had caused them few problems.

To fight them, the Americans had to find them. The PBYs couldn't fight effectively, but they could search and see—guide warplanes to their targets. Unfortunately, most of the PBYs dispatched initially went north over the Bering Sea. Only two searched in the right direction. The first found *Junyo's* combat air patrol instead of *Junyo*; the Japanese fighters shot it down. The second spotted the Japanese carriers, but atmospherics garbled the message the search team sent; Japanese fighters shot it down too.

The 11th Air Corps spent June 4 in a frustrating, uncoordinated effort to find and sink the Japanese carriers. It found them several times, but couldn't mount a coordinated attack. Luckily, the carrier force spent its day in equal confusion while its commander, Admiral Kakuji Kakuta, tried to decide what to do next. Intending to make a "softening up" attack on the proposed landing site at Adak, he initially steamed west—directly away from Dutch Harbor. Then, realizing that the weather would make an attack on that island impossible, at mid-morning he changed his mind, reversed course and headed back.

Finally, back in range, just before 3:00 p.m. on June 4, Kakuta launched 17 bombers and 15 fighters for another assault on Dutch Harbor. An hour later the combined force descended on its target.

The Americans had cleared the harbor except for the old ship *Northwestern*, deliberately beached and used as a civilian barracks. The bombers pounded the old ship and attacking planes found more targets on shore. Smoke roiled and flames darted, a steel building collapsed, one wing of the base hospital came down. When four fuel storage tanks went up, personnel at Umnak Island, less than a hundred miles away, heard the explosion.

This time the Japanese, too, suffered casualties. Fighters from Umnak shot down two dive bombers. The bulk of the Japanese force, though, once again escaped into the fog.

Even as the opposing forces in the Aleutians battled the weather and their own confusion on June 4, events at Midway, far to the south, took a dramatic turn. The American Navy destroyed four of Commander and Chief Isoroku Yamamoto's carriers that day. In shock, his grand strategy in shambles, the commander and chief of the combined Japanese fleet struggled. At first blush, the assault on the Aleutians looked like a waste of time. However, Japan still needed to defend its northern boundaries, and an Aleutian victory might help counter the effects of the Midway disaster on the Japanese public. The Aleutian operation would go on.

On the water in the North Pacific, Admiral Boshiro Hosogaya, commander of the invasion fleet forces, knowing that the American Air Force had planes on Umnak, in range of Adak, cancelled his plans for a landing there and steamed west to Kiska and Attu. Two days later, June 7, the enemy occupied Kiska and the following day troops invaded Attu. An estimated 2,500 enemy troops had taken the western Aleutians. They would remain until a bloody U.S. invasion dislodged them in May 1943.

At Dutch Harbor, taking stock on June 5, American commanders judged the battle of Dutch Harbor a draw—good enough. Four more days would pass before they learned that the Japanese had occupied Kiska and Attu—American soil. Clearly, Dutch Harbor and the Aleutians remained at risk, and they needed to make changes. On June 21, the Navy made an official statement to the press, "The enemy has occupied the undefended islands of Attu and Kiska..."

The attack, followed by occupation, galvanized public opinion in the United States. Millions of frightened and angry Americans had known nothing of the Aleutians or a possible threat to America's interests there—until an actual threat materialized, seemingly out of nowhere. The need for a land route to Alaska vaulted onto front pages and into newsreels, and the spotlight of public attention suddenly came to focus on the Alcan Highway Project.

On June 5, *The Salt Lake Tribune* headlined, "Coast Cities Redouble Vigilance Against Jap 'Sneak' Attack." The story reported, more or less accurately, dramatic responses up and down the west coast of the United States and Canada. The Canadian government had silenced radio stations and placed defense forces on high alert in British Columbia and the Yukon. American authorities had ordered radio silence along the entire Pacific Coast from Canada to Mexico, and placed all Pacific Coast civilian defense agencies on high alert. Civilians should use blackout curtains or, at least, window shades after dark along the western coast. The Army and Navy, the *Tribune* proposed, should expand martial rule in California's vital coastal military zones.

In a Washington, D.C. press conference, Secretary of War Henry Stimson declared, "I warn you this is not the only and last raid we may expect." A reporter asked him whether his warning applied to the Continental United States as well as to outlying possessions. He declined to place geographical boundaries on it.

On June 4, the *Santa Cruz Sentinel reported from Philadelphia:*

> An unidentified man, his face red with rage, stomped six blocks down dignified Chestnut Street last night, buying newspapers headlining the Japanese attack on Dutch Harbor and tearing them into shreds. Police said he was within his rights.

On June 20, a Japanese submarine torpedoed a Canadian lumber ship off the Washington state coast near Cape Flattery and shelled a telegraph station on Vancouver Island. On the 21st, it bombarded the naval base at Astoria, Oregon, and three days after that it shelled Fort Stevens, Oregon. If the fear and anger generated by Pearl Harbor six months earlier had abated, events in June brought it roaring back.

Finally, as word of the assault reached the frightened soldiers on the highway—in fragmented, incoherent and often inaccurate bits—they suddenly felt a whole lot closer to the action. This occurred just as decisions made far above them in the chain of command increased their isolation.

When the news of the Dutch Harbor attack reached the first battalion of the 340th Engineers, still in Skagway, it occurred to most that the Japanese might target them next. It even occurred to some that they might have to protect or even evacuate civilians. They had rifles, but no ammunition. A young lieutenant remembered that the ammo was being unloaded at the docks of Skagway, but he and several others couldn't find where it was stored. Luckily, the Japanese had no designs on Skagway.

In the 18th Regiment, working north of Whitehorse, frightened troops pictured the Japanese marching inland down the Yukon valleys and into the forests. The engineers had rifle butts and muzzles protected by arctic socks, wrapped in mattress covers. They hadn't unwrapped and actually fired the rifles in a very long time. Their training had been about road building, not combat, and they knew they couldn't defend themselves.

Warren Duesenberg was a partner in a contracting company that worked with the 97th Regiment in Alaska. He wrote in his diary on June 4, 1942, "War conditions much worse than people think. Army has complete control of all shipping. Eight bombers landed here. Planes are bringing back wounded from Dutch Harbor."

On June 7, the same day that Japanese forces occupied Kiska in the Aleutians, Duesenberg noted delays in shipping. Two days later he recorded an air raid false alarm.

...

PROBABLY MOST IMPORTANT TO THE soldier engineers on the ground from the Yukon Territory to Alaska, the high command stopped mail service. At first blush, the mail interruption may not seem a big deal. Yet, however tenuously, mail connected the isolated, frightened soldiers of the Corps to the outside world that gave their efforts meaning. When it stopped, morale plummeted.

When Chaplain Edward Carroll described the importance of mail to his 95th regiment, he described it for the other six regiments as well. "The men have a deep and abiding attachment for their homes," he explained. "When the mail comes in, the soldiers would leave the most luscious repast on earth to get it. Some read the letters right away. Others carefully husband them, opening one a day to make them last as long as possible."

Many of the 93rd enlisted did not know how to read or write. Sergeant Bollin and Pvt. Hamilton remembered helping their fellows write letters home, teaching them how to sign their names and reading their letters to them. All the companies had men like Bollin and Hamilton to help the soldiers with their mail. Mail for the 93rd came through the Carcross Post Office to H&S Company clerks, who sorted it by company. Constantly moving through the wilderness, companies worked out their own systems for keeping the flow of mail going. Now, for several weeks in June, that ground to a halt, devastating the isolated soldiers.

Lieutenant Timberlake was relatively immune to the effects of Dutch Harbor. In early June, he finally made it to the thick of the action, doing a difficult job he knew to be important and doing it well. For the first time, he didn't have to fret about the dream girl back in Somerset. He could relax and enjoy the dream. The attack, and the mail interruption, got Tim's attention but they didn't devastate his morale. He just kept writing.

His June 5 letter had mentioned the attack, but didn't focus on it.

> June 5, 1942
>
> Dearest Helen,
>
> ...Got your last letter about your last trip to Magnolia. So they have given you a drawer of your own huh! I am sure glad you are happy being there. Please go as often as you can.
>
> Wish I could talk to you Buzz—but no soap. In regard to your long letter ... I still say, You're the one, Buzz, Please wait. I get kinda disgusted now and then about things and sorta give up that's what makes me

write a letter like that, I guess.

If you have been watching the paper, you will note that some of those Jap Bombers have been getting very close by. Lets hope close and not here is the word.

…yesterday I received a radio from one of the forward parties on the job about 60 miles out. It was from a Captain that knows you write so often. The message was in regard to some machinery, and it began 'Timber Darling'—I have been getting quite a rib about it.

Bye and I love you Buzz, Turner

His June 12 letter merely notes the mail problem.

June 12, 1942

Dearest Helen,

Guess you have been waiting a long time for a letter but just can't seem to get one. Well in fact I haven't had any for a long time. The last letter I got from 505 was dated June 2, 1942 … Air mail service has sort of called it quits since the last air raids on the coast of Alaska. Service has been stopped altogether…

CHAPTER 9

DRIVE TO THE TESLIN RIVER

As May turned to June, General Hoge's most critical problem was getting Colonel Russell Lyons' white 340th to Morley Bay, where its assigned section of highway began. Lyons had over half of his regiment stuck in Skagway. On June 1, Lyons waited, chafing at the bit. The action centered squarely on the seventy miles of road from Carcross to the Teslin River and the men of the 93rd who fought to build it.

On the morning of June 4, as Japanese and American planes battled over Dutch Harbor, the men of the H&S Company of the 93rd boarded a convoy of trucks that would carry them from Carcross over the new road to Tagish. Colonel Johnson needed to get his headquarters out in the field, closer to the action. Squires and Tim and their NCOs rode with them. Colonel Johnson knew that bulldozers and other heavy equipment for the 93rd were already landing in Skagway and piling into Carcross. The Regimental Motor Pool would coordinate the effort to get the equipment out of the way and out to the field. The men who ran the Motor Pool were about to become, albeit temporarily, the most important men in the regiment.

Colonel Johnson needed a location in the field where his men could receive the equipment and supplies coming up, check it, sort it, and get it out to the line companies. He needed to locate a motor pool and a supply dump. Dead center in Johnson's area of operations, Jakes Corner offered the perfect location.

Moving rapidly east from Tagish, Company A of the 93rd dashed through the woods. On June 4, the same day the H&S Company came up from Carcross, Company A bivouacked just three miles short of Jakes Corner. Between June 4 and June 6, they raced through Jake's Corner, and the rough road in their wake provided access from Carcross through Tagish to the Motor Pool site— just in time.

...

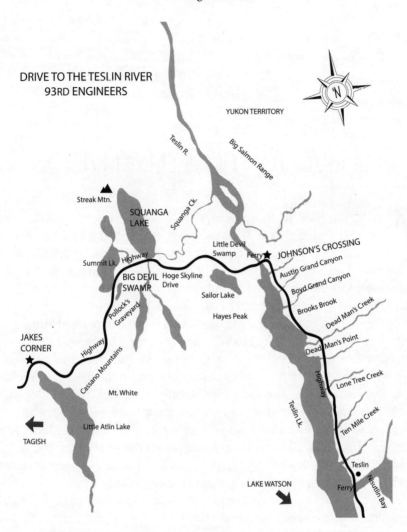

DRIVE TO THE TESLIN RIVER
93RD ENGINEERS

YUKON TERRITORY

Teslin R.

Big Salmon Range

Streak Mtn.

SQUANGA
LAKE

Squanga Ck.

Little Devil
Swamp

Summit Lk. Highway Ferry JOHNSON'S CROSSING

BIG DEVIL Hoge Skyline Austin Grand Canyon
SWAMP Drive

Sailor Lake Boyd Grand Canyon

Pollock's Brooks Brook
Graveyard Dead Man's Creek

Hayes Peak

JAKES
CORNER Highway Dead Man's Point

Cassano Mountains Lone Tree Creek

Highway

Mt. White

Little Atlin Lake Ten Mile Creek

TAGISH Teslin Lk.

Teslin

LAKE WATSON Ferry Nisutlin Bay

HEAVY EQUIPMENT OFF-LOADED ON THE Skagway docks, came up on the
WP&YR to Carcross. Precious trucks, jeeps, D8 dozers and graders moved
off the ships, on to rail cars, and up the White Pass. In the first week of June,
its arrival took chaos to a new level in Skagway and Carcross. The regiment
fought to get the precious machines out of Carcross and over the muck and
stumps of the primitive road, still under construction, to Jake's Corner and
from there, to the line companies that so desperately needed them.

As the Assistant Motor Officer for the 93rd, Tim Timberlake suddenly
found himself at the very center of the action. His June 5 letter to Helen
apologized for not getting around to writing sooner and explained the delay.

Friday June 5, 1942

Dearest Helen,

Things are kinda' screwed up and we are up to our ears in work. I am now in the rear echelon waitin' and assigning equipment as it comes in. We are still without about 40% of our equipment. Bye I love you Buzz, Turner.

Yukon Territory fought the equipment invasion with heavy rains and thick mud, but the engineers, sweating and cursing, prevailed. With a brutal schedule hanging over their heads, Hoge and his commanders needed the equipment in place and working. Their soldiers made it happen.

At Tagish River, the 73rd Pontoon Engineers' ferry staff operated 18 hours a day. In the first three weeks of June, the men moved 1,050 vehicles, including D8s, gas shovels and supplies. Lieutenant Squires vividly remembered watching a string of new D8's slew and grumble through Tagish toward Jakes Corner. "Now they could make headway." In his June 12 letter to Helen, Tim described how he is finally in place and an integral part of the 93rd's effort.

Friday June 12, 1942

Dearest Helen,

…This very minute I am sitting on a box with a portable typewriter with a gasoline light writing a peach of a gal a letter, and to be more particular I'll try to tell you where I am.

The highway we are building goes North toward Whitehorse and south to Atlin [Teslin Post] a distance of some 110 miles. To get to the place called Jake's Corner we built some 35 miles of road from Carcross where we came after leaving Skagway.

It is a lot of work. I live in a tent all by myself, 30 miles from the closest camp [Carcross] and 65 miles from the nearest town which has two houses and a dog team in it.[Skagway] I have my own Jeep, a radio command car and am set for the outside world, get all the war news every nite and even the ball scores.

Makes me feel funny when I hear them talking of the gas ration, no tires, no sugar and stuff at home, but oh those movies, newspapers, and etc. must make it rough. Love, Turner.

Out on the road, new equipment replaced a meagre stock of borrowed equipment. Johnson's lead companies raced through the wilderness—but it fought back—hard. Melting ice, snow and spring rains had turned rivers and streams into raging cataracts. Lakes had swollen into the surrounding woods. Deep mud covered the route of the highway. Daytime temperatures averaged 72 degrees and 29 degrees at night.

June taught the engineers more about muskeg. Patches of the nasty stuff lay in wait for unwary truck and dozer drivers and many fell prey to them. Engineers learned to look for stands of aspen and poplar because the roots grew on rocky soil or a firm gravel base, and to avoid spruce that grew, often leaning precariously, out of muskeg.

Hammering diesel engines powered heavy vehicles through the mud—skidding left and right, tires and tractor tracks alternately spinning and gripping, spitting mud at everything around them. Sooner or later, the mud won. Gripping would cease and spinning would simply sink the big tires deeper. Shifting into neutral and letting the diesel idle, a driver would climb out into the mud, unwind steel cable from the winch mounted on his bumper, drag it through the mud to a tree, wrap it around and secure it with a steel hook. Engaging the winch gear, he would rev up the diesel, wind the cable back in and pull the truck from the sucking mud. A stuck dozer, presented a more difficult problem. Winching a 23-ton dozer would move the tree instead of the dozer. Dozers had to be pulled free by other dozers.

The mosquito assault that had launched in May continued apace. Ten thousand mosquito nets had finally arrived, along with repellant, which levelled the playing field a bit. The battle raged into June. Lieutenant Walter Dudrow recalled, "You could reach up and smack the back of your neck and have fifty mosquitos in your hand." Truck drivers had to take care when following the hand and arm signals of a ground guide—he might be swatting mosquitoes instead of giving directions.

Heavy traffic over the primitive access road inevitably created problems. A new culvert collapsed near Crag Lake. Company E hurriedly rebuilt it. It had taken a monumental effort to get the regiments moving and nothing would be allowed to stop them now. In his memoirs, Hoge recalled, "You had to go every day ... we had to move ... we had to make speed." Mortimer Squires remembered, simply, "We moved so fast."

At the Jakes Corner Motor Pool, lieutenants Timberlake and Squires became first lieutenants on June 12. Their frantic mission, getting the heavy equipment through and out to the road, rapidly morphed into an equally frantic ongoing mission—supporting the line companies in maintaining and fixing the equipment once they got it.

Squires described the D8 bulldozer as "a good machine. It takes a high-class piece of equipment to clear the roads and deal with permafrost." He also noted that "the blacks" were trained in operating the equipment and became very proficient.

The men of the motor pool gradually turned into a team. Each player assumed a role and Tim was a key player. "Everybody liked Tim," Squires said. "He was very industrious. Didn't mind working. He got his hands into the job and he knew how to motivate men to get things done and to do it right. Never seen anybody that he couldn't get along with."

Differences between the attitudes and roles of lieutenants Squires and Timberlake emerged early. Tim's letters sparkle with amazement at his surroundings and with the thrill of his difficult work. Squires remembered very different feelings. He was not happy in the Yukon; he wanted to be out of there as fast as possible. "I went to Whitehorse as much as possible and stayed as long as I could," he wrote. "If there was ever an excuse to go to Whitehorse, I would go," he added, noting his first stop was at the Caterpillar Specialist office to check on the status of spare parts for trucks and dozers and his second was the liquor store.

...

COMPANY A OF THE BLACK 93rd drove out through rugged wilderness toward Summit Lake and Big Devil's Swamp. Sergeant Albert France remembered, "They had difficulty cutting down trees. Often we would dig down through green grass and then hit cakes of solid ice beneath the dirt." Back in a bivouac, at Jake's Corner just east of Tagish, Boyd's Company C built culverts while Company B cleared underbrush. Taking advantage of the midnight sun, his platoons worked in seven-hour shifts, stopping only during the hours of darkness between 11:00 p.m. and 2:00 a.m. for basic maintenance on their equipment.

The point of all this effort, as far as General Hoge and Colonel Lyons were concerned, was to get the 340th to Morley Bay so it could start building its assigned section of the road. General Hoge wasn't waiting. Lyons had already moved with his H&S Company over the river route to Morley Bay. Heavy equipment for the 340th would arrive at Skagway at mid-month and he had people in place to move it over the river route. The important thing now was to move his last four companies out of Skagway and onto the road to the Teslin River. General Hoge ordered Lyons to make it happen.

Led by their Company A, the 1st battalion of the 340th came up to Carcross on June 6. Eight hundred men moved through the little town and formed up in the woods, organizing themselves into a long train—jeeps, small trucks and marching soldiers wearing fifty pound packs. Moving out, they passed through and around Companies D, E and F of the 93rd, and on in pursuit of the black regiment's Company A, which was breaking trail.

By June 11, the head of the long 340th train had passed five companies of the 93rd and was at Summit Lake, closing in on Company A of the 93rd, which had reached the Johns River. There the 73rd Pontoon Engineers had floated two pontoon boats between two trestles—a 36-foot bridge that could support a 23-ton D8. Company A of the 93rd crossed it and forged on through thick woods toward Squanga Lake and Teslin River. The 73rd Pontoon Engineers raced with them, bringing a dock and a pontoon ferry. Quality control went out the window along with personal comfort, food, rest and a lot of other things normally considered essential. Company A of the 93rd gouged out that last 16 miles with the 340th hot on its heels.

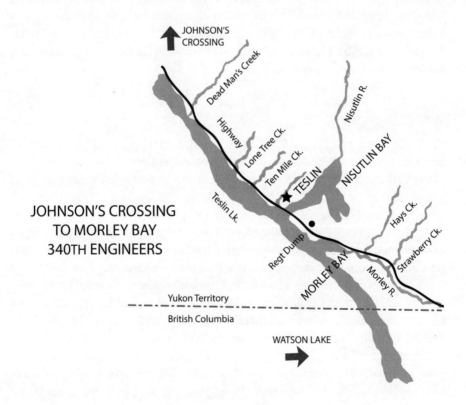

The trail-blazing men of Company A accomplished the primary mission of the 93rd, in the nick of time, all by themselves. The head of the 340th train caught up with it precisely as it reached the river. The First Battalion of the 340th boarded boats and ferries and floated down to Morley Bay on June 16 and 17. The place on the river where they boarded is known to this day as "Johnson's Crossing."

Behind Company A of the 93rd, Colonel Johnson and the H&S Company of the 93rd moved from Tagish out to Squanga Lake, closer to the action. Company B of the 93rd bivouacked at Squanga Lake. Companies D and C of the 93rd worked from Jakes Corner toward Big Devil's Swamp.

...

Teslin River Ferry, Johnson's Crossing, YT, at Teslin River.
Photo courtesy of the Signal Corps, CS 148494.

NORTH OF WHITEHORSE, AT THE beginning of June, the 18th Engineers occupied a 65-mile corridor from Whitehorse toward Champagne. By the end of June, Company F, cut a trail across the southern end of Kluane Lake and began building the Slims River Bridge.

Farther to the north, in Alaska, the 97th Engineers cleared Thompson Pass and began moving what equipment they had from Valdez toward Slana—two hundred miles away. The heavy equipment that started arriving in late June was the equipment which the unit had junked back in the States before leaving for Alaska.

In the southern sector, living off the land, recovering from serum hepatitis, waiting for its supply road, the 35th Regiment confronted Steamboat

Mountain, towering three thousand feet above the surrounding valleys 45 miles from Fort Nelson. Slick mud covered the steep, crooked road up Steamboat. A trucker preparing to use it geared up and raced into the climb as fast as he could. Within a few hundred yards, the truck began to lug and slow and the trucker downshifted through the gears until he got to first. The truck crawled along in first gear over the miles to the summit. The slick mud made going down worse than going up, creating a pile of wrecks that littered the bottom mile and a half. Behind them out of Fort Saint John, the 341st struggled to build a supply road.

At the end of May, Colonel David L. Neuman, a civil engineer from Columbia University, had brought his black regiment up from Fort Bragg, North Carolina. The 95th offered urgently needed qualities to the project—organization and training. In the full year of its existence, its men had trained for 13 weeks at Fort Belvoir, completed construction projects at Virginia's Camp A.P. Hill, and trained for ten more weeks at Fort Bragg.

No matter. When, on June 1, the 95th engineers arrived in the Southern Sector, their experience meant much less than their skin color to military planners. Many white officers believed—the Army *trained* them to believe—in the myth of black incompetence. They couldn't trust black men to learn or to think or to solve problems. Nor could they trust them to operate or care for sophisticated equipment.

However, some observers on the road learned differently. Harold Richardson wrote that many of the engineers only had "a few minutes" of instruction. "Yet some of the best operators both colored and white were boys that had never been on construction equipment until they arrived on the project." He wasn't just talking about the well-trained 95th.

Few hastily recruited "negro soldiers" brought experience operating heavy equipment with them to the Army, but building the Alaska Highway gave it to them. They became good equipment operators and they liked the job. A bulldozer was an expensive machine that manipulated and transformed wilderness into road. When an engineer learned to operate a D8 tractor, it gave him a sense of personal achievement and importance that ordinary physical labor lacked.

At some of the highest levels of command, however, the myth of black incompetence, despite all evidence to the contrary, never did go away. Asked, in a 1974 interview, which soldier, the black or the white, was best at his job, General Hoge responded:

> The blacks were nothing worthwhile at all. In many
> cases they were just a problem to have along. They could
> break equipment. They could break a drawbar that was

that big around [4-6 inches] on a carry-all. They could snap it off just like a pencil and when they did, they couldn't do anything. They would just lie down, build a fire and go to sleep and they'd wait for an officer to come along and get the thing straightened out. They could do pick and shovelwork and that was about all.

(G. W. Hoge 1974)

The 95th Engineers arrived in country a working team. The men knew their jobs. Moreover, their equipment followed close behind them. The Corps had provided a tremendous asset to Colonel O'Conner, who was struggling to reorganize his effort and recover from a disastrous May. The all white 341st regiment had arrived in country without heavy equipment; so, when the 95th's heavy equipment arrived at Dawson Creek, General O'Connor promptly handed it over to the 341st. The 95th, coming to the highway, was left with only with two bulldozers, one grader, a carryall, less than twenty small dump trucks—and hand tools.

The events of May had clearly demonstrated the inexperience of the white 341st. Nevertheless, O'Connor pointed the regiment and its stolen heavy equipment at the road and ordered the 95th to fall in behind to clean up the roadway with hand tools. The soldiers of the 95th swung picks, wielded shovels, hauled dirt with wheelbarrows and felled trees with axes and saws. "Morale was bad," Henry Roberts remembered.

Within a short time, work for the well-trained 95th actually began to run out. With little to do, the soldiers found themselves occasionally serving as stevedores and truck drivers for the "white rookies" of the 341st. More often they simply remained in camp, surrounded by mud, huddled under rain-soaked canvas. Colonel David Neuman, commander of the 95th, exacerbated the problem. Army censors began to notice a pattern in letters from enlisted men in the 95th. Private Dulin, for example, wrote simply that Colonel Neuman "...was a problem." Corporal Jonathan Welch wrote, "That old southern principal of keeping Negroes as slaves is still being practiced."

When Lt. Joseph J. Sincavage, a white officer in the 95th, recorded his disgust in a letter to his wife, the censors paid special attention. Some of his fellows were "dastardly punks ... it was disgraceful." Sincavage wrote his wife about one white officer who lolled in bed while his black platoon sergeant did his work. "The Army works for the officer, but the colored man is his slave," he concluded.

When General Sturdevant, back in Washington, D.C., read Sincavage's letter, the "shit," as they say, "hit the fan," but Neuman, who had injured his leg and secluded himself in his tent with a bottle, wasn't demoted. The Army sent him "home for his health." On July 19, Lt. Colonel Heath Twichell, executive officer of the 35th Engineers, assumed command of the 95th, and inherited its crushing morale problem.

...

BACK IN YUKON TERRITORY, THE triumph of reaching the Teslin River came and went, but Hoge's road still had a long way to go. Both the 93rd and the 340th redoubled their efforts. Johnson now had well over a thousand men in the woods that he had to provide for. In addition to requiring food, clothing and protection from bugs, their dozers and trucks gobbled fuel, grease, oil and spare parts voraciously. Thousands of gallons of diesel fuel, mountains of 55-gallon drums, had to get out to the line every day—without fail. Every box and every drum had to come through tiny Carcross—either a distribution center or a bottleneck, depending on your point of view.

Even with heavy equipment, General Hoge's battle with the folks in Seattle at the other end of his supply line raged through June. He had, several weeks earlier, urgently requested three quartermaster truck companies from the War Department: one to haul gravel and two to haul supplies. The first landed in Skagway during the first week of June without its trucks or any basic supplies. Hoge messaged Seattle not to send the other two companies without supplies, but they came anyway.

Back when the 93rd had first moved out of Carcross, a few soldiers from that unit and an 11-man quartermaster detachment transferred everything from train to truck. Truck drivers hauling supplies from Carcross to the line companies in those early stages endured an eight-hour round trip. A driver knew his destination company, but only its approximate location. Building from two to four miles of new road a day, the companies were, for the drivers, a moving target.

By the end of the month, one of Hoge's quartermaster truck companies, the 134th, made it to Carcross and set up a more efficient routine. As supplies came up to the depot, the 134th loaded them and moved them out on a "train" of 2 ½-ton tactical trucks. Drivers bounced over ruts and slid through mud for as many as 24 or even 36 hours, swatting at hordes of monster mosquitoes as they drove. If they got stuck, they walked to find a D8 to yank them out.

As soon as Col. Johnson got the 340th to Johnson's Crossing and out of the way, he began repositioning and repurposing his regiment. He had a primitive path as far as Johnson's Crossing, but it in no way met pioneer standards, and he had no road at all from Johnson's Crossing to Teslin Post or from Jakes Corner north toward Whitehorse.

Johnson moved his First Battalion companies onto the worst stretches. The most difficult stretch ran through Big Devil's Swamp. Company B of the 93rd had hurriedly traversed it once to reach Squanga Lake on the 16th. Now Johnson ordered the company to turn around and make it right. However, Yukon Territory served up a stretch of incredibly rainy weather to make the job nearly impossible.

Tim had great news for Helen in his letter of June 22.

> Dearest Helen,
>
> Well, Buzz, it's 1st Lt. Timber now and I am glad. I got it yesterday and it was dated June 12, 42 and that's the day of rank. It has been nine months and 28 days since I first went on active duty and ten months and 22 days since I received my commission.
>
> Well that's about the biggest news I have except the other day I got a letter from 3rd Army in San Antonio, Texas saying my transfer into the CE [Corps of Engineers] was awaitin' in WD [War Department] Adj at Washington … for it has been a happy weekend even in this mess.

He also told her about the incredible weather the Yukon Territory was visiting on the regiment.

> …It has rained here for 3 days and man you never saw such mud in your life seemed like it was miles thick. We just haven't had time to write. Going nite; and day. Honey, if you don't think I haven't seen a struggle well wait till I tell you when I get home. Love, Turner

Long stretches of road turned to thick sludge with the consistency of wet concrete. Sometimes an entire section would slide down a hill. In Big Devil's Swamp, during the four days following the June 16, the mud immobilized Company B's trucks one by one and they were pulled to the side of the road.

Successive morning reports record "…going was hard…" The weather was miserable and the "mosquitos bad." Finally, one precious bulldozer, growling through the muck, slipped into a muskeg bog. The operator threw his machine into reverse and accelerated, trying desperately to back away from the sucking mud. The great steel tracks spun and slung mud defiantly into the bog to no avail. Commander William Pollock dispatched another dozer to pull it out—too late. Big Devil's Swamp swallowed the D8 whole. Prodding deep into the mud with a ten-foot pole, a soldier tried to locate the machine by feel—no luck. The North Country swamp holds its giant mechanical hostage to this day. On Tim's map of the area one spot in the middle of Big Devil's Swamp is labeled "Pollock's Graveyard."

Bulldozer and carryall deep in muskeg.
Photo courtesy of the Timberlake Collection.

In the end, Companies B and C of the 93rd ganged up on the worst mile through the swamp. In addition to the D8, it swallowed over eight thousand trees for corduroy. Men carried these logs on their shoulders lest the swamp swallow more precious trucks and equipment. At one point, they had dumped three feet of gravel and dirt over a layer of corduroy and it seemed solid. In a few days under heavy truck traffic, the roadbed began to undulate: it became "Boyd's Rippling Rhythm Boulevard." The swamp took a second and a third layer of gravel, each two feet thick over the corduroy, before it could base a suitable road.

At the end of the month, the 93rd had finished the road from Carcross to Jakes Corner. Company A of the 93rd worked back west from Teslin River while Company B and Company C ganged up on Big Devil's Swamp. Company D approached the swamp from the east and Company E remained in Carcross.

Lyons and the 340th reached their base camp at Morley Bay in the nick of time. In the middle of June, the Skagway docks still convulsed with frantic activity as vessels bearing heavy equipment for the 340th arrived. Stevedores struggled to get the heavy equipment off ships onto the cars of the WP&YR and off to headquarters in Whitehorse. There it was wrestled onto steamers and secured for the laborious river passage to Morley Bay. At Morley Bay, the 340th had made little progress. In his June report, General Hoge claimed just twenty miles of new road built by the 340th.

Nearing the end of the month, some of the exhausted troops found opportunity to rest and clean up. At Squanga Lake, with the temperature in the 80s, Capt. Boyd decided he'd been enduring the smell of himself and his men long enough. Men had washed faces and taken sponge baths, but most of them, given a rare chance to rest, fell onto their cots wearing the road. Now, at the risk of polluting the lake, Boyd ordered an "allover" bath for all hands. Listening to his men, screaming, laughing and splashing, Boyd filled his helmet with water, let it warm in the sun, then stripped and poured the water over his body, soaped and shampooed. The enlisted watched as their commander dove into the cold water to rinse off. It was six feet deep and his feet hit the solid frozen icy bottom. The water was so cold that he turned a "dark blue—darker than about half of my soldiers." He heard the boisterous laughter as he tried his damnedest to walk on water back to the warmth of the sun.

CHAPTER 10

THE CORPS SETTLES IN

In the Southern Sector, Colonel Twichell, struggled to improve morale in the black 95th Engineers. He had operator's names painted on vehicles and equipment, making clear their responsibility to repair and maintain them. Should a soldier fall short, his name would be scratched off and replaced with another. Their status in the regiment at stake, the "catskinners" rose to the challenge.

Twichell needed more, something dramatic. Condemned to following the white 341st, which had taken its heavy equipment, the 95th fell heir to a lot of unglamorous work. Exploring, locating and clearing, the 341st led the charge while Twichell's troops were limited to picks and shovels. However, as the road approached the Sikanni Chief River, Twichell spotted an opportunity.

The glacial waters of the Sikanni Chief pour through a canyon between two mountains. The grade down to the river and back up exceeds ten percent. In 1941, a Canadian construction crew working on the Northwest Staging Route required three days to get ten sleds of equipment down the last mile to the river. Engineers at their desks in Whitehorse estimated two weeks to bridge the three hundred-foot wide river. O'Connor budgeted five days and reluctantly agreed to give the 95th a shot at building it.

The 341st, of course, had reached the river first. Company A of the 341st dynamited cuts into the treacherous hillside to create approaches. Company B hauled a "seemingly unending number of pontoons" down the steep hill to the shores of the river. On July 20, its Company C put a pontoon bridge across the river.

Now, Twichell brought his Company A—166 men from the 95th—to the site. He ordered them to build a trestle bridge across the river in just five days, and they delighted Twichell by raising the ante. Every man agreed to bet a month's pay that they could do it in four days. Obscure black regiment or not, the 95th got the attention of the rumor mill and word of the bet buzzed the length of the highway. The commander of Company A, Lieutenant Lee, sent two platoons out to serve as point for the effort. Constructing a raft of empty fuel barrels lashed to logs, Sgt. Brawley and Sgt. Price took a platoon to the north side of the river. Sergeant Tucker and Sgt. Bond took another to the south side.

Nervous, Lee had asked Sgt. Brawley, "Do you think we can do this in four days?"

Excited, Brawley replied, "Yesir, Lieutenant Lee, yesir! We can get it done in four days, you and me."

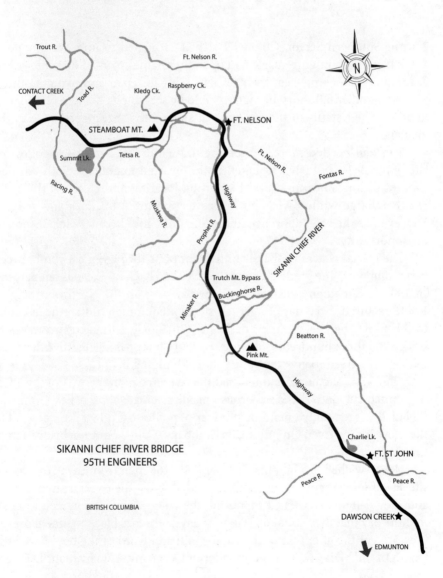

SIKANNI CHIEF RIVER BRIDGE
95TH ENGINEERS

BRITISH COLUMBIA

From the surrounding woods, Sgt. Harvey and Pvt. Hickens selected trees—monsters for trestles that would stand up out of the water and support the bridge; long, straight ones for bridging timbers that would run horizontally from trestle to trestle; and an endless number that could be turned into the decking that would span the bridging timbers and provide the roadbed. As fast as Harvey and Hickens could select them, their fellows swarmed to cut them down, lop off limbs and hew them into timbers and planks. As fast as bridge parts emerged from the raw timber, other men of the 95th dragged them down to the river bank. Private Dulin remembered his platoon "trimmed the trees, sawed them and made posts of the bridge. It was a big thing to do."

The point platoons anchored to the shore with ropes, waded, chest deep, icy water surging around them. They built cribs up from the bottom, floated the massive trestles to them and stood them upright, and filled the cribs with rocks to stabilize the trestles. The soldiers rotated into and out of the water. Numb and stiff, one group would struggle ashore to warm themselves at roaring fires, while others took their place in the torrent. When they had trestles in place, the men in the frigid water hoisted bridging timbers to span from trestle to trestle. Then, they spanned the bridging timbers with decking.

The whole area around the emerging bridge hummed with activity. The men in the woods made music; sang spirituals; kept time with their ringing axes. The work didn't stop when the sun went down. At night, a line of trucks cast their headlight beams into the darkness to illuminate the site.

Privates First Class Wilmore and Waldrum were bridge carpenters, and they worked thirty hours at a stretch. Sergeant Price supervised dynamite settings and blasted over twenty cuts into the mountain. Corporal George Hack built bridge abutments. While the men worked day and night, so did the cooks, who provided warm meals three times a day and midnight snacks of hot coffee and biscuits. Not five days, not even four days: in just three days the frantic activity ground to a halt. The 95th had bridged the Sikanni Chief.

Private Walter Henry drove a command car over the bridge. Lieutenant Lee and Sgt. Brawley commandeered a jeep and drove 324 miles, round trip to Dawson Creek for beer. Private Dulin remembers that "once they started drinking, guys were dancing with one another."

Twichell hoped that Sikanni Chief would wash away "the sullen resentment and passive resistance" of his troops. He made as big a deal as he could of the achievement. On Sunday, July 26, the regiment formally dedicated the bridge as part of Chaplain Edward Carroll's church service.

"…The progress of the work demanded that we move on," Twichell wrote in a letter. The soldiers packed up and drove their equipment over the bridge. They fixed approaches. It was a tricky job of road construction down the river canyon. They built some very substantial and handsome structures. Then they returned to following the 341st with picks and shovels. It was still a black regiment in a white army. *The Long Trail,* the published history of the 341st, contains not a single word to suggest that black engineers even participated in spanning the Sikanni Chief River.

The 35th conquered Steamboat Mountain, grappled with its ongoing problem of finding a route and arrived at Summit Lake on July 4, although its supply problem had continued unabated. Chester Russell remembers two soldiers dragging two mountain sheep into camp there—the first meat he had eaten in three months. The 341st and the 95th labored behind them, installing culverts and laying endless corduroy.

The engineers worked deep in the wilderness where survival sometimes required creativity. A story from the history of the 35th offers what might be the most extreme example: A trailblazing crew, including a soldier named Moore, happened to be following a D8 as it powered into the trees. A tree limb broke loose, flew back over the top of the dozer and struck Moore on the head. He fell to the ground, unconscious. A Medical Corps doctor named Stotts made his way to the scene and evaluated Moore's condition. "There is no way that we can get him out of here in time to save him … we can operate here."

Stotts cut through Moore's scalp behind his left ear with a razor blade, drilled a triangle of three holes with a wood brace and a 3/8-inch bit, cut between the holes with a hacksaw blade, took out the "plug," and removed a clot. Placing the soldier on a cot and erecting a tent over him, the soldiers left him in Stotts' care and returned to work. Four days on, Stotts' found Moore's lungs filling with fluid; he sucked it out with a rigged-up air compressor. Several days on, Russell visited Moore and found him sitting up and feeling pretty good. The story could have had a better ending. Finally evacuated by air to a Seattle hospital, Moore died enroute.

North of Whitehorse, the 18th worked northward around Kluane Lake, ferrying men and supplies across on two rafts built by the 73rd Pontoon Engineers, towed by two launches rented at Burwash Landing. The tragedy at Charlie Lake had taught the Corps about the apparently placid lakes of the North Country. Kluane Lake, like Charlie Lake, could boil up quite suddenly if the weather changed, but now cautious troops knew what to expect.

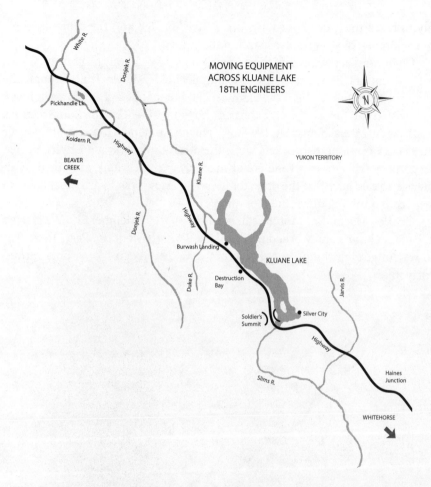

New rules decreed that personnel would ride on the launch, not the raft, but that didn't resolve the safety issue. Carrying a 23-ton bulldozer, a pontoon raft had little freeboard, rode very low in the water, and resisted the drag of the launch, pulling its stern deep into the water. Given the slightest turbulence, both vessels took on water.

Technician Rust remembers crossing Kluane Lake with his 23-ton bulldozer. He waited days for calm water. When he finally crossed, three pontoon engineers from the 73rd operated the ferry: one to steer, two to bail water. Forced to tinker with balky motors, falling behind with the bailing, the pontoon men asked Rust to steer so all three could bail. "It gave me a funny feeling to stand in that leaky little tub and look back a couple of hundred feet at my D8 riding sideways almost on top of the water."

Eight miles of road would one day carry vehicles along the southern shore of Kluane Lake to where it met the Slims River. The 18th struggled throughout

July to build the 1,044-foot-long Slims River Bridge and the difficult eight-mile approach over permafrost and mud.

Up in Alaska, the black 97th had worked its way 125 miles out from Valdez to the Mentasta Pass, the portion of the old Valdez-Eagle Trail through the Wrangell Mountains. There the engineers all but stopped. The old pack horse trail twisted and turned through the pass, hugging the sheer cliff. Some sections disappeared in washouts; sliding mud plugged others. Threading bulldozer tracks back onto their sprockets while the dozer hung over a precipice turned out to be a skill not everyone could master. Sergeant Monk explained in an interview years later that the operator "…got to know how to drop that blade to keep from tumbling down the mountain."

Charles Mason Sr., Motor Officer of the 97th, remembered, "We started at Slana on June 7 and worked up the Slana River to Mentasta Pass. There was no way of getting things in there. From June 7 to August 7 we only moved thirty miles."

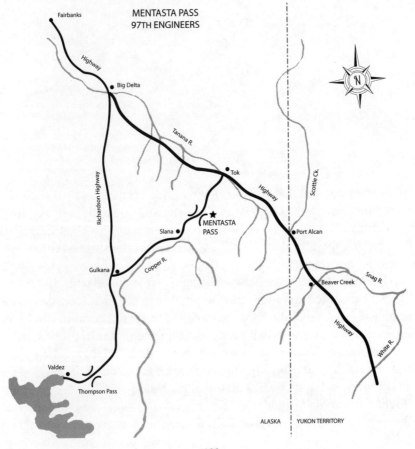

Lieutenant Timberlake, working in the 93rd motor pool, still at Jakes Corner, spent July consumed by his work. His alter ego, Tim, found time to make really good use of the three-cent love affair. His July 1 letter sets Buzz up for a surprise.

> Wednesday July 1, 1942
>
> Well Buzz be careful and don't be blue, honey, cause those dark clouds are plenty dark now—but wait—I'll make it worth your while. Nite and love, Timber.

Not part of the Army, not even from the United States, Canadian bush pilot Les Cook nevertheless continued to operate as a kind of one-man support unit for the 93rd and the 340th. He supported all seven regiments, but he concentrated in the center, and the 93rd and 340th thought of him as their own. He flew in good weather; more often in bad. Cook flew crews ahead of the road construction to build temporary bridges. Colonel Lyons of the 340th had Cook cache supplies of fuel and food along the banks of lakes and rivers ahead of his advancing troops. Lieutenant Herman Engel of the 340th led a 29th Topographic Unit reconnaissance party in advance of the 340th's lead company; Cook kept them supplied. Engel's men would build a smudge fire along a lakeshore so Cook could find them, and he would land on the lake. Cook would often carry Engel aloft to get a better view of the terrain.

On one of these occasions, Cook couldn't get his plane off the water. It was unusually calm that day, and calm water creates a suction effect under the pontoons of a small plane, holding it tight. Cook had Engel sit out on a pontoon, his feet roiling the lake as the plane accelerated across the lake; then he instructed Engel to jump inside at the last moment as the plane left the surface.

As General Hoge's headquarters grew, Whitehorse mushroomed into a small city, its population inflated not only by military personnel but also by civilians. The Caterpillar Corporation, for example, maintained an office in Whitehorse to supply parts and counsel for maintaining its equipment in the field. The Public Roads Administration maintained its own headquarters— offices, barracks and a cluster of machine shops—in Whitehorse.

The town also offered an Army hospital that administered a complex system for providing medical care to the troops. The men got sick—a lot. A sick soldier remained in his tent for a day or two. If he didn't get better, he went to an aid station, or field hospital. A doctor or medic would evaluate his condition and if necessary, admit him to the hospital in Whitehorse or even have him flown to a hospital in Seattle or Vancouver.

All the troops worked incredibly hard in cold, heat and incessant rain. The nature of the work subjected them to constant risk of injury. Moreover, they lived in close quarters. Illnesses such as pneumonia and influenza spread quickly. Some may even have contracted tuberculosis, which was endemic among the indigenous peoples. Mental stress was constant.

Black troops had entered the Army, joined their regiment, and been dispatched north with incredible speed. It's hard to imagine that the Army's screening had been very thorough. How many illnesses showed up only after they got to the North Country, we will never know.

James Lewis researched and wrote a report in the field in 1942 that provides a sense of what the black soldiers themselves thought on the subject. Many of them believed that each individual "stores up cold in his chest" that could only be removed by warm sunshine. The longer a man remained in a cold and dark place, the more subject he would become to rheumatism, tuberculosis, arthritis and losing his mind. The most common health complaints were bad feet, colds, measles, mumps and minor accidents.

Sharron Chatterton, in 2008, commissioned a study for the Teslin Historical & Museum Society called "The History of the Construction of the Alcan Highway Near Teslin." It noted that Carcross housed a small field hospital and dispensary with a medic toting a "large band aid box" with pain pills. According to a researcher, he would clean and tape cuts and bruises, but tended to miss more serious issues.. A problem like appendicitis might require three trips to the medic—along with forceful yelling or screaming and loud cursing to attract his attention.

Once the medic made a serious diagnosis, the patient typically travelled 12 to twenty hours on a truck, accompanied by a wrecker, over rough, bumpy roads to a distant field facility or to the hospital in Whitehorse. Sometimes the more severely afflicted caught a ride to the hospital with a bush pilot.

Whitehorse had barely adequate water, garbage and sewerage facilities before the Corps arrived. Residents dumped garbage and other waste in the Yukon, or "on" the Yukon in the winter—either way the river made it disappear. Sewerage went into privies, cesspools and poorly maintained tile fields. The Corps, multiplying the population and the demands on these primitive systems, turned Whitehorse into what Major Mendel Silverman called "one vast cesspool." In response to widespread dysentery and measles, authorities closed schools and theaters. They urged residents—and compelled restaurants—to boil or chlorinate water.

...

THE NORTH COUNTRY CONTINUED TO fight back, in July, by replacing the wet cold of spring with the wet heat of summer. According to WP&YR railroad records, total rainfall the week of July 5 broke a 31-year record. Morley Bay averaged highs of 90 degrees, Whitehorse, 82.

Getting to know his officers and their capabilities, Colonel Johnson tuned the organization chart of the 93rd during July. Black enlisted men of the regiment got promoted. In the early weeks of July, a number of privates became privates First Class, privates First Class became corporals, corporals became sergeants and sergeants became staff sergeants. The Corps had added new non-commissioned officer slots to the enlisted rank structure so more men could be non-commissioned officers, or NCOs. Technicians, Grades 4 and 5, equated to sergeants and staff sergeants respectively. The 93rd took advantage by promoting a number of men into the new grades. The promotions boosted morale, but morale boosting in general proved an uphill struggle in July.

The Land of the Midnight Sun kept the lights on 19 hours a day, and General Hoge in the Northern Sector, Colonel O'Connor in the Southern and their commanders made full use of all that daylight. Henry Geyer, a truck driver, remembered the reality on the road: "you worked until you dropped." Chester Russell of the 35th echoed Geyer: "We was working so hard that by the time you got through the night, you rolled your sleeping bag out underneath a tree or in the bushes and you crawled in it and sacked out."

Private First Class Fowler of the 340th remembered, "When we started building the highway, we slept on the ground with two blankets and a mattress cover. All of our extras, clothes, toilet items and writing things were kept in the mattress cover." When men awakened in the morning they put their things into a bedroll and placed it in a pile. At the end of the day, at a new campsite, they found their individual bedrolls in the pile that had accompanied them, unrolled them and promptly fell asleep. There were no tents or shelters.

For two months, the men of the 93rd worked endlessly. Like gypsies, they moved their bivouac every two to three days. Life boiled down to bone-tired exhaustion—driving a dozer, swinging a sledge or axe, slogging through knee-deep mud, or wading through icy water carrying pieces of a bridge or culvert. The schedule and the setting offered virtually no opportunities for recreation. Men hoped for furloughs but few got them. Sometimes weeks passed without letters and packages.

As the black regiments on the highway moved into the field, personal relations between the races subtly changed. As the 93rd moved out of Carcross, all the soldiers, black and white, suffered the same harsh conditions—the same cold, the same mud, the same mosquitoes. With the regiment finally making road, every unit was forced into teamwork. White officers and black soldiers slept and ate and drank separately, used separate outhouses, but they worked long hours together, sharing misery and solving tough problems. White officers couldn't build the road by themselves; they needed the skills of the black men who worked for them. To make use of those skills, they had to trust black troops and give them some autonomy. Lt. Squires particularly remembered Staff Sgt. Alexander Jefferson. They always put him at the rear of a convoy because he knew how to fix things.

Mechanics of the Regimental Motor Pool—Staff Sergeant Jefferson is second from the left. Photo courtesy of the Timberlake Collection

Former Lt. Walter Dudrow recalled a funny incident during an unannounced inspection visit by General Hoge to his troops in Carcross. A Master Sergeant (almost certainly Sgt. Wasp of the Motor Pool) lay on his back under a dozer, struggling with some mechanical problem. He heard footsteps, then a voice.

"Having a problem?"

"Yes, hand me that wrench lying in my truck."

The man behind the voice proved most helpful, and fetched several other tools. Only when, satisfied with his fix, Wasp struggled out from under the dozer did he recognize his helper—General Hoge.

If race relations improved, they didn't become perfect. A few of the young, white officers didn't change their minds or behavior at all, but that rendered them useless as managers on the road. Samuel Hargroves of Company F of the 93rd remembers one 1st Lt. so "mean" that the catskinners tried to run their bulldozers over him. He didn't last long; found himself bounced to a rear echelon job.

More important, if the relationship between junior officers and their senior black NCOs changed, that only widened the gulf between the NCOs and young privates like Leonard Larkins of Company A of the 93rd. It fell to the NCOs to control the men—to force them through cold and hunger to desperately long hours in the brush and muskeg. On the plantation, Leonard hadn't answered directly to white men. He had answered to "The Man on the White Horse" most often a black man, who ruled the fields. He hated that "Man on the White Horse". In Yukon, Leonard had little to do with officers. The men in his face—spewing profanity, pushing, harassing, squeezing every last ounce of work out of him—were black men. Remembering Company A's 1st Sergeant Ashel Honesty, Leonard recalled his "meanness". Had this been a shooting war, someone would have shot Honesty.

Kitchen crew with fresh food at Jake's Corner, YT.
Photo courtesy of the Timberlake Collection.

...

THE SOLDIERS FOUND WAYS TO recreate. The officers squeezed in poker. Mortimer Squires fondly recalled Frank Parren who, on Saturday nights, hosted poker games—graced with Canadian Club from the Whitehorse Liquor Store. The black enlisted men shot craps. Reporter George Yakulic remembered that if the soldiers stopped to shoot craps, "the smart officer damned well let them shoot craps." The game usually lasted ten to 15 minutes and then the men would return to work. We know that the officers, too, occasionally indulged in the game.

> Tuesday July 28, 1942
>
> Dearest Helen,
>
> Guess what I was doing when your last letter came, shooting dice, right now I am about 8 bucks ahead after sending $25.00 of my winnings home, but you got to use your head or down you go. Love Turner.

As a source of unrelieved misery, food topped the list. The 93rd, officers and enlisted, white and black, ate C-rations. Everything else—milk, eggs, potatoes and vegetables—came canned or powdered. Powdered vegetables tasted like cardboard. Monotonous and unsavory canned food—Spam, chili, Vienna sausage, corn beef hash and stew—didn't help. Years after the fact, the mere mention of the word Spam nauseated Tim. Fred Rust of the 18th Regiment insisted that the number of discarded Spam sandwiches could have paved the road. Corporal Anthony Mouton of the 93rd remembered corned beef hash as "shit on a shingle." Tim used that popular phrase to describe creamed chipped beef over toast. The 18th regiment knew Mouton's corned beef hash as "silage." "Big John" Erklouts of the 340th remembered, "There were two foods we classified as battery acid, lemonade powder and chili con carne, the worst food I ever tasted. It was so hot you couldn't eat it. The Army medics put a halt to it." Vienna sausages were everywhere despised as "Yukon Shrimp." The quartermasters sent bread to the regiments stuffed in mattress covers—keeping it fresh. Mattress covers or no, it arrived so hard the cooks had to saw off slices.

The Company's mess did have coffee, sugar, flour and salt. The cooks struggled to make the food as good as possible. Boyd boasted that Company C had good cooks and bakers. They made biscuits, bread, doughnuts and cinnamon rolls.

Nature could supply fresh food. One moose would feed a company in steaks, stews, brains and liver for several meals. Boyd and Lt. Hostetter borrowed a pontoon boat and outboard motor from the 73rd and caught 17 trout. Boyd boasted that the largest was 39 inches and the smallest 23.

Near the end of July, the food supply gradually began to improve. Butter and occasional fresh pork and ham appeared. Tim saved a photo of the first fresh food crates at Carcross Depot. They had no refrigeration, of course; but even in summer the lakes offered ice not far below the surface. They certainly had enough sawdust to preserve the ice after they cut it out. At Morley Bay, the men carved out a root cellar.

Tim thickened his plot on the 10th, noting Buzz's upcoming birthday.

> Friday July 10, 1942
>
> Dearest Buzz,
>
> We have been right busy here of late … mud is all over the place and it gets rough now and then however the road is in better shape and it takes more time for the road to get into bad shape.
>
> I have no idea on when we will leave or what will happen during the winter. There are a lot of theories

on the situation but facts are none too clear. It seems a sure fire bet that if we do not get this road thru we won't come home for it cost too much money to get us here in the first place.

I hope you kinda' like what will happen on July 20th. I had hopes of sending you a wire but no soap any more.

I hope mother makes a good pick of what you want. The thing what gets me most in the whole affair is that in all my life mostly everything I have tried to do is done by mail.

This damned three cent love affair isn't all it could be. I realize now that maybe at one time or another I said things I should not have said but being lonesome and seein' people and those you love makes you talk unusual at times … Barrels of love, Turner.

He had written his mother, asking her to purchase an engagement ring as a birthday surprise. On the 19th, far from home and thinking hard about the special birthday present, he wrote a birthday letter—one day early.

Sunday July 19, 1942

Dearest Buzz,

I guess you know what tomorrow is and I sincerely hope you like it. Mother has poor taste about some things but on others she is the tops, or even topper. I know that it's not the way it should of been done, maybe we both should have gone hunting together and wouldn't that be fun. But these unusual circumstances cause all these things.

I have written to your mother and dad about it, too. I hope everyone is pleased. Please Buzz just wait until I get home and I'll do my darndest to make you happy…. I never could make up my mind, now, I feel that I have and Buzz I believe I am one of the luckiest guys in the world.

When you receive this letter just stop and kinda "make believe" I was there and kinda think what I would say and you'll understand even if I am 4800 miles away. Love and someday it will be Mrs. H.M. Timberlake.

CHAPTER 11

BUILDING ROAD AND ADJUSTING THE PLAN FOR YUKON

From Dawson Creek to Tok,, the Alaska Highway had begun to emerge from the wilderness. "The Tote Road," "The Pioneer Road," "The Truck Trail," "The Alcan Highway," "The Long Trail," "The Oil Can Highway," "The Burma Road of North America".... The impressive and growing list of nicknames suggested that the story of the project had already been transformed into a modern epic.

The men of Company A of the 93rd, the heroes of June, bivouacked at Summit Lake on July 1, assigned to improve the road from Squanga Lake back to the village of Tagish. Colonel Johnson moved most of the rest of the 93rd to Squanga Lake, preparing to cross the Teslin River and build the road south from Johnson's Crossing to Teslin Post. Company B and Company C were already there. Company D was coming. Company E finally crossed the Tagish River and would get to Squanga Lake on July 21.

On July 11, Company C of the 93rd, accompanied by Colonel Johnson's H&S Company who set up headquarters at Johnson's Crossing, led the way across the Teslin River to attack the biggest obstacle on the road south to Teslin Post—Boyd Canyon, newly named after the unit's commander. Between Johnson's Crossing and Boyd Canyon lay the smaller Austin Grand Canyon. Company B crossed the river on July 15 to deal with first with Austin Grand Canyon. Both canyons needed very large culverts. The road couldn't simply descend into their valleys then ascend the other sides; the grade was way too steep. The rugged path of the road from Dawson Creek to Alaska routinely confronted the engineers with sudden elevation changes, and culverts were the solution of choice.

Filling the dip or canyon with packed dirt would provide a level roadbed; but the dip or canyon usually existed because a stream had dug it, and the stream continued to run along its bottom. Simply filling it would dam the stream.

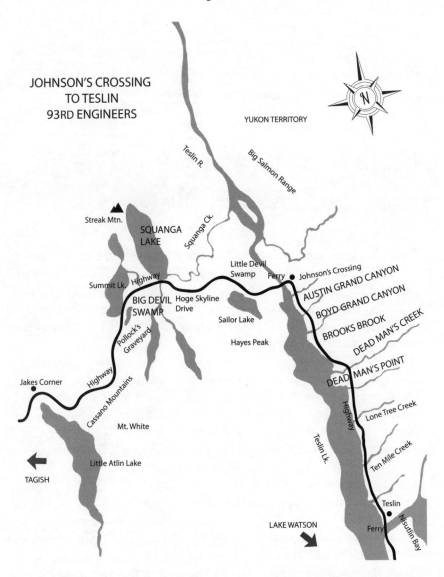

JOHNSON'S CROSSING
TO TESLIN
93RD ENGINEERS

YUKON TERRITORY

Teslin R.

Big Salmon Range

Streak Mtn.

SQUANGA
LAKE

Squanga Ck.

Little Devil
Swamp

Ferry   Johnson's Crossing

AUSTIN GRAND CANYON

Summit Lk.   Highway

BOYD GRAND CANYON

BIG DEVIL   Hoge Skyline
SWAMP   Drive

BROOKS BROOK

Sailor Lake

DEAD MAN'S CREEK

Pollock's
Graveyard

Hayes Peak

DEAD MAN'S POINT

Jakes Corner

Highway

Cassano Mountains

Lone Tree Creek

Highway

Mt. White

Ten Mile Creek

Teslin Lk.

Little Atlin Lake

TAGISH

Teslin

LAKE WATSON

Ferry

Nisutlin Bay

To avoid creating potentially dangerous dams, soldiers built a rough, square tunnel of logs and timbers—for the stream to flow through—then dumped dirt on top of it, packing and filling. In effect, the culvert and fill dirt combined to make a bridge.

A culvert needed sufficient height and width and a sufficient cross-sectional area to pass whatever amount of water the stream brought to it. Its length depended on the fill. The sides of the fill had to slope from a wide base to the roadbed on top; the deeper the fill, the wider the base and the longer the culvert, which ranged from thirty to one hundred feet.

Building a culvert.
Photo courtesy of the Timberlake Collection.

The men enjoyed constructing them. It was a break from the monotony of building featureless rutted road through the woods and the men of the 93rd got good at it. An outside contractor noted in his logbook that he had watched, impressed, as a black unit near Teslin Post built a 15-foot wide and forty-foot long culvert in 45 minutes.

Boyd's Canyon needed a very long culvert and very deep fill. To speed things up, the 73rd Pontoon Company ferried a dozer around on Lake Teslin to the south wall of the canyon so dirt could be pushed down from both sides.

At the culvert, the men ran out of the metal spikes they used to pin the timbers together. They resorted to drilling holes through the logs with a compressed air drill and shaping wooden spikes to drive in through the holes.

Major General Sturdevant, Commander Hoge's boss from Washington, D.C., happened to be in the Yukon Territory on an inspection tour and he chose to visit Company C's effort. An hour and a half before the scheduled VIP visit, Tech Sergeant Frank Hinkel on the far bank of the canyon got his dozer too close the edge and followed the dirt over. Hinkel tried to jump but banged his head and sat back down; he ended up riding his steel mount down to the floor of the canyon. Luckily, the dozer landed on its tracks.

Clambering down from his side of the canyon, company commander Robert Boyd found Hinkel shook up with a bump on his head.

"Who told you to drive that dozer over the edge of the bank?" he asked.

"Nobody, sir."

"Then what are you doing down here?"

"I really don't know, sir."

Boyd ordered Hinkel and his dozer back to work and when Sturdevant arrived with Colonel Johnson, he found a busy, normal work site.

Boyd's Canyon, about five miles south of Johnson's Crossing, YT.
Photo courtesy of the Timberlake Collection.

...

Tuesday July 28, 1942

Dearest Helen,

...a week ago, it was raining, we had two big machines stuck in the mud so bad that the drivers couldn't sit on the seats. For 50 hours we worked getting them out and I mean when we were done I just about reached the end of my rope.

Its funny however, most of the officers have the same thing in mind, that is "anything to win the war" and all joking aside that's the way everyone feels even if shells aren't bursting in the air here.

Love Turner

As Company B worked on from Austin's Canyon toward Teslin Post, Lt. Robert P. Brooks' third platoon had encountered the brook that still shows on road maps as Brook's Brook. The muskeg and mud there had tried hard to suck two of Lt. Brooks' dozers into its depths, and Tim and men from his motor pool had helped rescue them.

Company D of the 93rd crossed the Teslin River on July 20, travelled to join Company B at Brook's Brook. One Platoon of Company B moved to Teslin Post on Jul 27 and by July 31 all of Company C of the 93rd had joined them.

To the south, during the first half of July, the 340th Engineers struggled to get going. Commander F. Russell Lyons finally had his regiment in one place—

the right place—but he confronted the same problems Colonel Johnson and the 93rd had dealt with moving out of Carcross back in May. Lyons had two battalions—over a thousand men—stumbling all over one another at Morley Bay, struggling to get organized and out on the road. His inexperienced companies and their commanders confronted Far North realities, for the first time—mud, muskeg and all the rest. Like the officers and men of the 93rd, they would figure it out—but it would take time.

Back in June, two platoons from Second Battalion of the 340th had started building highway from Morley Bay west toward Nisutlin Bay. This was Milepost 0 for the 340th, and they struggled for weeks to complete that seven miles. The road wound through rugged mountains, then descended abruptly, curved sharply to the right and ended at the icy water of the Bay.

First Battalion of the 340th officially started work on the highway on June 25. But a week later, on July 2, Company A bivouacked just three miles east. Only two Company A platoons worked on the highway; the other two struggled to corduroy the single mile from Morley Bay out to their bivouac.

Company C of the 340th worked out toward Strawberry Creek, just sixteen miles from the Bay. During the first days of July, they encountered a swamp and a clay hill with a twenty percent grade. They managed to bury a dozer there in the swamp. By July 14, they bivouacked one mile east of Strawberry Creek.

General Hoge had long since figured out that getting the 340th anywhere close to "on schedule" would require drastic changes. The regiment's destination, Lower Post, lay a disheartening 185 miles east of Morley Bay. On July 15, Hoge officially changed the route of the highway—and his strategy for building it.

The Alaska Highway would one day go from Teslin Post through Johnson's Crossing to Jake's Corner and then north to the McClintock River and Whitehorse—but not in 1942. For now, the 93rd's road from Jake's Corner to

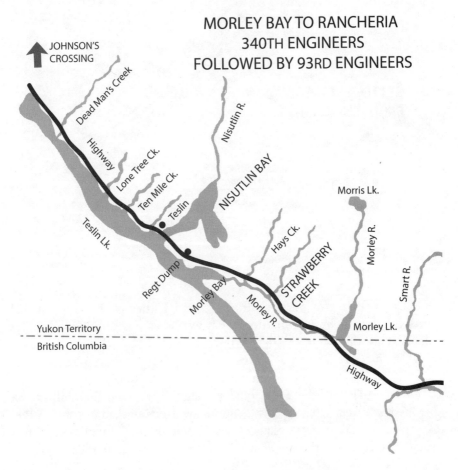

Carcross and Lt. Dudrow's wagon road from Carcross to Whitehorse would serve and building toward the McClintock River would be would be left for the PRA. The Second Battalion of the 93rd, freed up by this change, would go back to Carcross and upgrade Lt. Dudrow's wagon road to Pioneer Road.

Hoge ordered Colonel Lyons and the 340th to abandon the standards for a Pioneer Road from Strawberry Creek and to push a rude, single-track trail east from there as fast as it could. He demanded four miles a day. The 29th Topo Engineers had specified a 130-mile route from Teslin Post to where the Rancheria River flows into the Upper Liard River valley. Hoge wanted that road built, standards be damned, by late August. The First Battalion of the 93rd would complete its road from Johnson's Crossing to Teslin Post and then cross Nisutlin Bay and follow the 340th east, upgrading their road to Pioneer Road standards.

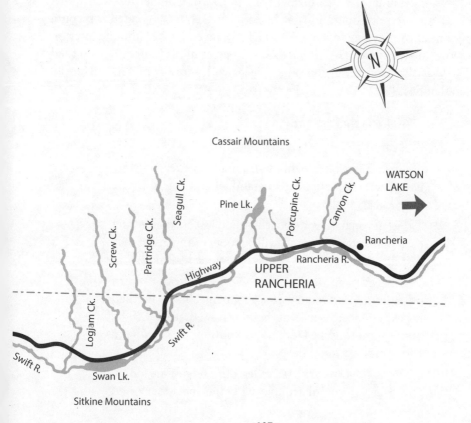

Morley Bay, about ten miles south of Teslin, YT.
Photo courtesy of the Bureau of Public Roads, 42-5024 National Archives

...

Mortimer Squires and Tim Timberlake, with the mechanics of the 93rd Regiment, had worked out of Jakes Corner for weeks, but in August the line companies they supported would disperse. Over a hundred miles of rough road would separate the two elements of the 93rd. Colonel Johnson didn't close his motor pool operations at Jakes Corner, but he created a second, larger one at Morley Bay in late July, and Tim moved farther into the interior.

When he wrote to Helen on July 28, a big piece of his future finally settled and he was thinking about the other pieces with more confidence. He told Helen that he is "107 miles out" of Carcross.

> Tuesday July 28, 1942
>
> Dearest Helen,
>
> Gosh I am sure behind in letters to everyone, we have been right busy moving and all and you don't get much sleep at all...
>
> Helen you have yourself a husband just as soon as I get back in the states. I hope it will be soon, in any case it may be a little hasty for what comes up no one really knows.
>
> If we ever hit the states we will be sent out to form other outfits and start new regiments that have had no experience. It is being figured now that we will be home sometime in December, I sure hope so, what a Christmas we could have...
>
> Right now we are 107 miles out and we are doing OK. Having lots of trouble with the machinery and

stuff, but I am getting great experience fixin' it up and keepin' it rolling…

I believe the war will take about 15 years of our life away, its rough, hours of worry, and a real struggle if I ever saw one, but we'll do OK … Love Turner.

On July 30, he followed up with a bit of explanation.

Thursday July 30, 1942
    Dearest Helen

We are making fair progress, of course we are all awaitin' that day when we can all come home. Any day now it may get colder than the devil.

As far as the road goes we should reach our main goal sometime next week. That's where we hit a section another outfit is building. Nite and Love, Timber.

…

IN MID-JULY, THE 340TH REGIMENT received nine additional D8 dozers, doubling its production, and moved out, implementing Hoge's new instructions. By the middle of August, lead elements of the 340th were building road 77 miles out from Nisutlin Bay. To put even a single-track trail in place, Lyons had all his companies working close behind Company A, but the going was rough. Company E overturned an Osgood Shovel and had the devil's own time getting it back upright in the mud. At Strawberry Creek, slick clay, a twenty percent grade and a rough culvert stuck in the memories of the men of the 340th. On to the east at Morley River, Company F overturned a carry-all.

The 73rd Pontoon Company came up to help the 340th. It installed a pontoon ferry across the Morley River that allowed the regiment to move heavy equipment across and get on with it. Company D of the 340th worked on a bridge to replace the ferry. That done, it moved ahead to upgrade a temporary bridge at the Smart River, but managed to bury a D8's tracks and a carryall's rear wheels deep in thick mud.

Out in front on August 16, Company A of the 340th and the First Battalion Headquarters of the 340th moved to the vicinity of the Upper Rancheria River. They didn't bother bridging the Upper Rancheria, just forded it and moved on. They ended the month 140 miles from Nisutlin Bay and just 45 miles from Lower Post and the oncoming 35th Regiment.

The Second Battalion of the 340th raced close behind. By the time Second Battalion Headquarters crossed the Lower Rancheria River, Second Battalion Troops had built a two hundred-foot bridge over it.

August 1 found much of Colonel Johnson's 93rd Engineers concentrated on the critical 32-mile road between Johnson's Crossing and Teslin Post. Company E of the 93rd moved from Squanga Lake and crossed the Teslin River on August 3.

On August 6, Company C of the 93rd crossed Nisutlin Bay and went to work on the 340th's road. Bivouacked at Morley River from August 7 through August 11 they lengthened culverts and widened the road out from the Bay.

...

THE 93RD REGIMENTAL OFFICIALLY COMPLETED the ninety-nine miles of road from Carcross to Teslin Post the week of August 10. Colonel Johnson began moving more companies off that stretch and into position to implement General Hoge's new plan. Companies A and B crossed Nisutlin Bay on August 11. Company E came down from Squanga Lake and crossed on August 24. Positioning themselves along the way from Nisutlin Bay to Seagull Creek, Johnson's companies spent the rest of August bringing the 340th's road up to pioneer standard.

Excited by the sudden appearance of thousands of soldiers bulldozing at and around them through the woods, the residents of Teslin Post marveled at the transformed landscape. When the bulldozers pushed through to Fox Point and roared into Teslin Post, little Dolly Porter hid in panic from the massive machines pitching trees in every direction through her world. The engineers pressed local river boats into service wherever feasible, hiring paddle and steam boats to carry gear from Johnson's Crossing and Timber Point to Morley Bay. The sternwheelers and barges steamed constantly up Teslin Lake delivering equipment, and some villagers in small boats or canoes traveled down Teslin Lake to monitor the action. Tom "Bosum" Smith remembered that the rumbling power of the dozers disturbed and upset the adults in his village.

When Company C of the 93rd moved to bivouac at Teslin Post, ready to cross the bay and follow the 340th, its black troops caused consternation. The RCMP ordered their commander to keep his men out of the settlement. Captain Boyd complied and instructed his NCOs to keep the Indians away from their bivouac, but he "was sure there was some co-mingling of the soldiers and the Indian belles."

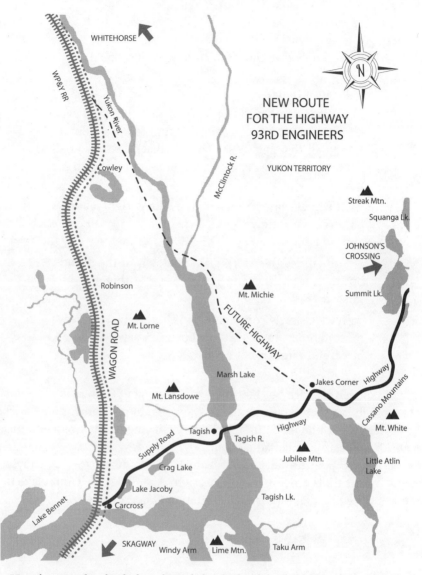

Hoge's new plan had also altered the path of the highway, routing it from Jakes Corner to Carcross and from there north to Whitehorse. That meant that the wagon road between Carcross and Whitehorse needed an upgrade to become a pioneer road. On August 11, Johnson sent Company D to make that happen. Company D travelled a hundred miles that day and landed six miles north of Carcross. On August 18 and 19, Company F and Second Battalion Headquarters travelled to join them.

...

TIM, IN THE MOTOR POOL at Morley Bay, scrambling to keep up with increasingly heavy demands for support as his regiment redeployed and scattered, checked in with Helen on Saturday, August 8.

> Dearest Helen,
>
> …Since you have been wearing that ring (and even if I haven't seen either you or the ring) I have a different feeling all together. It seems now that I loved you all the time and didn't have brains enough to make up my mind….
>
> …Things have been coming along right good. I haven't been feeling as well here of late, but will come around I guess.
>
> Sometimes this work gets me down in the dumps, but then we all have to remember that this may end this war.
>
> We are slowly coming to a finish or rather where we meet another outfit [340th]. Love and say hello to all, be careful Timber.

Tim missed his girl, but his alter ego, Lieutenant Timberlake, had fallen into a tough job that played to all his strengths. In his element, he "worked the problems" and he made things happen. On August 11, Colonel Johnson made it very clear that he had noticed.

Earlier, Lt. Squires had moved from H&S Company to Company A—assigned to its third echelon motor shop. On August 11, Lt. Timberlake took over as the Regimental Motor Transportation Officer.

> Tuesday August 11, 1942
>
> Dearest Helen,
>
> Well, today I came up another notch in the 93rd. I have been made Regimental Motor Transportation Officer and Heavy Equipment Officer.
>
> The best part is that the job calls for a Capt. And it is known as a position opening (that is after six months if everyone likes your work) you automatically get your Capt. Bars. Six months is a long time away, but it would sure be great if I could make a success of it.
>
> Tomorrow I am going to take a 150 mile plane hop

to a nearby place to look over some machinery and you have to take a bed roll and stuff. Gosh it is getting cold here, and nasty, but I believe we are on our last leg and I hope we get home. Nite and loads and loads of love, Timber.

...

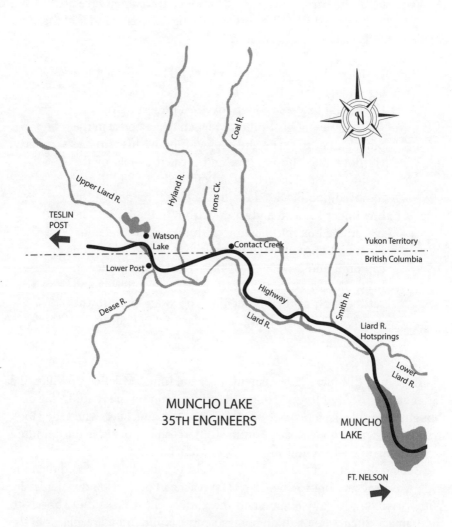

DYNAMITE PLAYED A LARGE ROLE in building the road. To the south, the 35th plowed through Summit Lake and moved on, pretty quickly, until it hit Muncho Lake. A wide, flat trail offered an easy path around that body of water, except for the place, about half way, where a sheer rock cliff descended from high in the sky directly into the deep blue water. The engineers backed up and built a primitive work trail up the mountain behind the cliff. From the top, they proposed to bulldoze rocks and dirt into the water below, building a ledge between the water and the cliff. For five days, the massive blades of the D8s shoved landslides down the wall of rock, tons of rock and debris. On the sixth day, watching a giant spruce sail over the edge, fall through space, smack the water and disappear into its depths without a trace, they gave up.

Enter Lieutenant Mike Miletich. Colonel Ingalls, commander of the 35th, recalled Miletich's extraordinary effort.

> Below the sheer cliff, the waves and ice had cut holes big enough for a box of TNT … Miletich sent a man up the cliff to fasten a long rope to a projecting rock … After removing his clothes, Miletich tied a noose in the other end of the rope and slipped it under his arms … He dove into the icy lake and located a hole of the right size. He removed the lid off the box of TNT and removed one block and laid it aside … he placed the box under his arm and swam with it to the hole … he placed the box into the hole with the opened side out. He took the spare stick of explosive, placed a blasting cap on it and a waterproof fuse. Placing the device in his teeth, he lighted it, and with the fuse sputtering and set to go off at the proper time, he swam back to the box. He placed the charge and swam out of danger.
>
> (Twichell 1992)

Repeating this incredible maneuver several times, Miletich provided the 35th enough roadbed to get around the cliff and on up the road. In the end, though, it would take a massive effort by the 341st and, later, when they took over the road, the Public Roads Administration—and more than one hundred tons of dynamite—to vanquish the cliff at Muncho Lake.

Behind the 35th on the road to Fort Nelson, came the 341st and then the 95th, widening and improving. The 341st reached Fort Nelson on August 26. With virtually no heavy equipment, the 95th wielded picks and shovels to cut drainage ditches open, drain plugged culverts and drain low places in the road bed.

North of Whitehorse, the 18th completed the Slims River Bridge and opened the road around Kluane Lake during the first week of August. For the most part, the path north to the Big Duke River followed the lakeshore, and along the lake the 18th encountered frozen ground—in August. At Destruction Bay, dozer blades skidded with mammoth futility over icy dirt. They also had to negotiate the steep lakeside mountain at Soldiers Summit; they used 110 cases of dynamite to blast a roadbed out of solid rock.

At mid-month, the lead elements of the 18th finally left the forty miles around Kluane Lake behind and headed for their next challenge at the Donjek River, just one hundred miles short of Alaska.

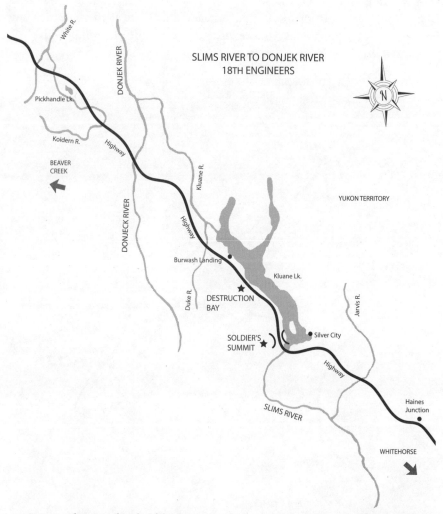

Far to the north, the black men of the 97th had finally escaped from Mentasta Pass and forged on toward the Tok River. Colonel Lionel Robinson, who had replaced Colonel Whipple in Command in mid-July, sped things up significantly when he decided to build a one-way instead of a two-way road to Tok. Once they got there, the 97th would build the Alaska Highway south and east toward Canada, but right now they were building a mere access road.

On August 14, the 97th crossed the Tok River just 12 miles from the Tanana River. A few days later, from its new base camp at the Tanana, the regiment finally turned to the south and east to build its portion of the Alcan. PRA contractors had moved in behind it, gravelling and improving the road through Mentasta Pass and on toward the Tok River. Deusenburg Construction worked on the short stretch of the Alcan from Tok north to Delta. The Alaskan troops were finally headed for the Canadian border one hundred miles distant, where they expected to meet the oncoming 18th

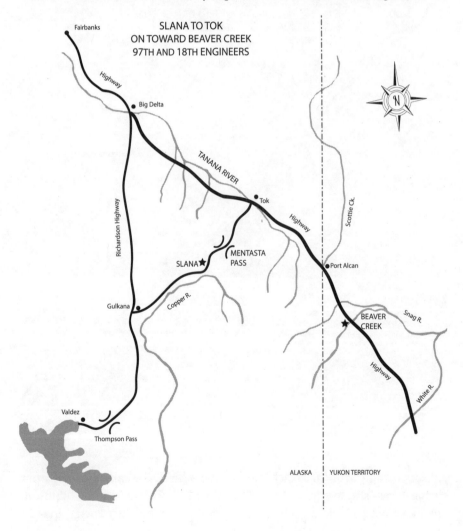

CHAPTER 12

DOING THE JOB

y the first of August, the engineers, white and black, had worked in the woods for weeks; they knew the job and endured its hardships. The racial issues that plagued the black regiments hadn't gone away, but by August they lurked in the background. The road emerged, threading its way through the vast wilderness. Everybody focused on completing it and going home.

The mosquitoes disappeared in August, but the Far North had more than one creature up its sleeve. Swarming gnats, accompanied by "no-see-ums," replaced the mosquitoes and made the them seem almost gentle by comparison. Small, built for speed, a gnat uses its tiny mandibles to attack and eat a man's flesh, leaving behind a swollen, itching clot of blood. Gnats especially favored ears, but they weren't picky and clothing offered no protection. One surveyor, eyes swollen and ears bloody, found six more gnats in his navel.

The North Country finally dried out in August, but that, too, offered the troops only temporary relief. The endless mud dried into endless red dust that swirled to cover duffle bags, pack the creases in fatigues and abrade vital machine parts. Soldiers of the 93rd, convoyed by truck to Teslin Post, arrived unrecognizable, their faces totally obscured by red dust.

Life in the woods rendered simple things like keeping clean complex and difficult. "Big John" Erklouts of the 340th, dealt with icy cold rivers and streams by washing half of his body at a time—"quickly wash the top half of yourself, put on some clothes, then wash the bottom half." Norman Bush of the 341st gave up bathing altogether. If he didn't bathe, it made no sense to change clothes, so he didn't do that either. After four months, he itched everywhere and the soles of his boots disintegrated.

The soldiers despised their monotonous and dismal meals, but they ate them. Men who eat, to put it somewhat delicately, eliminate. Companies in the field had to get rid of garbage and "eliminations." Chester Russell of the 35th described the problem:

You've got a regiment of men up there, no water, no
toilet facilities and you've got to make up this camp,
toilet facilities, garbage pits. And you've got to dig
through this ice, and you've got one air compressor, and
all the rest is picks. And you hit that old ice with a pick
and it just bounced back in your face. Every time you
moved, they had to dig out the garbage pits ... and then
when they move again they'd cover them all up and put
a sign up, saying what it was garbage pit or a latrine.

(PBS video, American Experience: Building the
Alaska Highway, Interviews) 1992

Every bivouac site left buried garbage behind and bears immediately dug
it up. They could paw through four feet of dirt, topped with rocks.

Given the working conditions, the food, the standard of personal care and
the sanitation, it should come as no surprise that injury and illness remained
a problem in the field. Soldiers exchanged germs with the local population
and, more often, with one another. Everybody experienced dysentery—and
some jaundice. The dangerous work lacerated skin and fractured bones on a
regular basis.

The soldiers drove vehicles with cannibalized parts, sometimes without
brakes. They patched broken tools together with wire, tape and ingenuity. They
worked brutal hours swinging axes, felling trees, piloting vehicles through
mud and along steep mountainsides. Soldiers at war, they got wounded and,
in the most dramatic cases, they died.

On August 9, 1st Lt. Small of the 18th wrecked his jeep. His men found
his body, back broken, under the jeep. Two soldiers in the 35th died when
they rolled their grader over a bank. A cook in the 340th torched himself by
pouring gas on a lit stove burner; he died on route to the hospital. Tech Sgt.
Max Richardson of the 340th died in his wrecked truck. An unknown officer,
probably a second lieutenant, training his men to field strip a machine gun,
accidentally shot Staff Sgt. Whitfield of the 340th.

Regimental histories, interviews, memoirs and letters contain examples
of death on the highway. There are no exhaustive records. The three black
regiments were ghosts in this as well. Black men made the ultimate sacrifice,
but their deaths are largely absent from the fragmented history of death on
the highway.

Not where they wanted to be, not comfortable, but getting the job done
and making the best of it, the troops soldiered on. On August 10th, Tim
interrupted a gathering in his tent to report the proceedings to Helen.

Monday August 10, 1942

Dearest Helen,

This is what is happening in our tent right now. The boys (that is my tentmates) are now opening a bottle of the Neh Plus Ultra (better than the best), we are having a party for one of the boys who got a promotion a long time ago.

Capt. Egge, the dump commander, [Regimental Supply Officer] greatest blocking end the south has seen in years, so he says, (spread that stuff where the ground is poor) is now pulling the cork from the bottle (co-plunk), just a minute honey while a poor of a little this juice now my short elbow, ah fooled you its coffee, believe me, ha, ha.

Anyway we are now having a midnite bite and it's a little light yet, but its getting colder that the dickens, and its real fall.

Say, I have it all figured out, when I get home I'll get some leave and we can get married. We'll figure out some way to have a church wedding so the folks can be there, we'll have to dope it all out before I get the leave. Love and be careful honey, Timber.

...

WORK IN THE FIELD CENTERED on bulldozers—especially the D8 Caterpillar Bulldozer, the indispensable, all-purpose weapon of the Engineers. The Caterpillar Company called their monster machine a crawler, "a bucket of olive drab."

The D8 weighed in at 23 tons. Its six-cylinder, air-cooled, diesel engine moved it over the ground at 5.8 miles per hour. Its starter, itself a 24-horsepower gas engine, only operated in warm temperatures; during winter, the machines ran 24/7. Most regiment had 20 D8s and an assembly of smaller tractors— D4s, D6s and D7s. They worked 20 to 22 hours a day, seven days a week. Theoretically they stopped for two hours each day for maintenance—minor repairs and lubrication. "Catskinners" regularly diverted from the path to rescue other dozers—and trucks and jeeps—mired in mud. They also diverted to drag carry-all scrapers and non-motorized graders through the woods.

The dozers forded small streams, were ferried over rivers. On the ground between the waters, they gouged a continuous 60- to 90-foot wide right-of-way through the woods. The 10-foot tall monsters, pushing a 21-foot blade, pulling a 15-foot body, lumbering, often in tandem, through the woods, came to epitomize the Alaska Highway project.

Catskinner pilots his D8, pulling a carryall over a culvert.
Photo courtesy of the Timberlake Collection.

As the proud Catskinners worked the levers, D8 engines roared, spewing black smoke, and giant tracks ground through dirt and mud, alternately spinning and catching. Out front, giant blades pushed down trees; gouged out dirt and stumps. Men swarmed around them, cutting and milling trees for bridges and culverts, burning the 'slash' or stockpiling it for corduroy. From his platform, the Catskinner couldn't see over the engine and the giant blade to the ground immediately in front. Stories of commanders' jeeps squashed and buried by marauding D8s fill the annals of the road.

The D8s had no cabs. As a tree went down, its top could break and fall back toward the dozer. Leonard Cox, Catskinner with the 340th, watched "the top 10 to 12 feet of the tree." Sometimes he hurriedly bailed off. "It was very dangerous." A member of the 340th saw a Catskinner stand to back up his dozer, failing to notice a long sapling caught on the blade. When the sapling broke loose and sprung back, the very tip of it caught one of his testicles and "flicked it out as clean as if a surgical knife had been used."

The appetite of the great dozers for fuel posed the single biggest supply challenge on the highway. A D8 dozer burned roughly ten gallons of diesel fuel per hour, and more when working over rough terrain, mud and muskeg. If a machine burned through 200 gallons a day, the engineers had to get about four 55-gallon drums to it. A regiment moved 90 drums a day over hundreds of miles of rough road.

The condition of the road demanded tactical vehicles, designed for off-road travel; the ubiquitous army deuce-and-a-half (tactical 2 ½ ton flatbed) trucks crawled the road, singly and in convoy, burning their own gas as they went. The deuce-and-a-half, minus its familiar canvas bed cover, carried 25 drums, but it burned roughly three gallons of gasoline for every four gallons of diesel it delivered to the trail head. Under especially difficult conditions even the deuce-and-a-half couldn't negotiate the terrain. When that happened, D4s hauled the drums on towed sleds.

The dozers, trucks and other equipment that moved around them required more than just mountains of 55-gallon fuel drums. Tracks and rollers broke. Truck axles broke. Tires wore out and blew out. A serious number of heavy trucks operated without brakes. Mud had sucked every hydraulic hose in the regiment loose from its fitting—some of them many times.

Each company assigned "mechanics" as the first line of defense against equipment problems. Typical of these men, John Bollin of Company F of the 93rd had never clapped eyes on equipment like this before he came north. "He was an asphalt and concrete city boy and didn't know nothing about this heavy equipment." He learned fast, on the job and in a hurry. "We were able to overcome what we did not know by trial and error," he recalled.

Mechanics from the Regimental Motor Pool made the tougher repairs—what the Corps called second and third echelon maintenance. The pool had brought enlisted mechanics, senior non-commissioned officers, from Louisiana, but those few men couldn't possibly handle the overwhelming workload by themselves. If a man anywhere in the regiment had mechanical experience, the Motor Pool NCOs would, sooner or later, find and grab him. These men learned on the job.

Unknown Motor Pool welder poses next to his portable arc welder.
Photo courtesy of the Signal Corps.

Writer John Virtue reported a memory of a 2nd Lt. named Schnurstein who served with the black soldiers of the 93rd. "The guys would get out there and get on those tractors and would pull them apart and do all sorts of things.... I don't know how they did it, but they fixed them. They were good."

Some of the most serious repairs had to be made on site—deep in the woods. If the repair required a Motor Pool mechanic, he had to get himself and his tools, often including a welding rig, through the woods to the distant site. The trucks and trailers the Motor Pool used broke and got stuck just like everybody else's. In the end, like every other soldier on the project, the mechanics made do with what they had and, somehow, got it done.

In addition to supplying mechanics, the Motor Pool struggled to acquire and distribute parts as the regiment chewed through its inventory. Truck drivers carried spare parts, scavenged from broken equipment abandoned by other drivers along the road—tires, axles, anything useable. A driver who left even a useable truck unattended might well return to find a stripped hulk.

All along the road, every steep hill or canyon featured debris scattered at its bottom. Broken-down and wrecked trucks lay everywhere—over banks, in ditches. Ten-ton wreckers couldn't keep up with demand for their services and the Motor Pool didn't waste time on junk. Scattered along with the wrecks were lumber, cement and especially, the empty fuel barrels that gave the road one of its best names—"the Oil Can Highway." One black soldier told Cyril Griffith, a PRA trucker, as they careened down a steep hill, "Don't worry boss, Uncle Sam has lots more trucks and lots more 'nigga' boys to drive 'em."

Lines of junked and cannibalized vehicles waiting for parts, sprouted and grew across the yards at the Regimental Motor Pools. Parts orders overwhelmed the Caterpillar offices in Whitehorse and Fort St. John. Orders for tires overwhelmed G.K. Allen, who operated tire supply facilities in Fort St. John and Whitehorse. An order for 1,250 tires might result in delivery of 250.

The men working the machines needed sustenance, too. The thousands scattered through the woods consumed mountains of rations. They needed underwear, boots, coats, winter coats, sleeping bags and toilet paper. Headquarters used tables, chairs, filing cabinets, pens, pencils and typewriters. Kitchens needed stoves and gas, cookware, seasonings. Medics needed bandages and drugs, dental supplies and tools, surgical tools, intravenous fluids...

In July, General Sturdevant changed the Corps' plan of attack. In the original plan, the Corps, would push the road through as quickly as possible. The PRA would follow them with civilian contractors to build the permanent highway, upgrading some sections, completely bypassing others. The PRA and its contractors would replace the Corps and its supply and support structure allowing the military to move on to urgent missions elsewhere.

That plan wasted a lot of resources. In effect, much of the road would be built twice. The Corps could get its job done much more quickly if the civilians came in to help. On August 7, Sturdevant announced that PRA contractors would move in now to support and supplement the work of the regiments, and it would not be required to build to permanent road standards. Sector commanders and project engineers would work together.

Eventually, five management contractors and 47 construction contractors—a total of 7,500 civilians—worked on the road. The civilians had the same logistical and supply problems as the Army. Although they supplied themselves, they did it over the same routes and through the same bottlenecks.

In August, Dowell Construction, with its equipment and supplies, arrived in Carcross. Project Superintendent George Wagner set up headquarters near Squanga Lake. Among other things, Dowell would construct two-way bridges over Tagish River, McClintock River, Teslin River and Nisutlin Bay. Dowell, like other PRA contractors, found the Corps' cumbersome supply system intensely frustrating—it's no surprise that the soldiers in the field felt much the same way. All too often, using the system meant circumventing it; and, if everybody circumvented the system, that made the system even more cumbersome and difficult.

For General Hoge's Northern Sector, supplies came up from Prince Rupert or Seattle to Skagway or Valdez on tug-towed barges supplemented by every other kind of craft that might serve, including yachts. Frequently, some of the motley collection of vessels negotiating the perilous coastal waters didn't make it. Tragedy came often.

Port battalions at Skagway and Valdez harbors stockpiled fuel, supplies and equipment until trains could get them out of Skagway and trucks could get them out of Valdez. Either way they arrived at their destination, far inland, on the ubiquitous deuce-and-a-half—unless especially difficult terrain required a sled or crawler wagon towed by a dozer.

To the north, material for the 97th made its way from Valdez 125 miles along the Richardson Highway over Thompson Pass to Gulkana and 128 miles further over Mentasa Pass to Tok. For the 18th, material hauled on the WP&YR to Whitehorse continued 200 miles up the road to Kluane Lake and then made its way at first on ferries and barges over the lake, later, around the lake and over the Slim's River Bridge.

The 134th Quartermaster Truck Company brought supplies for the 93rd from Carcross to Teslin Post, crossing the Tagish and Teslin rivers on ferries. The long trip offered gumbo mud or dust, corduroy sunk in endless swamp, and road sections that slid away down steep hillsides. The dozers sometimes came out to pull trucks like "strings of barges."

Material for the 340th came up to Whitehorse on the WP&YR, then moved on barges via the Yukon River, the Teslin River and Teslin Lake to Morley Bay. From Morley Bay the inevitable deuce-and-a-half convoys carried it out to the field.

Pilot Les Cook remained a minor, but dramatic part of the supply effort, flying when and where no one else could. One way or another, he would get it done—but his methods didn't always yield the results he hoped for. Delivering a four pound D8 transfer pump, he found the target dozer deep in the wilderness. Placing the pump in a loaded mail bag, he dropped the bag to the road below where it bounced and rolled several feet before coming to rest. The pump survived the drop, but it turned the mail into confetti.

Leonard Cox of 340th Company D remembered another Cook delivery. He "brought us a quarter of fresh beef. Now just imagine throwing a beef quarter out the door of a plane which is going one hundred miles an hour. After bouncing several times, the beef was in bad shape. The cooks were lucky to salvage half of it."

On another occasion, after several passes, Cook dropped several cases of steel drift pins along with several cases of canned vegetables—including beets. He had made several passes before pushing the cases out the door, but all of them burst open when they hit the ground. Flying drift pins penetrated deep into the trees with blood-red beet juice dripping around the penetrations. Observers described the combined effect as the perfect set for a deep-woods horror movie.

…

TWO MONTHS AFTER PEARL HARBOR, Army Chief of Staff General George C. Marshall and his civilian boss, Secretary of War Henry L. Stimson, had reorganized the Army into three major commands, one of which was Army Services and Supply. They appointed General Brehon Somervell to command ASF which included the Quartermaster Corps, the Ordnance Department, the Corps of Engineers, the Medical Department and the Signal Corps.

Somervell turned his command into a personal empire. Heath Twichell who commanded black troops of the 97th described him as a "sleek, good-looking and well-dressed [man] with a soft-spoken manner that concealed a gnawing ambition, a violent temper and a mean streak. Those who knew him called him "Dynamite in a Tiffany Box." For many of his fellow officers, the mention of his name had the effect of a red flag in front of a bull.

On August 17, Lt. General Somervell came to Whitehorse with his subordinate, General Reybold, Chief of the Corps of Engineers. Four days before their arrival, the commander on the ground, General Hoge, learned that at least some of his troops would have to stay in the woods to keep the road open through the winter. Hoge had promised his men they would winter in the States. Worse, the tent bivouacs that served in August would not serve through a North Country winter. Building something better would take time, and Hoge didn't have time.

His plan for several sites with wooden-floored, double-walled tents didn't satisfy Somervell, who demanded installations of permanent barracks, each to house two thousand men plus forty to eighty officers in Whitehorse, Dawson Creek and Fairbanks. And, by the way, Hoge needed to extend his highway north from Fairbanks to Nome, he added.

Clearly the imperious General Somervell understood little of the reality facing Alcan builders on the ground. Hoge, who understood it very well, had a road to build and open before winter. The orders he followed had been issued by General Reybold, who now stood beside Somervell and uttered not a peep. Somervell expected accommodations befitting his exalted rank, and Hoge didn't have time for that either. Whitehorse offered but one hotel, and locals, soldiers and the civilians of the PRA crammed it full. The hotel rented rooms in three eight-hour shifts. Guests ate meals standing up. Whitehorse had few facilities for entertaining the egotistical and self-absorbed.

The exalted general slept in a room in the small house the Corps had constructed for Hoge and his wife; ate simple meals prepared by that accommodating lady; and left insulted. In an interview years after the fact, Hoge remembered, "It wasn't a big enough show or spread. All of his life he wanted to be connected with the biggest, most expensive enterprise. This did not suit him. He called himself a 'mean son-of-a-bitch', and he was."

At the end of August, the project was coming together and a ribbon of highway was emerging across the North Country map. But Somervell, the new "head knocker," puffed up and headed back to Washington, D.C., poised to amputate the project's head.

On August 24, Tim updated Helen, with devastating news.

> Monday August 24, 1942
>
> Dearest Helen,
>
> Just to let you know what is in a day here, I'll make a short summary of today. Up at seven and in a plane for a 150 mile ride to sector headquarters [Whitehorse] to look over some equipment and then a return trip back to a bay some 60 miles from our supply base to look at a couple of bad tractors and then a flying trip back to our

base here by 4:30. Gosh this country is sure something from the air and you can look down on the road and see it for miles.

It is still a rumor, but according to actions taken place here we are staying all winter. This all winter thing has sort of taken the wind out.of my sails. It has just about knocked everyone here for a loop and let me tell you, it might get right bad here if we do. How these men will take it and all is yet to be seen, but it won't be fun you can bet your last dime on that.

The weather turned cold. On the night of August 31st, it snowed and the promise to return all troops to the states before winter went by the wayside.

CHAPTER 18

CHANGE OF COMMAND

The 340th and the 35th plunged toward each other through the rugged mountains of the Mackenzie-Yukon Drainage area. Their imminent, climactic meeting would open the road all the way from Dawson Creek to Whitehorse.

On September 24, an advance crew from Company E of the 340th, loaded a D8 with extra drums of fuel and pushed ahead of everybody to the west bank of Contact Creek. Here the men waited, hearing the dozers of the 35th coming through the woods, closer and closer, until they watched them burst from the thick woods and lumber down the bank and into the creek.

From both sides of the little creek, wildly happy soldiers competed to see who could yell the loudest and the woods rang with profane arguments about who got there first and who built the most miles. Major McCarty rode the lead dozer from the 35th and Colonel Lyons clambered up on his regiment's lead dozer. The machines lurched forward until their blades touched and the road officially reached from Dawson Creek to Whitehorse.

The man who had done more than any other to make this happen, General William Hoge, wasn't around to see it. On September 4, General Somervell combined the Northern and Southern Sectors into a new Northwest Service Command which would report not to General Reybold of the Corps of Engineers, but directly to Somervell himself. A disinterested observer might have expected that Somervell would put General Hoge in charge of the Northwest Service Command as a reward for his hard work during the preceding seven months, but he chose General James A. O'Connor. Bill Hoge was fired. On September 12th, 12 days before the triumph at Contact Creek, Hoge regretfully relinquished his command.

As the men of all seven regiments and their PRA partners moved through the woods in September, serious problems loomed for October and November. Sturdevant, Hoge, the PRA—they had all known that the 1,500 miles of road they had put in place were a mess—some of it nearly up to pioneer standards, more of it just a single-lane truck trail, weaving and winding crazily around and over

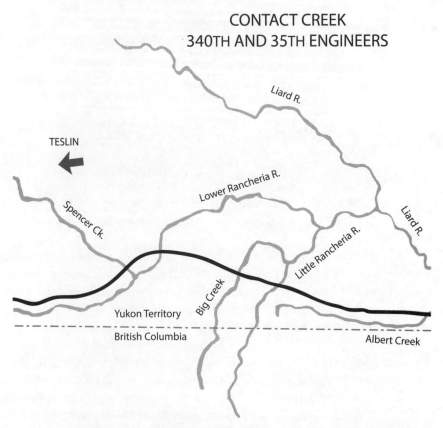

CONTACT CREEK
340TH AND 35TH ENGINEERS

steep mountains, through unbridged streams, through muskeg bogs. Abandoned trucks and equipment, empty oil drums, trash and garbage littered the entire way. They knew they still had a hell of a lot of work to do and had planned for that.

Somervell had expanded the scope of the project, however. He wanted the road to go all the way to Fairbanks, he wanted a cut-off to Haines, Alaska, and he demanded progress on a" so far neglected" side project to build a road from Johnson's Crossing up to the oilfields at Norman Wells. The Corps—and the PRA—would remain in the Arctic into the winter.

Thousands of men were in the deep woods still sheltered in tents inadequate for the looming weather. Frigid temperatures threatened already abused heavy equipment and trucks. The jerry-rigged supply operation that had grown into place behind the troops during the summer wouldn't work in winter. Truck drivers bringing supplies would confront a whole new set of problems when ice and snow re-entered the equation. Finally, morale plummeted as men who had dreamed of being home for the holidays realized that they would be spending the winter on the road.

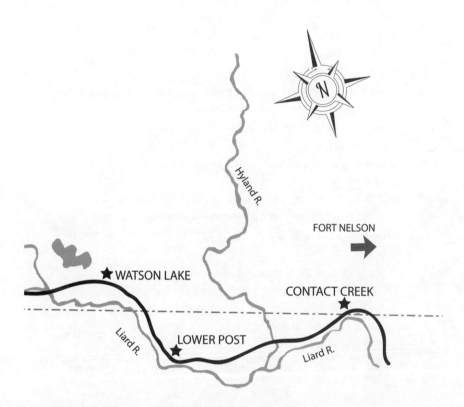

General O'Connor knew the problems he faced, probably as well as Hoge had, but he had snared Hoge's job precisely because he was a commander who danced to his boss's tune. Somervell, who would be making plans and decisions for the project, knew virtually nothing of the realities of the North Country. His new plans, especially the expansion of the project and the decision to stay in the North into the winter, would flow unaltered through O'Conner and down the chain of command. Men on the ground, especially the black men in Yukon Territory and Alaska, would suffer serious, unnecessary consequences.

Rain fell on the northern sector for the first twenty days in September. Water levels rose and flooding streams washed out bridges thrown in place during the rush of the summer. The mud came back. The temperature occasionally dropped and turned the rain to snow. Successive snows piled a bit higher and stayed on the ground a bit longer. Temperatures for September ranged from a high of eighty degrees to a low of twenty degrees.

The apprehensive men in the field knew what lay ahead, even if Somervell didn't.

Sept 20, 1942

Dearest Buzz,

I guess you have been worried, but the weather has been so bad and the roads are terrible that mail has become a luxury. It's been just three weeks ago today that I received a letter.

Well we are still unaware as to what is going to happen this winter. We may come home and we may not. I sure hope some arrangement will be made so that we might come home if only on a 30 day leave or something, but I have my doubts. I haven't seen some of the folks for a long time now and a good peep at them would be good for the soul …. How is the job coming on? The responsibility of mine is sure preying on me. I worry about it all the time. Kinda' gets me down now and then. Gosh it gets cold here. We have already had snow…

Nite, Bye and Buckets of Love, Timber.

93RD ENGINEERS WORKING BEHIND THE 340TH

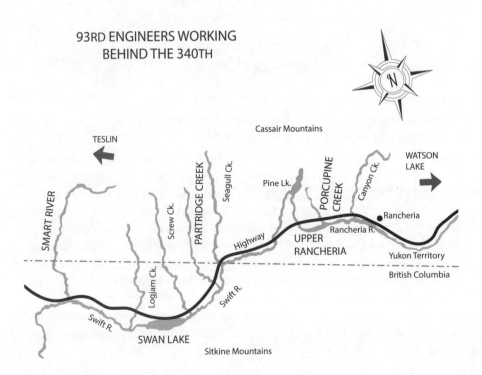

Most of the 93rd had moved into position behind the 340th during August, working to upgrade and improve the trail. Companies D and F of the 93rd had labored through August to upgrade the Carcross-Whitehorse road and finished the job. Now, on September 2, Company D joined the rest of the regiment, using the brand new—if still rough—Alaska Highway to move 150 miles to Swan Lake, 55 miles east of Nisutlin Bay."

Colonel Johnson had put Captain Pollock's Company B in the lead and positioned the rest of the 93rd along the road behind them. By the end of September, Company B worked near the Lower Rancheria River while Company C worked near Porcupine Creek. Company D ended September near Partridge Creek, and Company E operated a Sawmill at Milepost 44 between Morley Lake and Smart River.

After September 24, though, with Contact Creek in the rear view, Lyons and his H&S began pivoting the 340th to head it back toward Teslin Post. ,As the 340th turned to upgrade its own road, in October, it would effectively displace most of the 93rd.

In the Northern Sector, the wilderness between the 97th and the 18th presented some of the most difficult engineering problems of the road—but the regiments steadily closed on each other, working through the problems. General O'Connor ran the entire project out of Whitehorse. In a contemporary newspaper article, writer Morley Cassidy compared the impact of the Alaska Highway Project to that of the turn-of the-Century gold rush that had spawned the town. Economically, the highway had a far greater impact, but socially Cassidy found Whitehorse wanting. "No girls. No liquor. No water. No noise. No dancing. This is a hell of a boom town."

Soldiers packed the streets of Whitehorse. Jeeps and trucks, olive drab and marked with a white star, charged up and down Main Street. Uniformed MPs carrying wooden clubs kept order. Canadians swelled the squatter settlements of Whiskey and Moccasin Flats. Contractors jammed their offices in and among old business buildings and compact wooden Native houses. Machinery, vehicles, supplies and equipment packed vacant lots. "An isolated and seasonal community exploded from a sleepy river depot to a major military and construction complex," the journalist noted.

During an interview many years later, Lt. Squires laughed at one memory of Whitehorse. "I'll never forget watching a D8 bulldozer tow an airplane down Main Street. It was the funniest thing I had ever seen."

Tim's best friends—Audrey and Ted Laputka—
pose in front of the Depot in Whitehorse, YT.
Photo courtesy of the Timberlake Collection.

Enlisted men occasionally got detailed to Whitehorse, but most in the field—especially black enlisted men—rarely saw Whitehorse unless they became sick or ran afoul of Army regulations. As the primary conduit for instructions flowing from senior officers to the field and for information flowing from the field to senior officers, junior officers found themselves in town on a regular basis. As Regimental Transportation Officer, Tim spent a lot more time there. In late September of 1942, he was at headquarters when his old friend from Camp Lee and Camp Claiborne, Ted Laputka, walked in. Ted had been assigned to the Northwest Service Command in Whitehorse.

> Sept 29, 1942
>
> Dearest Helen,
>
> Gosh I got to get a letter off to you today and I'll be darn if we aren't right up to our necks in work and worries.
>
> But I have some news for you that to me is really news.

The other day I flew to the main base [Whitehorse] and since my last visit some new units have come in, well, I was in talking to the Colonel there and while I was in the office guess who came in, just guess—Ted Laputka. Well we just forgot about the Colonel and you can just guess what was said.

Ted and I were at Lee together, then I went to Livingston and he went to Clayborne only 30 miles away and me way up here and then way up here, Ted.

Ted is at this base however and it's a right big town in fact it has a movie [theatre]. Audrey [Ted's wife] is here also, well you can just dream how homesick when I saw that pair. I went to the hotel to see Mac [Audrey] and do you know she sure was tickled to see me, in fact kissed me right in the darn lobby.

She is to have a baby in March and they sure are a happy couple. She has a room in this hotel and here board and room cost 110.00 dollars a month.

Ted had joined the 141st Quartermaster Truck Company assigned to the 18th Regiment. Transferred senior officers routinely brought their wives along; junior officers, not so much. Ted's enterprising wife, Audrey, though, had formed the right friendship with the right senior officer's wife, and when Ted landed in Whitehorse, she landed with him.

Laputka and his smiling, gorgeous and pregnant wife temporarily tossed Tim into an emotional turmoil, but having them nearby made him happier than he had been in a long time. He would spend every minute he could with the Laputkas until Audrey, wanting her baby to be born at home, left on November 7.

Tim's September 29 letter admitted

> ...gosh sometimes I really get home sick and right now I sure am, darn seeing Ted and Audrey really made me think. But I couldn't make up my mind then, darn it. Ted looks great And he got his silver bars this month [he's now a captain]. Audrey looks fine too and she is sure a swell egg and they are really in love.
>
> Well sixteen more days and I have been here six months.

Wonder what the next six months will bring....

A few days later, back home at the 93rd Regimental Motor Pool at Morley Bay, Tim's emotions had calmed. His first October report to Buzz is the most reflective letter of the entire three-cent love affair series.

October 4, 1942

Dearest Buzz,

I am sitting on a box with a portable Underwood smoking a Wm Penn cigar, in a pair of coveralls, with a short hair cut writing a letter to the bestest gal in the United States.

Boy the northern lights were really shinnin' last nite. In twelve more days the forces of our Unc [Uncle Sam] have been here six months. In six months we built some 240 miles of road over land even trappers hadn't traveled, over land that even timber couldn't make a stand, over land that wasn't land, it was just something to fool you and make believe.

Two weeks ago I traveled some 155 miles of that road in a Jeep and we went that distance in a little better than seven hours counting time it took to wrestle three ferries across rivers that have not been bridged.

Its an engineering feat, a feat that even the Canadian government hadn't dared to try. You know Unc [Uncle Sam] screws up the works now and then, but when Unc trys or starts to do something it gets done and that's why Unc is our Unc.

The first truck has already come from the US to a point 165 miles above us [Whitehorse] ... Its Sunday night and lots, lots colder. We had our second snow last nite and this morning the mountains were covered with the ole white stuff.

Seems funny that even away up here where the population of this entire territory is not as big as Bel Air, Maryland [his home] that Sunday is Sunday, God is God and Hitler is Hitler. Even here people talk of our country and our problems like they were problems of their own just so they can say we are with the Allies, the side that says Sunday shall be Sunday, God shall be God and people shall be people.

Things are pretty well settled now as to what we will do and that is we are to stay. I guess we are going to be 'Sour Doughs' (that is a person that stays here the entire year around, in addition he must have shot a bear and date a squaw). I can do them all but the last. Maybe if these squaws would use Lux [soap] I could do that…

Ted came down the other day and we went for a little hunt, shot about eight rabbits and missed a heck of a good chance to get a bear.

Looks like the Russians are holding out and if the Germans don't get Stalingrad well they better fold up cause they have thrown in every effort they could make to take the Volga River town.

Well, Buzz, guess I better sign off station BLAB tonite and get thee into bed. Got a little flying to do tomorrow and need my rest … Love, Timber

…

THE COLDEST WINTER EVER RECORDED across northwest Canada and Alaska commenced in earnest in October. By December and January, the temperature routinely dropped to sixty below zero—a stupefying cold that none of the troops had ever experienced. Everybody suffered. A few died.

Cooks "opened eggs only to find crystals of ice in the shell. Potatoes were ribbed with frozen strips that looked like Italian marble." Placed in a pot to boil, iron-hard potatoes took longer to thaw than to cook. Returned laundry arrived in a solid chunk that had to rest beside the stove for days before underwear or a sock could be pried loose. Private Francis, of the 93rd, tossed a frozen egg against a tree—only the shell cracked.

Soldiers in the field wore down-filled parkas 24/7. Climbing into his "double mummy" sleeping bag—down-filled sleeping bag plus two blankets and a comforter—at night, a soldier wore arctic underwear, gloves, a sweater and socks. Once he brought his body, the only source of heat, to his nest, it took a half an hour or more for it to warm. He slept with his boots to keep them warm and pliable in the morning. Yet none of this really protected him from the bone-cracking cold.

Black soldiers from semi-tropical Louisiana and Mississippi suffered horribly. A crane operator in the 97th remembered, "We wore three pairs of socks with galoshes instead of shoes because leather would freeze." Those with fur mukluks or fabric galoshes stuffed them with layers of socks. A few used evergreen needles stuffed in their socks for insulation. Shoes had to be big because "tight shoes meant frozen feet."

Boos, a soldier in the 340th, spent evenings with his four tent mates huddled next to a little stove that struggled gamely to warm the tent, warming but one side of each man at a time. Another 340th engineer named Hayes remembered, "The outside of the tents were sparkling with frost all the time. Tent ropes were covered with ice. Even the inside of the tents were sparkling white with frost."

Mouton of the 93rd got his foot stuck in deep permafrost. When, with the help of his friends, he managed to free it, he had to immerse the frozen foot in a bucket of snow to slow the thawing process and avoid permanent damage. At forty below, skin froze in seconds. Soldiers kept an eye on one another's faces, looking for white spots. Ice crystals formed on eyelashes and beards, and men lost toes to frostbite.

Billy Connor, a civil engineer, remembered the greatest danger—travelling the pioneer road. "If your vehicle breaks down, walking a few miles can actually cost you your life." And the horrendous cold increased the probability of a breakdown.

Travelling the winding, twisting, often single-lane highway, drivers faced constant blind curves. They preferred to drive at night when oncoming lights would reveal the presence of opposing traffic. However, at night, temperatures fell, and a truck that failed its driver in the dark put him in serious jeopardy.

A black truck driver, serving with the 97th, broke down at the Slana Cutoff in Alaska. He gathered brush and built himself a fire, but with the surrounding air at 66 degrees below zero, the fire didn't help much. Abandoning it, he tried to walk the 14 miles to camp. He didn't make it.

On the way to Fort Nelson, PRA trucker Oscar Albanati ran into a convoy of Army trucks stopped along the road. He approached a stalled truck.

> There was a black swamper in the cab. I thought he was sleeping. The other [black soldier] had the hood up and was leaning against a fender peering into the engine. I tapped the boy on the shoulder and he fell over. He was dead, frozen stiff. He was trying to repair something. The man inside was so cold he couldn't move, but he wasn't dead.
>
> (Schmidt 1991)

The bitter cold killed softly, even kindly, but very, very quickly. "Soldiers who have handled such cases say the dead men look as if they have just peacefully and even pleasantly, sunk down in the snow for their long rest," an observer commented.

The fundamental racism that permeated the project could elevate suffering into peril for black soldiers. In Alaska, an ignorant white officer ordered ten black men into the back of an open truck for a 130-mile ride from Big Delta to Fairbanks. Knowing the ride would possibly kill and certainly cripple them, the soldiers refused. Instead of cashiering the officer, the Army court-martialed the ten soldiers for mutiny. The result? All ten men were convicted and sentenced to twenty years at hard labor. Eventually a staff judge advocate reviewed the case, freed four of the men and reduced the sentences of the other six to ten years.

Beyond the danger of frostbite and freezing to death, the treacherous winter road caused wrecks that killed and maimed. Relatively good traction in severe cold disappeared when temperatures warmed toward freezing. "I have seen tools, chains, men and even trucks sliding down [a hill] faster than a man could run," one observer wrote.

Some got really good at negotiating the perils of the winter road. A driver named Lee McMillan pulled feats on icy hills that most others couldn't duplicate. "They called him lucky, but his 'luck' came from skill and experience. Lee's trucks ran for him; and, when they didn't, he could usually fix the problem with some tape, rope or wire," a company mate insisted.

A soldier's truck didn't usually kill or maim him; but sooner or later, it would roll to the side of the road and refuse to continue. Truckers carried motley collections of scrounged tires and spare parts, and they made major repairs on motors, transmissions and rear ends there on the side of the road. At twenty, thirty, or forty below zero, metal broke, fuel lines froze, oil and grease congealed. When bulldozers and diesel trucks were required to stop, their drivers knew not to shut them down. Engines continued to rumble under covering tarps. That usually kept the engine running, but cold threatened more than just engines.

Diesel fuel congealed into gel, causing oil lines and screens to clog. A small amount of gasoline or kerosene mixed with the diesel fuel solved that problem. In the frigid fuel tank, tiny droplets of moisture condensed and then travelled through fuel lines, freezing at choke points like the carburetor intake.

Other parts of the machines—transmissions, drive lines, rear ends—all worked in lubricating fluids that severe cold thickened into gluey sludge. Sometimes, drivers had to get underneath a truck with a blowtorch and heat up the transmission and the rear axle before it would move. Some placed lighted lanterns or even built open fires under idling machines. Others salvaged large empty tomato cans from the mess, filled them with sand and saturated it with gasoline. When lit and placed under a truck, the can heaters kept lubricating fluids fluid. However, lubricating fluids tend to be extremely flammable. Lanterns, open fires and cans proved a less than satisfactory solution. All too often, idling equipment suddenly burst into spectacular flame.

Radiators presented especially difficult problems. Prestone antifreeze worked—if you could get it—but in extreme temperatures even Prestone would freeze. During December and January when the temperature along the White and Donjek Rivers hit seventy below, antifreeze froze hard in its containers. Radiators didn't require airflow to keep coolant cold, so every driver stuffed something in front of his radiator to block it. "Steam cabooses," small, wood-burning boilers, generated live steam for thawing out vehicles in a convoy.

Surprisingly, snow didn't present much of a problem. When it came, bulldozers and graders could remove it relatively easily. Ice, though, was a different matter. At more than 250 places between Watson Lake and the Alaska border frequent icing caused delays. In the North Country, ice and permafrost lie only a few inches below the surface of the ground even during summer and during winter, they come to the top.

Ice doesn't form in the current of swift-flowing streams but on the sides and bottom, narrowing the channel and raising the bottom until the water overflows, forming new channels. Ice completely buried approaches to bridges built back in the summer. When spring arrived in 1943, floods washed the bridges away. One bridge on the highway was rebuilt seven times.

In frigid northern culverts and ditches, freezing water created "mushroom ice." Water freezes, the current bleeds through and more water freezes. Ice builds in layers. Eventually, huge blocks of honeycombed ice grew to block roads. Troops had to burn oil to thaw out culverts, and they had to repeat the process every few hours.

At the middle of October, resigned to his fate and clearly back in something approaching good spirits, Tim penned a vivid description of a slice of his life as it moved on into a North Country winter.

> October 17, 1942
>
> Dearest Buzz,
>
> There is no one else here tonite, but Lt. Parker (the Asst Supply Officer) and myself. We are now in the process of heating up our tent so we can take a shower in our home made shower which consists of a gas barrel cut in half with a valve on the bottom. We have the barrel up in the air about 7 feet and we have a step we

climb up on so you can pour in the hot water. Some stuff, huh!

Its Saturday too and when I think of all the things we use to do on Saturday nite well I just get home sick. Parker and I are figuring on a big game of checkers after our shower and then to bed about ten.

Gee, we haven't had any mail for over a week now. Sure seems rough but when it does come its plenty ok. Your last letter was dated Sept. 23rd.

Tomorrow I got a big tractor job coming up. My job as Equipment Engineer really keeps one going. Three times this week we were out repairing machines at ungodly hours and you really get tired.

Wait a minute honey I got to put some wood on the stove. Darn you know I haven't had much Xmas since I have been out of college. Last year never got home. This year is just as bad and plenty worst. Boy if I could get home for New Years would we have a time boy oh boy. However no one has any news on our going home.

We have completed our mission of building a road and we are now digging in for all winter.

Tim in front of his very cold tent at Morley Bay.
Photo courtesy of the Timberlake Collection.

CHAPTER 14

THE EXTRAORDINARY ROAD

The project had brought sickness to the Natives. Outsiders had always brought sickness. Few societies on earth developed in an isolation as profound as that of the indigenous people of the North, and that isolation set them up for recurring bouts with diseases transmitted by strangers.

In 1942, when illnesses began to appear in the Native population, the Army and PRA physicians who came with the Corps offered their services, but Canadian bureaucracy made that difficult. Territorial authorities, protecting existing private medical practices, required Canadian licensure for physicians treating Canadian citizens. As illness spread and the death count rose, this requirement languished. The Whitehorse Army Hospital provided services to Canadian civilians—except for those with tuberculosis. Not equipped to handle TB isolation, the physicians feared the medical facility would do more harm than good by increasing the spread of that disease.

Carcross suffered epidemics of chicken pox, measles, whooping cough, jaundice and dysentery. Millie Jones remembered the Royal Canadian Mounted Police piling her and her friends into a truck and delivering them to the Army dispensary for immunizations to help avoid an epidemic of diphtheria.

Ida Calmegane, age 14 when the soldiers came to Yukon in 1942, recalled the epidemics in Carcross. Her mother, a nurse, spent night after night sitting with sick neighbors. One woman lost her husband and two children within hours of each other. Ida lost her sister. Teslin Post had become a major center of operations in the interior of Yukon Territory and disease hit the village as hard as any community along the route. Teslin suffered eight epidemics in 1942.

> November 2, 1942
>
> Dearest Helen,
>
> ...one of the Indian villages they all got measles.
> Five people died. Seems they get some kind of trouble
> in their head and it kills them...

Two strains of measles, Rubeola and then Rubella, had plagued Teslin since September and Whitehorse General Hospital sent young nurse Corinne Cyr there to care for the victims. With less than three years of experience, Corinne headed out with a supply of blankets, aspirin, cough syrup and penicillin. The parting advice from a physician at the hospital: "Use your common sense. Good luck."

Virtually every resident had measles. Corinne visited their homes every morning and again every evening with the help of the Mounties. A Catholic priest turned his house into a makeshift infirmary and an Anglican minister did the same with his church. Frank Morris, a Native surveyor, supplied the Anglicans with fresh water and fire wood and practically lived at the small church. Officers from the 93rd and 340th came by regularly to help.

Once the September meeting at Contact Creek had linked the road from Dawson Creek to Whitehorse, engineers transitioned from building road to improving it. At the beginning of October, Company A of the 93rd traveled the rough new highway 335 miles north through Whitehorse and on to the Stockton Bridge over the Aishihik River. The move took 12 days. The white soldiers of the 18th needed winter quarters, so the black men of Company A would spend October building them.

On October 8, Company B of the 93rd left its bivouac near Swan Lake to move to Kluane Lake behind the 18th Regiment. Their morning report notes "Road very bad. Weather very cold." They arrived at Kluane on October 11, pitching their tents in falling snow. The white soldiers of the 18th needed winter quarters there too. The black soldiers of Company B would build them.

On October 22, Company C of the 93rd started on the first forty miles of the Canol Road, north from Johnson's Crossing toward Norman Wells and its oil fields in the sub-arctic of Canada's Northwest Territory—the road General Somervell had made a priority. Company D remained near Partridge Creek throughout October. Company E operated its sawmill during October, moving it at mid-month to Carcross.

Colonel Johnson left the 93rd on October 16, reassigned to command the 18th. Lieutenant Colonel Walter Hodge took his place and found his troops scattered over hundreds of miles of highway—building winter quarters for white regiments, building the Canol Road and doing "odd jobs."

Further north, two regiments labored to close the last gap in the Alcan Highway. Moving up from the south, the 18th grappled with ice, permafrost and deteriorating weather. Its men built three bridges, one eighty feet over Lake Creek Ford and two—fifty and 245 feet—over the Koidern River. The rest of the regiment laid corduroy and built culverts.

As winter settled in, the 18th loaded supplies on sledges and towed them with D8s. Fred Rust recalled the scene as a "…mudway twisting and turning up a wooded valley with a dozer convoy dipping and twisting along like a roller coaster in slow motion" through "Christmas trees and brush." When two platoons from Company B crossed the White River on October 10 the mercury hovered near 35 below.

Colonel Lionel Robinson's 97th black regiment, working alongside Duesenberg Construction Company, moved south out of Alaska to the Canadian border where it expected to meet up with the 18th. Arriving to find no connecting road and no sign of the missing white regiment, the Alaska battalion marched into Canada and kept on building south. Duesenberg Construction brought additional men, dozers and equipment to the assault. Supplies for soldiers and civilians alike had to come all the way from Valdez—and over the fearsome Thompson Pass. Snow piled high, threatening to close the supply route. Colonel Robinson also worried about winter quarters for his men, but the 18th had promised to have portable barracks for them at the White River.

On October 25, Corporal Refines Sims of the 97th worked his dozer through the trees near Beaver Creek, branches snapping at his cold cheeks. Lieutenant Walter Mason remembered, "...the 18th cat heard him from a distance and came overland without any trail cutting to meet Sims' cat." H.W. Richardson, editor of *Engineering News-Record*, had spent the night in Mason's tent and was on hand to witness and photograph closing of the Alcan Highway's last gap.

On November 1, Richardson sent the following telegram to his boss:

> In a murky arctic snow storm at Beaver Creek ... in the wilds of the Yukon, the climax of building the Alcan Highway was reached at four p.m. Sunday Oct. 25, when the advance tractor crews from east and west came together, closing the last gap in the trail route.
>
> After seeing trees fall away from him in weeks of swamping out the advance cut, Corporal Refines Sims, Jr., negro, 'catskinner' of the crew working down from Alaska, frantically, retreated with his diesel bulldozer as trees ahead started falling his way, not realizing the meeting was imminent. In a few moments, the lead bulldozer of the Yukon crew burst through the last patch of timber and brush, piloted by Private Alfred Jalufka.
>
> (Duesenberg 1994)

Mind you, the 18th had only "holed through" the trail from the White River, so the 97th and Duesenberg still effectively had thirty miles of road to build.

The regiments actually brought their roads to Beaver Creek on November 2. The promised winter barracks for the black regiment did not materialize.

On the north bank of the White River, an enlisted surveyor of the 29th Topo unit suffered abdominal pain. Captain Guardino of the Medical Corps diagnosed appendicitis and had the patient carried by litter across the river on planks connecting the gaps in the incomplete trestle-balk bridge, loaded into a waiting ambulance and driven to the Donjek River base camp. Doctors at the base camp requested an evacuation plane early the next morning. It failed to show up, so they requested two surgeons and medical instruments—urgently. As the weather rapidly deteriorated, Les Cook and two surgeons agreed to make the flight through valleys and over mountains in the howling dark. They made it. The soldier lived. Like many of pilot Cook's exploits, the story raced the length of the highway.

One month later, Cook again made news, devastating the troops—especially those of the 93rd and 340th who thought of him as their own. The flyer had finally pushed his luck and skill too far, crashing his plane to die on a street in Whitehorse.

However, the road was open from Dawson Creek to Fairbanks, and the Army would celebrate that. Soldier's Summit in Canada, one hundred miles east of the Alaska-Yukon border, was selected for the ceremony. Predictably, the weather interfered. The ceremony, scheduled and rescheduled, finally happened on November 20. Deluxe barracks and a mess hall for two hundred invited guests sprouted near the Slim's River Bridge at the south end of Kluane Lake—fully equipped with stoves for heat, generators for lights and aromatic spruce planks. The North Country graced the event with temperatures 15 degrees below zero and a snowstorm. Bonfires crackled, sending plumes of smoke into the gray overcast. While dignitaries spoke and listened and ate and celebrated, the thousands of men who had made it happen, still stationed throughout the wilderness along the road, endured.

Tim's Motor Pool at Morley Bay struggled to support a regiment scattered over hundreds of miles of Yukon Territory. For the most part, "support" meant collecting worn and broken equipment. His two October letters show us a miserable, homesick young man, longing for his girl and his home.

> October 11, 1942
>
> Dearest Helen,
>
> My oh my but I wish I could get home for Xmas, but guess we are snake bit. For right now we are figuring on digging in. Some of our outfits are making homes or log cabins now. Guess I'll be a sour dough after all.

Yesterday we had another snow and today it's colder than Hell. I'll bet from now on it continues that way...

He can't bring himself to let go of his faint and fading dream of making it home for Christmas.

> October 16, 1942
>
> Dearest Buzz,
>
> Today is an ungodly day here. It has snowed and then turned into rain. The ground is muddy and wet. Just sloppy as can be.
>
> Gosh Buzz news on coming home is still ain't. Sure wish it was soon. I seem to be getting homesick now for some reason.
>
> Boy that old rain is really coming done now. News around here is mighty slim. Things just don't happen. Nothin' but work and seven days a week 30 days month after month. It gets kinda tiresome. Be glad when I can get a job where you work five or six days a week and decent hours.

On November 2, he responded immediately to mail from home, changing the salutation in recent letters—"Dearest Helen" on October 11, "Dearest Buzz" on October 16.

> November 2, 1942
>
> Dearest Helen May,
>
> Gosh honey you should be here now. The temperature is just five points below zero and the darn thing won't stop going down. Last nite she was colder than heck and tonite its getting set for another rough session with ole man winter leading the way.
>
> Got some mail yesterday and I was sure tickled. Mail is like a dose of good whisky in this winter gale. It peps you up.
>
> Looks like we'll be a seein' xmas from way up here. Ain't no sign of going home.

He shared with Helen May a tiny portion of his misery. She had written about the annual 4-H conference. He "missed all the ole 4-H gang and almost bawled when he read her letter about them." Then, on November 10, he received a whole packet of letters and the strong young man was back in his response.

November 11, 1942

Dearest Helen May,

Yesterday quick like a rabbit I received letters 1,2, 3 and 4 and also an unnumbered letter, but just the same I was tickled pink.

Well, honey the ink is even froze. All last week it was below zero, Anywhere from 8 to 26 and let me tell you it was cold. I took a little trip in a jeep and you know with all our winter clothing on it wasn't so cold.

The cold here is funny, but it will freeze you up in a hurry. Some of the boys can't take it when you consider they never saw snow before...

By the middle of November Tim had accepted the reality that he's going to winter in the North Country.

November 14/15, 1942

Dearest Helen May,

Indeed ain't much news. But I have been reading plenty of stuff here of late and honey those paper clipping of the world series and the football games. Sure made me feel at home.

Things are just going along slow. Everyone is busy getting ready for the winter. Ole man winter has been howlin' too around the corners at 26 below.

Well Buzz looks like Xmas isn't going to see us together. Gee I would give a 100 bucks to be able to run up the back steps at home with you tucked under my arm callin' 'Hey, Mom', for that one act alone.

Through November, Hodge gradually assembled his 93rd back at its old stomping grounds at Squanga Lake. Leaving Kluane Lake in early November, Company B made its way back to Whitehorse. Several men suffered from frozen feet during the move. On November 15, Company A left Stockton Bridge to join them. They paused in Whitehorse to construct winter barracks for North West Service Command, but by the end of the month both companies were back at Squanga Lake.

> November 24, 1942
>
> Dearest Buzz,
>
> Ain't had no mail for ten days now, but I'll wait and you know I'll be a getting about five or six from you.
>
> Gee darling I am getting plenty homesick and golly day I am pining for you. Honest if I ever see you again I'll never let you out of my sight. These darn leaves are not definite and I'll be darn if I know when I'll ever get one. But in any case, I think I should be home sometime before March.
>
> Well guess you have been reading about the official opening of the road. It was a great thing and a great engineering feat, but it has been tough and plenty rough.

On Thanksgiving Day, Tim wrote at length about the feast the Army managed to provide at Morley Bay.

> November 26, 1942
>
> Dearest Helen May,
>
> Well today is thanxs day and can't see much in sight. It is about 9:30 now in the morning and I just finished telling my crew of 110 men that today would be a holiday and that one of our boys who is a minister will conduct a service for my men at one today. At two we are going to have dinner.
>
> Its not going to be such a bad Thanxs day. Last nite we went down to the Bay and with a sled, transferred a load of turkeys, candy, cakes and fixings from one truck and brought it over the ice to another truck. The River has frozen over but the ice is not safe for high axle loads. Our cooks got up at five this morning and began boiling the turkeys in hot water to thaw them out.
>
> Considering being away up here Uncle Sam did a

nice job of fixing up for our holiday. But Buzz I sure wish I could see you. Boy its loney here and I ain't taking it so good. Oh yes it was a mere 26 below this morning among other things.

Well its after dinner now and I am still trying to finish this letter. We had turkey, dehydrated potatoes, mints, olives and hot cocoa. It was swell. There was plenty for all and we were thankful to get a nice meal. We still have some left so guess we'll have it today for supper.

Gee I hope you all had a fine time. Today you know for the first time since I have been here that I actually prayed. I love you more than ever. Bye, Love, Nite.

PS In your words lets say

We have each other dearly, Buzz and Timber.

Someone took photographs during that Thanksgiving dinner at Morley Bay. One, which survived only in Timberlake family legend, showed a sea of black faces—Tim's face one of a few white dots among them. Remembering the day his father strode onto a Maryland baseball diamond and marched his humiliated son off the field, Tim scrawled a message on the back of his copy of the photo and mailed it to his dad.

"Dear Pop," the message read, "Let's see you get me out of this one."

AFTERWORD

B y December 10, the 93rd Engineers had completed its work on the Alcan Highway. Into December, Company C, joined by a detachment from Company B, struggled with the Canol Road until their single operational dozer broke through the ice into a stream. Back at Squanga Lake, in search of another dozer to pull his free, Boyd discovered that the 35th Engineers had inherited the Canol project. His Company C and the Company B detachments were returned to the frozen winter camp at Squanga Lake.

Christmas was a dismal affair for the men of the 93rd. Most of them still lived in frigid tents. There were plenty of evergreens in the region and icicles decorated the tents. Unfortunately, the trees and icicles represented misery, not Christmas.

> December 17, 1942
>
> Dearest Buzz,
>
> …Well honey child let me tell you it was plenty cold this AM and don't let me kid you, something like 54 below, and mixed with a little bit of wind, it just about takes your breath away. Right now I am all but sitting on the stove and if I could without getting my bottom section burned I would do that.
>
> …Are all the stores all trimmed up for xmas and stuff, guess they are … Nite, Love and Bye, Timber

On Christmas Eve, Tim wrote a Christmas letter to his family.

> December 24, 1942
>
> Dearest Mother and Folks;
>
> Tonight is Christmas Eve. Tonight is the night that years ago I waited eleven months and 23 days for. Tonight is the night that sort of ties a rope around the families of America so we can say that we are bonded together. Best of all, tonight is the night that mother and dad will do their darnndest to make those kids dash

down the steps at six in the morning with joy and glee that somehow just bespeaks the nature of our family.

I wish I could be home, folks, but tonight I'll just sit here and have a Christmas smoke dream, dreaming of those times of joy that each year would, without fail, drown our home in a mist of greeting and good cheer for all. Golly and how Pop used to just lie in bed waiting for those rascals to get up and with joy he would be pulled from his covers and carried downstairs just like he was a kid of old.

But tonight somehow, folks, Christmas is different. All the fellows are gathered around talking of the times they had and the wonderful things they received, but tonight we are all gathered here just waiting for either a chance to make America have more seasons of joy or a chance to say, "Well, we tried."

But really, Folks, we aren't down hearted. We are just thinking of you all back home. And what more in this world could a man want than the right to think of home and what his home meant to him. It's wonderful, Folks.

…I hope and pray with all my heart that this Christmas makes you proud and gives you the right to say "Well our boys are doing their part."

To All a Merry Christmas. Love, Turner

Privileged to have a relatively warm place to "gather around," the young officers of the 93rd had a much less dismal Christmas than the black men they commanded. Antony Mouton of Company A remembered beef hash for Christmas dinner—and loneliness. Mouton and another soldier, John Lockott, spent the day in their tent listening to one cracked record, played over and over. *Serenade In Blue* by Paul Whiteman and Helen Forrest which reminded them of home.

It wasn't until after Christmas that the 93rd was finally relieved of highway duty. December 26, Company A sailed from Skagway to Chilkoot Barracks in Southeastern Alaska near Haines, and by January 3, the entire regiment had joined them. Here the men finally moved into heated barracks—a glorious luxury after months in dilapidated tents.

Temporarily, the regiment left Lt. Tim Timberlake and Capt. Lowry in Whitehorse. The Corps planned to send the 93rd to Cold Bay and Unmak near the Aleutian war front, and the two motor pool officers spent much of January at headquarters, arranging to replace damaged heavy equipment and organizing its shipment north.

> January 18, 1942
>
> Dearest Helen May;
>
> Golly day honey, I sure am stranded now, darnnit. I am at Whitehorse and our outfit his gone to parts unknown and I am to join them later. As a result my mail has been out of the picture ... Nite, Bye, and Love Timber

Tim received no mail in Whitehorse. Worse, his frantic efforts to arrange for leave got nowhere. His luck finally turned when he joined the regiment at Chilkoot Barracks near the end of January.

> January 26, 1943
>
> Dearest Buzz;
>
> Well I finally joined the outfit [Chilkoot Barracks] and do you know I got 51 letters and 12 were from you, just think of it 12 letters all in one shot. They were all about xmas and New years and all your presents and honey child I sure was glad to read them...
>
> ...I'll let you in on the potent news. Here it is. Leaves have been cancelled, but I have been chosen to do some stuff in Seattle, and I'll be there about a month and Buzz you just got to come out. I will arrive sometime in the early part of Feb. and stay until late in March...
>
> I'll wire when I arrive and give you all the dope and stuff, but my duties there will not permit me to leave Seattle. Ain't it grand honey, why its wonderful. Boy I am tickled pink. I'll wire you from various points starting about the next five days before you get this letter.
>
> Nite, Love and Bye, Timber

Given even a little time to think about it, Tim figured out that Seattle offered more than just an opportunity to *see* his lady. Like a good engineer, he saw the opportunity, prepared a plan and a "to do" list and went for it.

> January 29, 1943

Dearest Buzz,

This is a hurried letter but I got to give you the dope. As to my arrival in Seattle, it depends on the weather, but I'll wire as soon as I get there. As I wrote before, my duties there will not permit me to leave.

So how's this for an idea … maybe see if someone can't arrange that you fly out. It will cost a lot, but Buzz I am tellin' you this may be the last time we'll be together for one long time and I mean a long time.

Here's what we have to do—that's if you want to get married. One is have our marriage certificate made in two copies, so I can get the additional pay [soldiers, including officers, received extra pay for dependents] … Then I'll make an allotment to you…

I know its not the way our families had it figured out. Its not the way I wanted it and it won't be near as nice. That's getting married in Seattle, I mean.

Now Buzz, its all up to you. If you want to get married that way here is one guy who is ready. See what your mother and dad have to say…

It's a mighty big jump honey. But Buzz, I love you and you love me—and if we don't do it when we have a chance it just won't be done. Maybe its not the right thing to do at all but its all up to you.

You're the boss, Buzz. Nite, Love, Bye Timber

The engineer's proposal did the trick. Throughout the three-cent love affair, in the face of Tim's worries and doubts, Helen had been absolutely committed, thoroughly in love. Offered the ultimate prize—Tim as her husband—she apparently valued it enough to ignore the ungainly proposal. But a week later, his arrangements hit a breath-stopping temporary snag.

February 6, 1943

Dearest Buzz,

…Somehow, somewhere there is a big screw up in the orders …. It is definite that my trip to Seattle is not off, however there is a delay …. When I get my first definitive dope, I'll write …. I sure hope this Seattle trip

doesn't peter out. It would break me. Nite, Bye, Love
Timber

It's not hard to imagine the impact of this on the excited and nervous girl packing her trousseau back in Somerset. The daughter of George Bryan, however, was made of stern stuff. Helen stayed packed, and she waited.

...

FINALLY, TWO DAYS BEFORE THE men of the 93rd boarded the *SS Chirikof* for transport to the Aleutians, Lt. Timberlake boarded a plane for temporary duty in Seattle. On February 16, 1943, Western Union brought Helen a telegram. "Arrive in Seattle soon ... Love, Turner."

She boarded a Baltimore and Ohio train in Washington, D.C. on February 19. Four days later, tears flowing, she stepped into Tim's arms on a platform in Seattle. The figure that had graced his dreams for 14 months, actually stood, warm and real, in the circle of his arms, her wet cheek pressed to his.

Helen had a friend who lived in Seattle—Lois Preston—who would be her bridesmaid and her temporary hostess. Lieutenant Paren, a resourceful friend of Tim's, got them a marriage license and a waiver of the usual waiting period. On the evening of February 25, 1943, at the Chapel On The Hill at Fort Lawton, Tim and Helen marched to the altar and exchanged vows. Tim finally got to kiss his bride. That night they moved together into a room at the Ben Franklin Hotel.

Tim wasn't the only military man taking advantage of leave time in Seattle. Helen recorded the arrivals and departures of young officers and their wives and girlfriends at the Ben Franklin—the lunches and dinners, movies and dancing at the Olympic Bowl. They had a really good time. Helen even made a guarded reference to an afternoon "tussel" in their hotel room. A quiet desperation lay just below the joyous surface. On March 3, Helen noted that Lt. Paren shipped out. His wife, Skooter, left on Thursday. On March 20, Lt. Schmidt and Lt. Wells departed.

Tim and Buzz counted anniversaries in weeks. On their fifth-week anniversary, Tim gave his new bride camellias. On their sixth, he gave her red carnations. They talked about everything but "the elephant in the room"—his impending return to the regiment in the Aleutians. On April 5, Buzz did a big wash and ironed Timber's shirts and pants. They dined at the American Oyster House, took in a movie and strolled the long way back to the hotel.

Newlyweds taking the first tremulous steps into intimacy, they tried hard to ignore the inexorable march of time. April 12, 1943 brought the inevitable.

At 7:15 pm, they got the call. Timber would leave the next morning. She pressed his uniform and he packed his foot locker. They fooled around and played. Timber was in one of his crazy moods. They finally got to bed about 1:00 a.m. On the way to be married at Fort Lawton, they had marveled at majestic Mt. Rainier. Their early morning trip to the airfield on April 13 offered the same nostalgic view. Tim's plane lifted off promptly at 8:00 a.m.

The 93rd would do the necessary but unglamorous work of building and maintaining runways, hangers, barracks and other facilities for Alaska Defense Forces in the Aleutians until the middle of 1944—an assignment that made the Yukon look like the Riviera. In addition to wild temperature variations, the Aleutians offered freakish winds—sixty or even 120 miles an hour—constant thick fog, and endless rain and snow.

Tim's journey from Seattle to Cold Bay took a while, occurring in stages, and he reinstated the three-cent love affair en route. Two days out, he noted one more anniversary—the seventh week. He counted forty hours since he had seen and held her. It felt like forty weeks. His letters ached with missing her.

On April 28, Tim walked down to the Cold Bay dock into snow and a high head wind—back into his regiment. "The boys" gave the "old married man" a hard time, he wrote. "Seattle is a memory now."

The marriage that began in Seattle in 1943 lasted until Tim Timberlake's death in 2001—58 years. When the couple said goodbye on April 13, the three-cent love affair would be all they had for a very, very long time. Two and a half years passed before they saw each other again.

The performance of the 93rd Engineers and other black Alaska Highway builders not only helped win World War II, but changed the course of discrimination in America. General Simon Bolivar Buckner—who had originally protested having black troops sent to his Alaska command—ordered the 93rd dispatched to fight in the Aleutians. Other units got excellent reviews as they manned war fronts around the world.

It should also be noted that the Army was the first agency in the U.S. government to integrate—an idea that many deemed impossible when the Alaska Highway builders were first sent to the Far North.

Captain and Mrs. Timberlake.
Photo courtesy of the Timberlake Collection.

Acknowledgments

In the three and a half years it has taken us to complete this book, a lot of people have participated and helped us. Among them, no one deserves our heartfelt thanks more than our two mentors—Heath Twichell and Lael Morgan.

On the 2013 trip to Canada and Alaska that jump-started our project, Heath's *Northwest Epic* was our guide and bible. Chris' dog-eared copy rode in the front seat with us the whole way. When someone led Heath to our blog and he contacted us, we were star struck, and his encouragement was a major factor in our decision to write this book.

Heath reviewed early drafts, helped us sort things out and find a focus, and encouraged us every step of the way. When we finally met him in person at his home in Rhode Island in 2015, he formally signed on to the effort to help us find a publisher and he has been tireless in that effort ever since.

On that same trip to Canada and Alaska, we found ourselves in the archives at the University of Alaska, Fairbanks, looking at the collected papers of Lael Morgan. We knew of Lael, of course. She has been writing about the North Country and other things for many years. We did not know, though, about her heroic efforts to correct the historical record and bring to light the participation of black soldiers in the construction of the Alaska Highway. Among other things, Lael had found and interviewed a number of veterans of the black regiments. Her interview notes were an invaluable resource.

When we sent her our "completed" manuscript a year ago, she called us. "There's a book in there somewhere," she said. And she offered to help us find it. In the course of a frantic three months last summer, Lael conducted via phone and email what amounted to a post-graduate seminar in how to write a book. And the volume in your hands is the book she helped us 'find'.

BIBLIOGRAPHY

The authors have made every effort to provide an accurate and up-to-date bibliography in this text. The websites listed herein are not affiliated with the authors and the authors make no guarantee that the website addresses or their content will not change or remain visible to the public.

1942. *11 February 1942 for President Roosevelt. On February 11, 1942 you approved a joint proposal of the Secretaries of War, Navy and Interior for construction of the Highway.* Memorandum, Archived at U.S. Army Corps of Engineers Office of History, Humphreys Engineer Center, Fort Belvoir, Virginia.

1942. *13 February 1942, to the Chief of Staff. Subject: International Highway. Authorized expedited construction. Notified Secretary of State and letter to Pierrepont Moffat from Secretary of State.* Memorandum, Archived at U.S. Army Corps of Engineers Office of History, Humphreys Engineer Center, Fort Belvoir, Virginia.

1942. *14 February 1942, to Chief of Engineers from Secretary of War. Orders to construct a pioneer type road from Fort St. John, Canada to Big Delta, Alaska.* Memorandum, Archived at U.S. Army Corps of Engineers Office of History, Humphreys Engineer Center, Fort Belvoir, Virginia.

1942. *16 February 1942, from Secretary of War to Secretary of State, authorizing construction of International Highway approved by president.* Memorandum, Archived at U.S. Army Corps of Engineers Office of History, Humphreys Engineer Center, Fort Belvoir, Virginia.

2,000 Colored Reserve Officers Are Available. 1940. "The Pittsburgh Courier." October 5: Newspapers.com website.

1942. "24 April 1942, from Brig. Gen. Sturdevant to Brig. Gen. Hoge, dividing highway into the Whitehorse Sector and the Ft. St. John Sector assigning O'Connor to the southern sector." Letter.

1942. *27 March 1942, from Major A.C. Welling to Colonel Hoge.* Memorandum, Archived at U.S. Army Corps of Engineers Office of History, Humphreys Engineer Center, Fort Belvoir, Virginia.

1942. *4 March 1942, from Adjutant General in War Department to Colonel Hoge to travel to Ft. St. John, B.C.* Orders, Archived at U.S. Army Corps of Engineers Office of History, Humphreys Engineer Center, Fort Belvoir, Virginia.

Administered by Parks Canada. 2008. "Caribou Hotel." *Canada's Historic Places.* Accessed September 2013. www.historicplaces.ca/en/rep-reg/place-lieu. aspx?id=9834.

n.d. *Alaska and Polar Regions Collections.* Elmer E. Rasmuson Library, University of Alaska, Fairbanks, AK.

n.d. "Alaska Natives Before Statehood." *PBS.* Accessed July 2014. www.pbs.org/wgbh/americanexperience/features/alaska-natives.

2017. "Alaska's Heritage: Road Transportation." *Alaska History and Cultural Studies, Chapters 4-10.* Accessed December 2014. www.akhistorycourse.org/articles/article.php?artID=175.

n.d. "All About Testudo." *University of Maryland Mascot.* Accessed July 2014. www.umd.edu/testudo.html.

Allard, Dean C. 2008. "The North Pacific Campaign in Perspective." In *Alaska at War 1941-1945: The Forgotten War Remembered,* by editor Fern Chandonnet. Fairbanks: University of Alaska Press.

Allen, Jeanette Thomas. 2016. "Daughter of Clarence L. Thomas, 93rd Engineers Company B." Email to author.

n.d. "America's Territory: Overland Routes Develop." *Alaska History and Cultural Studies.* Accessed December 2014. www.akhistorycourse.org/americas-territory/overland-routes-develop.

n.d. "American Experience: Building the Alaska Highway, interviews." *PBS.* Accessed July 2014. www.akhistorycourse.org/articles/article.php?artID=230.

n.d. "American Experience: Building the Alaska Highway, transcript." *PBS.* Accessed August 2014. www.pbs.org/wgbh/americanexperience/features/transcript/alaska-transcript/.

Austin, Finis Hugo. 2000. "Obituary." *Archived at Toledo-Lucas County Public Library, Ohio.* May 17. Accessed January 2015. www.toledolibrary.org/obits/request_submit.asp.

—. 1986. *Why We Behave Like Negroes.* New York: Carlton Press, Inc.

Bailey, J.R. "Bill". 2009. "1941 Louisiana Maneuvers: The Big One." *The Military Trader.* January 7. Accessed October 2013. www.militarytrader.com/military-trader-news/1941_louisiana_maneuvers-the_big_one.

Baskin, Gertrude. 1946. *Hitch-hiking the Alaska Highway.* Toronto: The Macmillan Company of Canada.

Blasor-Bernhardt, Donna. 1992. *Before ... the Tent in Tok: Early Stories of the Alaska Highway and the Pioneers Who Built It.* Fairbanks: Graphic North.

—. 2004. *Pioneer Road: Recollections of the Pioneers Who Built the Alaska Highway.* Las Vegas: ArcheBooks Publishing.

Bollin, Jr., John. n.d. "American Experience: Building the Alaska Highway, Interview." *PBS.* Accessed August 2014. www.pbs.org/wgbh/americanexperience/features/interview/alaska-interviews/.

—. 2007. "Maryland Generations." *The War, Veteran Profiles.* Accessed June 2010. ww2.mpt.org/thewar/profiles/bollen.html.

Bonnell, Ray. 2013. "A Wilderness Airstrip Serves the History of Interior Alaska." *Fairbanks Daily News-Miner.* December 21. Accessed March 2014. www.newsminer.com/features/sundays/sketches_of_alaska/a-wilderness-airstrip-serves-the-history-of-interior-alaska/article-1ce675aa-6a83-11e3-b66d-0019bb30f31a.html.

Boyd, Robert Platt, Jr. 1992. *Me and Company C.* Library of Congress Catalogue Card #92-90656: Self published.

Brady, Jeff. 2013. *Skagway, City of the New Century.* Skagway: Lynn Canal Publishing.

Brig. Gen. Clarence L. Sturdevant. 1942. *September Monthly Report of Operation, Alcan Highway.* Military report, Archived at U.S. Army Heritage and Education Center, Carlisle, Pennsylvania.

Brig. Gen. Hoge. 1942. *17 April 1942, from Brig. Gen Hoge to Brig. Gen. Sturdevant. Requesting a seventh regiment to follow the 341st.* Letter, Archived at U.S. Army Corps of Engineers Office of History, Humphreys Engineer Center, Fort Belvoir, Virginia.

Brig. Gen. L.T. Gerow, Asst Chief of Staff; Brig. Gen. R.W. Crawford; G.C. Marshall, Chief of Staff; Lt. Col. R. M. Young, Asst. Sec. War Department. 1942. *For the Chief of Staff, Discussion and action recommended for the International Highway, February 6.* Memorandum, Archived at U.S. Army Corps of Engineers Office of History, Humphreys Engineer Center, Fort Belvoir, Virginia.

Brigadier General Hoge. 1942. *12 September 1942, Commendation from Brigadier General Hoge to all personnel of the Whitehorse Sector, Alcan Highway.* Humphreys Engineer Center, Fort Belvoir, Virginia: Archived at U.S. army Corps of Engineers Office of History.

Brigadier General Sturdevant. 1942. *From Brigadier General Sturdevant to Colonel W. M. Hoge, Construction of the Canadian-Alaskan Military Highway under command of Col. Hoge, March 3.* Letter, Humphreys Engineer Center, Fort Belvoir, Virginia: Archived at U.S. Army Corps of Engineers Office of History.

Bureau, U.S. Census. n.d. www.quickfacts.census.gov/qfd/states/02000.html.

Bush, Norman. 2008. "The Alcan Saga, 1942 - 1943." In *Alaska at War 1941 - 1945: The Forgotten War Remembered*, by editor Fern Chandonnet. Fairbanks: University of Alaska Press.

Calverley, Dorothea. 2017. "Early Forts on the Upper Peace River." *South Peace Historical Society.* Accessed August 2014. www.calverley.ca/article02-009-early-forts-on-the-upper-peace-river/.

—. 2017. "Knox McCusker Guide and Surveyor with the Mary Henry Expedition." *South Peace Historical Society.* Accessed August 2014. www.calverley.ca/article/03-013-knox-mccusker-guide-surveyor-with-the-mary-henry-expedition/.

—. 2017. "The Fort Nelson Trail and E.J. Spinney." *South Peace Historical Society.* Accessed July 2014. www.calverley.ca/article/03-030-the-fort-nelson-trail-e-j-spinney/.

2017. "Carcross." *Sights and Sites of the Yukon.* Accessed September 2013. www.sightsandsites.ca/south/site/carcross.

2017. "Carcross Desert." *Sights and Sites of the Yukon.* Accessed September 2013. www.sightsandsites.ca/south/site/carcross-desert.

2015. "Carcross Historic Buildings: A Walking Tour." *Montana Mountain.* Accessed September 2013. www.tc.gov.yk.ca/publications/2015carcrossWTweb.pdf.

n.d. *Caribou Crossing Adventure Company.* Accessed August 2012. www.destinationcarcross.com/ccacprofile.htm.

Carroll, Chaplain E.G. 1942 - 1943. *A Visitation to Whitehorse: We have fought the road.*

Cassell, Captain J.L. n.d. *Diesel Engine Experiences on the Alcan Highway.* Lecture, Archived at US Army Corps of Engineers Office of History, Humphreys Engineer Center, Fort Belvoir, Virginia.

Cassidy, Morley. 1943. "Whitehorse boom outdoes '98 gold seekers." *The Nebraska State Journal,* June 27: Newspapers.com website.

Chandonnet, Fern, editor. 2008. *Alaska At War 1941-1945: The Forgotten War Remembered.* Fairbanks: Univeristy of Alaska Press.

Church, William D. MSC. 2009. "The North Atlantic Area, Northwest Canada." *Preventative Medicine in WWII Series, Vol. VIII, Ch. 6. U.S. Army Medical Department Office of Medical History.* August 26. www.history.amedd.army.mil/booksdocs/wwii/civilaffairs/chapter6.htm.

Coates, Ken S. and William R. Morrison. 1968. *Land of the Midnight Sun.* Edmonton: Hurtig Publishers.

Coates, Kenneth. 1985. "The Alaska Highway and the Indians of the Southern Yukon. 1942 - 50: A study of Native Adaptation to Northern Development." In *The Alaska Highway Papers of the 40th Anniversary Symposium,* by editor Kenneth Coates. Vancouver: University of British Columbia Press.

Cohen, Stan. 1981. *The Forgotten War: Volume One.* Missoula: Pictorial Histories Publishing Company.

—. 1988. *The Forgotten War: Volume Two.* Missoula: Pictorial Histories Publishing Company.

—. 1979. *The Trail of 42: A Pictorial History of the Alaska Highway.* Missoula: Pictorial Histories Publishing Company.

—. 1980. *The White Pass and Yukon Route: A Pictorial History.* Missoula: Pictorial Histories Publishing Company.

Coll, Blanche D., Keith, Jean E. and Rosenthal, Herbert H. 1958. *United States Army in World War II: The Corps of Engineers: Troops and Equipment.* Washington, D.C.: U.S. Government Printing Office.

Colonel Heath Twichell Sr. 1942. Letters, Archived at U.S. Army Corps of Engineers Office of History, Humphreys Engineer Center, Fort Belvoir, Virginia.

Commission, Yukon Anniversary. 1991. *Those Were The Days.* Archived at University of Alaska, Fairbanks, AK, Alaska and Polar Regions Collections, Elmer E. Rasmuson Library.

Conner, Billy. n.d. "American Experience: Building the Alaska Highway." *PBS.* Accessed August 2014. www.pbs.org/wgbh/americanexperience/features/transcript/alaska-transcript/.

Correspondent, Yank Field. 1943. "Hail Army Engineers for Alcan Highway: Broke all records." *The Pittsburgh Courier,* February 27: reprinted from a field correspondent from Yank Magazine.

Costello, John. 2002. *The Pacific War 1941 - 1945.* New York: Perennial, Harper Collins Publishers.

Cruikshank, Julie. 1985. "The Gravel Magnet: Some Social Impacts of the Alaska Highway on Yukon Indians." In *The Alaska Highway Papers of the 40th Anniversary Symposium*, by editor Kenneth Coates. Vancouver: University of British Columbia Press.

D.C. Recruiting Office Turned Down 569 Negroes. 1940. "The Pittsburgh Courier." October 10: Newspapers.com website.

Dahl, Robert A. 2013. *After the Gold Rush: Growing Up In Skagway.* Self published.

n.d. "Delta Junction: Official End of the Alaska Highway." *History Alaska Highway*. Accessed March 2014. www.alaska-highway.org/delta/alaska-highway.html.

Dhenin, Rene. 1942. "Memory Letters archived at North Peace Museum." Letters, Ft. St. John, British Columbia, Canada, British Columbia.

Dickson, Andrea. 2013. Letter, Private collection.

Dobrowolsky, Helene and Linda Johnson with Bob Cameron, John Firth, Michele Genest, Ty Heffner, Rob Ingram, Marilyn Jensen, Ingrid Johnson. 2013. *Whitehorse: An Illustrated Hisotry*. Vancouver: Figure 1 Publishing.

Driscoll, Joseph. 1943. *War Discovers Alaska*. Philadelphia: J.B. Lippincott Company.

Dudrow, Lt. J. Walter. 1942. *June 8 Memorandum*. Memorandum, Archived at University of Alaska in Fairbanks, AK, Alaska and Polar Regions Collections, Elmer E. Rasmuson Library: Lael Morgan Collection.

Dudrow, Lt. J. Walter. 1991. *Letter of Memories*. Letter, Archived at University of Alaska in Fairbanks, AK, Alaska and Polar Regions Collections, Elmer E. Rasmuson Library: Lael Morgan Collection.

Duesenberg, H. Milton. 1994. *Alaska Highway Expeditionary Force: A Roadbuilder's Story*. Clear Lake: H & M Industries.

Dziuban, Stanley W. 1990. *Military Relations Between the United States and Canada, 1939-1945*. Washington, D.C.: U.S. Army Center of Military History.

Elson, R.T. 1942. "U.S. Engineers Rush Alaska Highway Job." *The Winnipeg Tribune*, March 12: Newspapers.com website.

Emmets, Katie. 2013. "Skagway's Medical History: A Community Health Profile." *Skaguay Alaska*, Summer.

2017. "Esler Field (ESF), near Alexandria and Pineville, Louisiana." *History of Esler Airfield*. Accessed 2014. www.alexandria-louisiana.com/esler-field-louisiana. htm.

2014. "Experience the Tagish Lifestyle." *Southern Lakes Yukon*. Accessed November 2014. www.southernlakesyukon.com/tagish.htm.

Faculty, The Judge Advocate General's School. 2002. "The General Officer Aide and the Potential for Misuse." *The Army Lawyer, Department of the Army Pamphlet 27-50-355*. Accessed 2014. www.loc.gov/rr/frd/Military_Law/pfd/08-2002.pdf, 36 - 42.

Fetrow, Karla. 2014. "The Incredible Alaskan Bush Pilots: Those Multi-Tasking Pilots." *Subversify Magazine*. February 12. Accessed March 2014. www.subversify. com/2014/02/12/the-incredible-alaska-bush-pilots.

2017. "Field Facilities for Human Waste Disposal." *U. S. Army Study Guide.* Accessed July 2014. www.armystudyguide.com/content/army_board_study_guide_topics/ field-sanitation/field-facilities-for-human.html.

Flather, Patti. 1992. "Memories of a Tlingit Elder." In *The Optimst*, Vol. 18, #2. Archived at University of Alaska in Fairbanks, AK. Alaska and Polar Regions ·Collections, Elmer E. Rasmuson Library.

Ford, Corey. 1943. *Short Cut To Tokyo: The Battle for the Aleutians.* New York: C. Scribner's Sons. Acknowledgment made to The Crowell-Collier Publishing Company for permission to reprint certain sections of this book which first appeared in Collier's Magazine.

Fowle, Barry W, editor. 1992. *Builders and Fighters: U.S. Army Engineers in World War II.* Fort Belvoir, Virginia: Office of History U.S. Army Corps of Engineers.

Garfield, Brian. 1969. *The Thousand Mile War: World War II in Alaska and the Aleutians.* Fairbanks: University of Alaska Press.

General Buckner. 1942. *April 1942, from General Buckner to Brigadier General Sturdevant. Lael Morgan Collection.* Letter, Archived at University of Alaska, Fairbanks, AK, Alaska and Polar Regions Collections, Elmer E. Rasmuson Library.

Gibson, Truman K., Jr. with Steve Huntley. 2005. *Knocking Down Barriers: My Fight for Black America.* Evanston: Norhwestern University Press.

Gifford, Bill. 1993. "The Great Black North." *Washington City Newspaper, Vol. 13, No. 40*, October 8: www.washingtoncitypaper.com/article/130090171/great-black-north.

Gilman, William. 1942. "Cold Weather Was Help To Alcan Road." *The Fairbanks Daily News-Miner*, November 17: Newspapers.com website.

—. 1942. "Ghost Town Awakened by Alcan Road." *The Fairbanks Daily News-Miner*, November 19: Newspapers.com website.

—. 1942. "Sub-zero Weather Prevailed at Alcan Highway Dedication." *The Fairbanks Daily News-Miner*, November 23: Newspapers.com website.

Godsell, Phillip H. 1944. *Romance of the Alaska Highway.* Toronto: The Ryerson Press.

Gordon, John Steele. 2007. "Why did Russia Sell Us Alaska So Cheap?" *Free Republic.* October 18. Accessed May 2014. www.freerepublic.com/focus/f-news/1913255/ posts.

Grafe, Willis. 1992. *An Oregon Boy in the Yukon: An Alaska Highway Story.* Altona: D.W. Friesen and Sons.

Greenwood, John T. 1985. "General Bill Hoge and the Alaska Highway." In *The Alaska Highway: Papers of the 40th Anniversary Symposium,* by editor Kenneth Coates. Vancouver: University of British Columbia Press.

Griffith, Cyril. 1989. *Trucking the Tote Road to Alaska: 1942-43: Memories of the early days of the Alaska Highway.* Saskatchewan: Self published.

Griggs, William E. n.d. "American Experience: Building the Alaska Highway." *PBS.* www.pbs.org/wgbh/americanexperience/features/transcript/alaska-transcript/.

Griggs, William E., photographer, and Merrill, Philip J, editor. 2002. *The World War II Black Regiment That Built the Alaska Military Highway. A Photographic History.* Jackson: University Press of Mississippi.

Guest, H. 2015. "Teslin." *The Canadian Encyclopedia.* www.thecanadianencyclopedia. ca/en/article/teslin.

Haigh, Jane. 2001. *The Alaska Highway: A Historic Photographic Journey.* Whitehorse: Wolf Creek Books, Inc.

Haman, Ray C. 1945. *Adventure on the Alcan (Alaskan) Highway: a Diary.* Self published.

Hargroves, Samuel, interview by author. 2016. *T/5 Company F 93rd Engineers*

Harrold, E.W. 1943. "Whitehorse Now Ain't What She Used To Be." *The Winnepeg Tribune*, October 5: Newspapers.com website.

Hendricks, Charles. 2008. "Race Relations and the Contributions of Minority Troops in Alaska: A Challenge to the Status Quo? In Alaska at War 1941 - 1945." In *The Forgotten War Remembered*, by editor Fern Chandonnet. Fairbanks: University of Alaska Press.

Hoge, General William M, interview by Lt. Col. George Robertson. 1974. *Archived at U.S. Army Heritage and Education Center, Carlisle, Pennsylvania* (January 14 - 15 and April 16 -17).

Hoge, General William M. 1942. *Progress Reports, May to September 1942.* Military report, Archived at University of Alaska in Fairbanks, AK, Alaska and Polar Regions Collections, Elmer E. Rasmuson Library: Jane Haigh Collection, Walter E. Mason file.

Huntley, Theodore A. 1945. *Construction of the Alaska Highway. The First Year - 1942.* Public Road Administration report, Washington, D.C.: Archived at US Army Corps of Engineers Office of History, Humphreys Engineer Center, Ft. Belvoir, Virginia.

Jackson, Sam. 1943. "Illness Hits Heavily At Army in the Yukon." *The Kane Republic*, March 10: Newspapers.com website.

Jones, Millie, interview by author. 2013. *Resident of Carcross and Whitehorse, Yukon Canada* (Summer).

Jones, Sherron, published by, and prepared by Donna Clayson. 2007. "1929 Fokker Super Universal (CF-AAM): George Simmons, pilot, Carcross." September 7. Accessed 2014. www.ruudleeuw.com/pdf/1929%20Fokker%20Sept%202007.pdf.

K. Bisset & Associates. 1995. "Action on Waste Program Arctic Environmental Strategy (AES) Indian and Northern Affairs." *Research of Former Military Sites and Activities in the Yukon.* April. emrlibrary.gov.yk.ca/cw/c1995.

Kay, Leon. 1941. "American Army Successful in Stopping 'German' Advance in Gigantic Southwest War Maneuvers." *Amarillo Daily News*, August 19: Newspapers.com website.

—. 1941. "Noted War Correspondent at Louisiana Maneuvers." *The Marysville Tribune*, August 22: Newspapers.com website.

Kelly, John. 2012. "Yes, the University of Maryland has Traditions." *The Washington Post*, August 29: Newspapers.com website.

Kennedy, David M. 1999. *Freedom From Fear: The American People in Depression and War, 1939–1945*. New York: Oxford University Press.

Kupperberg, Paul. 2009. *Building America Then and Now: The Alaska Highway*. New York: Chelsea House.

Lane, Albert Colonel. 1945. *Letter, Jane Haigh Collection*. Letter, Archived at University of Alaska in Fairbanks, Alaska, Alaska and Polar Regions Collections, Elmer E. Rasmuson Library: Jane Haigh Collection.

Lane, Albert Colonel. October. "The Alcan Highway: Road Location and Construction Methods." In *The Military Engineer, Vol. XXXIV*, 492–499.

Lanks, Herbert C. 1944. *Highway to Alaska*. New York: D. Appleton-Century Company.

Laputka, Donald and Audrey, interview by author. 2012. *Son and Wife of Capt. Ted Laputka*

Larkins, Leonard, interview by author. 2016. *Pvt. Company A 93rd Engineers*

Lee, Ulysses. 1963. *The Employment of Negro Troops*. Washington, D.C.: U.S. Government Printing Office.

Lemoine, Dan. n.d. "Memories of Alexandria Friends." Accessed October 2013. www.alexandria-louisiana.com/other-alex-06.htm.

Lewis, James L., Lt. Col. n.d. *Notes on service with the ninety-third Engineer Regiment GS in extreme cold and in wet cold climates*. Notes, 1-16, NARA Section 3.3, NIIID735044: Lael Morgan Collection. Archived at University of Alaska, Fairbanks, AK, Alaska and Polar Regions Collections, Elmer E. Rasmuson Library.

LiDrazzad. 1940. "Army Doors of 7th Corps Area Opened to White Soldiers, But Negroes Are Compelled to Wait for Draft." *The Pittsburgh Courier*, October 19: Newspapers.com website.

Livingston, Camp. 2017. "A WWII abandoned military camp located in Grant parish, Lousiana." *Camp Livingston*. April 20. www.camp-livingston.winnfreenet.com.

Lloyd, John K, editor. 1992. *Alcan Trail Blazers*. 648th Topographic Engineers Memorial Fund.

1942 - 1943. *Location of Troops Engaged in Construction of Alaska Highway*. Military report, Archived at U.S. Army Corps of Engineers Office of History, Humphreys Engineer Center, Fort Belvoir, Virginia.

LoLordo, Ann. 1992. "Black GI's helped carve a road across frozen hell." *The Baltimore Sun*, July 4: www.articles.baltimoresun.com/1992-07-04/news/1992186045_1_alaska-highway-rubber-galoshes-nolan.

Lytle, Wallace. n.d. "American Experience: Building the Alaska Highway." *PBS*. Accessed August 2014. www.pbs.org/wgbh/americanexperience/features/transcript/alaska-transcript.

MacDonald, Joanne. 1992. "Fighting a measles epidemic in Teslin, 1942." *The Optimst*, June: Vol. 18, No. 2, Archived at University of Alaska in Fairbanks, AK. Alaska and Polar Regions Collections, Elmer E. Rasmuson Library.

MacGregor, Morris J. 1985. "Integration of the Armed Forces 1940-1965." In *World War II: The Army Defense Studies Series.* Washington, D.C.: Center of Military History, U.S. Army.

Marchand, John F. MD. 1943. "Tribal Epidemics in the Yukon." *J.A.M.A.*, December 18: Vol. 123, No. 16, 1019 - 1020, www.jamanetwork.com/journals/jama/fullarticle/265440.

McBride Museum of Yukon, Alaska Highway Project. n.d. "Polly, the Foul Mouthed Sourdough Parrot." *Yukon News.* Accessed September 2013. www.yukon-news.com/letters-opinions/polly-the-foul-mouthed-sourdough-parrot.

McClellan, Catharine with Lucie Birckel, Robert Bringhurst, James A. Fall, Carol McCarthy and Janice R. Sheppard. 1987. *A History of the Yukon Indians: Part of the Land, Part of the Water.* Vancouver: Douglas and McIntyre Ltd.

McGuire, Phillip. 1988. *He, Too, Spoke for Democracy: Judge Hastie, World War II and the Black Soldier.* New York: Greenwood Press.

McGuire, Phillip, editor. 1983. *Taps For A Jim Crow Army: Letters From Black Soldiers in World War II.* Lexington: The University Press of Kentucky.

Mikell, Franklin O. n.d. *Memories of Alexandria Friends.* Accessed October 2013. www.alexandria-louisiana.com/other-alex-04.htm.

Millett, John D, auithor and Kent Roberts Greenfield, editor. 1954. *United States Army in World War II. The Organization and Role of the Army Service Forces.* Washington, D.C.: Office of the Chief of Military History, Department of the Army.

Mills, David. 2008. "Documenting and Interpreting the History and Significance of the North West Mounted Police Peace-Yukon Historic Trail." *NWMP Final Archival Report*, June 11: www.muskwa-kechika.com/uploads/documents/cultural/NWMP/%20trail%20Final%20Archival%20Report%20-%20June%2012%202008%20NWMP%20Trail.pdf.

1942. *Minutes of Permanent Joint Board on Defense, 26 February 1942, Military Highway to Alaska-Canada-United States.* Meeting notes, Archived at U.S. Army Corps of Engineers Office of History, Humphreys Center, Fort Belvoir, Virginia.

Morehouse, Maggi M. 2000. *Fighting in the Jim Crow Army.* Lanham: Rowman and Littlefield Publishers.

Morgan, Lael. 1992. "Writing Minorities Out of History: Black Builders Of The Alcan Highway." *Alaska History, A Publication of the Alaska Historical Society*, Vol. 7, No. 2, 1 - 13.

Morgan, Lael. 1991 - 1992. *Collection of interviews and notes, 1991 - 1992.* Archived at University of Alaska in Fairbanks, AK, Alaska and Polar Regions Collections, Elmer E. Rasmuson Library.

1942 -1943. *Morning Reports, 340th Engineers, 1942 - 43, Company A, H/S, 1st and 2nd Battalion Headquarters.* Military report, Archived at The National Personnel Records Center, St. Louis, Missouri.

1942 - 1943. *Morning Reports, 93rd Engineers, 1942 - 43. Company A, B, C, D, E, H/S, and 1st and 2nd Battalion Headquarters.* Military report, Archived at The National Personnel Records Center, St. Louis, Missouri.

Morrison, William R. 1998. *True North: The Yukon and Northwest Territories.* Toronto: Oxford University Press.

Motley, Mary Penick. 1987. *The Invisible Soldier. The Experience of the Black Soldier, World War II.* Detroit: Wayne State University Press.

Mulhillvil, Carl, interview by author. 2013. *Resident of Skagway, Alaska* (Summer).

Neuberger, Richard. 1943. "Behind the Scenes at the Alcan Opening." *Alaska Live,* February: 9 - 12.

—. 1943. "Highballing at Sixty Below." *The Saturday Evening Post,* November 27.

—. 1944. "Yukon Adventure." *The Saturday Evening Post,* February 19: 18 - 21, 101 - 102.

—. 1942. "Biographical Sketch Brigadier General J.A. O'Connor. Officer in Command U.S. Army Here." *The Whitehorse Star,* October 16.

Neuberger, Richard,. 1943. "Alcan Epic." *Yank Magazine,* February 10: 20 - 22, www.unz.org/Pub/Yank-1943feb10-00020.

New Yorker Refused in Air Corps. 1940. "The Pittsburgh Courier." October 17: Newspapers.com website.

1942. *Notes on Cabinet Meeting, 16 January 1942, with Secretary Ickes, Secretary of War, Navy and Interior to confer and agree on necessity for the Highway and which route.* Meeting notes, Archived at U.S. Army Corps of Engineers Office of History, Humphreys Engineer Center, Fort Belvoir, Virginia.

Oland, Dwight D. 1985. "The Army Medical Department and the Construction of the Alaska Highway." In *The Alaska Highway: Papers of the 40th. Anniversary Symposium,* by editor Kenneth Coates. Vancouver: University of British Columbia Press.

Palfreyman, Major W. C. 1943. *History of the Whitehorse Sector of the Alcan Highway.* Report from Headquarters Whitehorse Sector Alcan Highway, Seattle Washington, Archived at U.S. Army Corps of Engineers Office of History, Humphreys Engineer Center, Fort Belvoir, Virginia.

Parker, Ted, interview by author. 2015. *Son of Lt. Charles Parker* (September).

Peace River Block News. 1942. "U.S. Army Engineers Hint Strongly of Alaska Military Highway Through Dawson Creek: Lay Groundwork for Accommodation of 3000 American Engineering Troops and Storage Space." February 26: Newspapers.com website.

Perry, Mark. 2008. "Louisiana Maneuvers 1940 - 1941." *History Net.* November 25. Accessed October 2013. www.historynet.com/louisiana-maneuvers-1940-41.htm.

Personnel Rosters, 340th Engineers. 1942 - 1943. *Lower Post or Freeze.* Archived at U.S. Army Heritage and Education Center, Carlisle, Pennsylvania.

1942 - 1943. *Personnel Rosters, 93rd Engineers, 1942 - 43. Company A, B, C, D, E, F and H&S.* Archived at The National Personnel Records Center, St. Louis, Missouri.

Philadelphia United Press. 1942. "He Can Do It." *Santa Cruz Sentinel,* June 4: Newspapers.com website.

Police, Royal Canadian Mounted. 1942. *Conditions at Carcross, Yukon Territory, June 9.* Memorandum, www.alaskahighwayarchives.ca/en/chap2/3sectiongallery. php?im=6.

n.d. "Population urban and rural by province and territory." *Statistics Canada.* www. statcan.gc.ca/tables-tableaux/demo62a-eng.html.

Potter, John. 1966. "Opening of Fort (Camp) Lee in 1941 Recalled." *The Progress-Index,* January 24: Newspapers.com website.

Prattis, P.L. 1941. "Brutal White MP's Stir Trouble in Army Camp: Race Soldiers Beaten Without Provocation--Many Reported Killed by Southern Military Police at Camp Livingston, LA." *The Pittsburgh Courier,* June 12: Newspapers. com website.

—. 1941. "Raw Recruits Get Army Fundamentals At Virginia Camp, Camp Lee, VA." *The Pittsburgh Courier,* May 10: Newspapers.com website.

—. 1941. "Sample of Work of White Military Police in Southern Army Camps; Staff Sergeant Joe White, Camp Livingston, La: Has Been in the Army 24 Years-Here's His Record." *The Pittsburgh Courier,* June 12: Newspapers.com website.

President Roosevelt Speeches and Statements. 1941. "President Franklin Delano Roosevelt address over the Radio on Navy Day concerning the attack upon the destroyer U.S.S. Kearny." October 27: www.usmm.org/fdr/kearny.html.

Press, San Francisco United. 1942. "Coast Cities Redouble Vigilance Against Jap 'Sneak' Attack." *The Salt Lake Tribune,* June 5: Newspapers.com website.

Press, Washington United. 1942. "Coast Alert After Raids: Radios Are Silent and People Are Warned of Possible Attack." *The Daily Chronicle,* June 4: Newspapers. com website.

Raines, Rebecca Robbins. 1996. *Getting the Message Through: A Branch History of the U.S. Army Signal Corps.* Washington, D.C.: Government Printing Office.

Rainey, Froelich. 1943. "Alaskan Highway an Engineering Epic." *The National Geographic Magazine,* February: Vol. LXXXIII, No. 2, 143 - 168.

1941 - 1945. *Regimental History of the 93rd Engineers.* Archived at National Archives, College Park, Maryland.

Reid, Alison. 1992. "For Native people, life changed forever." *The Optimst,* June: Vol. 18, No. 2, Archived at University of Alaska in Fairbanks, Alaska. Alaska and Polar Regions Collections, Elmer E. Rasmuson Library.

—. 1992. "Women and the Alaska Highway: Ida Calmegane remembers Carcross. Highway brought romance, epidemics." *The Optimst,* June: Vol. 18, No. 2, Archived at University of Alaska in Fairbanks, Alaska. Alaska and Polar Regions Collections, Elmer E. Rasmuson Library.

Relations, War Department Bureau of Public. 1942. *War Department Established Northwest Service Command.* Press release, Archived at U.S. Army Corps of Engineers Office of History, Humphreys Engineer Center, Fort Belvoir, Virginia.

Remley, David A. 2008. *Crooked Road: The Story of the Alaska Highway.* Fairbanks: University of Alaska Press.

Reybold, Maj. Gen. 1942. *6 March 1942, from Maj. Gen. Reybold, Chief of Engineers to Brig. General Fleming, Administrator, Federal Works Agency. Requesting services of the Public Roads Administration.* Letter, Archived at U.S. Army Corps of Engineers Office of History, Humphreys Engineer Center, Fort Belvoir, Virginia.

Richardson, Harold W. 1944. "Alcan-America's Glory Road." In *Bulldozers Come First: The Story of U.S. War Construction in Foreign Lands*, by Waldo G. Bowman, Harold W. Richardson, Nathan A. Bowers, Edward J. Cleary and Archie Carter. New York: McGraw-Hill Book Company, Inc.

Richardson, Harold W. 1942. "Alcan-America's Glory Road: Part I- Strategy and Location." In *Engineering News-Record*, 859 - 872.

Richardson, Harold W. 1943. "Alcan-America's Glory Road: Part III-Construction Tactics." In *Engineering News-Record*, 63 - 70.

Richardson, Harold W. 1942. "Alcan-America's Glory Road: Part II-Supply, Equipment." In *Engineering News-Record*, 907 - 914.

Riggs, Thomas. 1942. *24 February 1942, from Thomas Riggs to Secretary of War, Recommends Route A.* Letter, Humphreys Engineer Center, Fort Belvoir, Virginia: Archived at U.S. Army Corps of Engineers Office of History.

Robb, Jim. 2007. "It's Johnny Johns, of course." *Yukon News*, October 30: www.yukon-news.com/business/its-johnny-johns-of-course.

n.d. "Robinson Roadhouse." *Eh Canada Travel.* www.ehcanadatravel.com/...yukon/.../carcross/.../5542-robinson-roadhouse-historic-site.html.

Roosevelt, Franklin D. 1942. *From Franklin D. Roosevelt to Secretary of War, Allocates $10,000,000 for the Construction of the Highway, March 3.* Letter, Humphreys Engineer Center, Fort Belvoir, Virginia: Archived at U.S. Army Corps of Engineers Office of History.

Russell, Chester L. 1999. *Tales of a Catskinner: A Personal Account of Building the Alcan Highway, The Winter Trail and Canol Pipeline Road in 1942–43.* North Bend: Wegferds' Printing and Publications.

Rust, Fred Technician 5th Grade, Regimental Historian. 1944. *Role of the Eighteenth Engineer Regiment: April 1942 to January 1943.* Archived at U.S. Army Corps of Engineers Office of History, Humphreys Engineer Center, Ft. Belvoir, Virginia: U.S. Army.

Rutty, Christopher PhD and Sue C. Sullivan. 2010. *This is Public Health: A Canadian History, 1940 - 1949*, Published by Canadian Public Health Association: Chapter 5, www.cpha.ca/en/programs/history/book.aspx.

Samuels, Barbara. "Marks 40th Anniversary of the 1968 Baltimore Riots and Fair Housing Act". "Segregation and Public Housing Development in Cherry Hill and Westport: Historical Background." *ACLU of Maryland.* www.aclu-md-org/uploaded_files/0000/0172/chpresentation.pdf.

Schmidt, John. 1991. *This Was No DYXNH Picnic.* Calgary: Gorman and Gorman.

Shirley, Craig. 2001. *December 1941: 31 Days That Changed America and Saved the World.* Nashville: Thomas Nelson.

n.d. "Soldier's Summit." *Sights and Sites of the Yukon.* www.sightsandsites.ca/south/site/soldiers-summit.

Spletstoser, Frederick M. 2005. *Talk of the Town. The Rise of Alexandria and the 'Daily Town Talk'*. Baton Rouge: Louisiana State University Press.

Spotswood, Ken. 2008. "The History of Carcross, Yukon Territory." *Explore North.* Accessed September 2013. www.explorenorth.com/yukon/carcross.

—. 2008. "The History of Tagish, Yukon Territory." *Explore North.* Accessed November 2014. ww.explorenorth.com/yukon/tagish-history/html.

Squires, Mortimer, interview by author. 2013. *1st Lt., 93rd Engineers* (Spring).

Staff, Caterpillar Tractor Company. 1954. *Fifty Years On Tracks.* Chicago: Photopress, Inc.

Stimson, Secretary. 1942. *Secretary of War with Secretary of Navy, Secretary of Interior and Brig. Gen R.W. Crawford to obtain route surveys and survey of possible equipment for road building and report back in one week.* Meeting notes, Archived at U.S. Army Corps of Engineers Office of History, Humphreys Engineer Center, Fort Belvoir, Virginia.

Sturdevant, Brig. Gen. 1942. *10 October 1942, from Brig. Gen Sturdevant; Hoge's Papers.* Letter, Archived at U.S. Army Heritage and Education Center, Carlisle, Pennsylvania.

Sturdevant, Brigadier General. 1942. *From Brigadier General Sturdevant to Asst. Chief of Staff, War Plans Division, War Department General Staff: Outline of a plan for construction of supply road to Alaska submitted February 4.* Memorandum, Archived at U.S. Army Corps of Engineers Office of History, Humphreys Engineer Center, Fort Belvoir, Virginia.

Sturdevant, Brigadier General. 1942. *From Brigadier General Sturdevant to General Buckner, April.* Letter, Archived at University of Alaska, Fairbanks, AK, Alaska and Polar Regions Collections, Elmer E. Rasmuson Library: Lael Morgan Collection.

The Corpus Christi Caller-Times. 1941. "Army Expects 236 Deaths, 70,000 Casualties in Record Peace-Time Maneuvers of Troops." September 11: Newspapers.com website.

The Daily Chronicle. 1942. "Coast Alert After Raids." June 4: Newspapers.com website.

The Daily Inter Lake. 1946. "Billings Man Named Director of Tire Dealers Association." October 18: Newspapers.com website.

n.d. "The Early Years of Bushflying." *Canadian Bush Plane Heritage Center.* Accessed 2014. www.bushplane.com/data/uploads/education/downloads/support/The%20Early%20Years%20of%20Bushflying.pdf.

The General Synod of the Anglican Church of Canada. n.d. "Chooutla School." *Carcross, Yukon Territory.* Accessed November 2013. www.anglican.ca/tr/histories/chooutla-carcross.

2007 - 2008. *The History of the Construction of the Alcan Highway Near Teslin.* Teslin: Commissioned by Teslin Historical and Museum Society, George Johnston Museum, Sharron Chatterton, Manager.

The Jackson Sun. 1960. "Examples of Jim Crow Laws: Maryland." orig.jacksonsun.com.

The Lethbridge Herald. 1942. "Another Alaska Highway Force Heading North." March 14: Newspapers.com website.

The Ottawa Journal. 1942. "Heroic Indian Girl Died Fighting Measles Epidemic." December 19: Newspapers.com website.

The Pittsburgh Courier. 1942. "10 Soldiers Killed. Report Charges. Claim Sawed-Off Shotguns Used in Alexandria Riot." February 7: Newspapers.com website.

The Pittsburgh Courier. 1942. "5 Wounded in Riot at Alexandria." January 17: Newspapers.com website.

The Pittsburgh Courier. 1940. "Asked To Report for Air Corps Duty; Then Barred." November 7: Newspapers.com website.

The Pittsburgh Courier. 1940. "No Negroes Being Trained by Army Air Corps, Says N.A.A.C.P." October 24: Newspapers.com website.

The Pittsburgh Courier. 1941. "Race Soldiers at Camp Livingston Contribute Hard Labor, Fine Skill and Technical Knowledge to U.S. Defense." August 16: Newspapers.com website.

The Pittsburgh Courier. 1941. "Strikes Must Be Pitched by Men." August 14: Newspapers.com website.

The Pittsburgh Courier. 1942. "War Department Probing Louisiana Riot. General Davis Investigating Clash Between Soldiers and White M.P.'s." January 24: Newspapers.com website.

n.d. "The Village of Teslin." *Gateway to the Southern Lakes.* Accessed 2014. www.teslin.ca.

Timberlake, Turner G. 1914 - 2001. "Private Collection."

Timberlake, Turner. 1941. "Terrapin Talks sports column, and Hall of Fame." *Diamondback, Newspaper of the University of Maryland.* Private collection, April 4.

Timberlake, Turner with Earl A. Crouse, Betty Beachy, Jacke Gaither. 1948. *History of the Maryland 4-H Club All Stars.* College Park: 4-H Club, University of Maryland.

Timeline, University of Maryland. 1800s - 2000s. www.umd.edu/timeline.

Twichell, Heath. 1992. *The Northwest Epic: The Building of the Alaska Highway.* New York: St. Martin's Press.

U.S. Army, 340th Engineer Regiment. 1944. *Lower Post or Freeze: 340th Engineer Regiment on the Alaska Military Highway, 1942 - 1943.* Archived at U.S. Army Heritage and Education Center, Carlisle Barracks, Pennsylvania., Charlotte: The Herald Press Inc.

U.S. Army, 341st Engineer Regiment. 1943. *The Long Trail: 341st Engineers on the Alaska Military Highway, 1942 - 1943.* Archived at U.S. Army Heritage and Education Center, Carlisle Barracks, Pennsylvania, Charlotte: Herald Press Inc.

University of Maryland, Turner Timberlake editor-in-chief. 1940 - 1941. *"M" Book, Student Handbook.* Student Government Association.

Vancouver Newspaper. 1942. "Trapper Saves U.S. Engineers." May 23: Newspapers.com website.

Virtue, John. 2013. *The Black Soldiers Who Built the Alaska Highway: A History of Four U.S. Army Regiments in the North, 1942 - 1943.* Jefferson: McFarland and Company Publishers.

Waldvogel, Robert. 2015. "Narrow Gauge to White Pass Summit." *White Pass & Yukon Route.* Accessed October 2013. www.wpyr.com/sight-sounds/narrow-gauge-to-white-pass-summit.

n.d. "Watson Lake History-Gateway to the Yukon." *Yukon Info.* Accessed August 2014. www.yukoninfo.com/watson-lake-history.

Webber, Bert. 1993. *Aleutian Headache: Deadly World War II Battles on American Soil.* Central Point: Webb Research Group Publishers.

website, Ancestry.com. n.d.

1955. *Westinghouse Electric Bulletin, No. 5, Vol. VIII.* Private collection.

n.d. "What's Cool at the Yukon's Carcross Desert." *Canada Cool.* Accessed September 2013. www.canadacool.com/location/yukon-carcrossdesert.

Wheeler, Herb. 1942. *The White Pass and Yukon Railroad.* Archived at University of Alaska in Fairbanks, Alaska, Alaska and Polar Regions Collections, Elmer E. Rasmuson Library: Jane Haigh Collection.

Whitney. 1991. "Reunion planned for heroes who built Alaska Highway." *The News Journal,* December 3.

Williams, Lt. G.A. 1943. "Winter Maintenance Problems on the Alaska Highway, Roads and Bridges."

Williams, Lt. General Arthur, interview by Lt. Col. George Robertson. 1974. *Engineer Memoirs: General William M. Hoge, Archived at Office of History, U.S. Army Corps of Engineers* (January 14 - 15 and April 16 - 17).

Wolf, Tom. 1942. "Alcan Highway Pioneers Battle Bears, Skeeters." *Freeport Journal-Standard,* December 26: Newspapers.com website.

Wooldridge, Robert Corp. 1942. *Alaska Highway Expeditionary Force: A Roadbuilder's Story.* Letter, Clear Lake: H & M Industries.

Wormser, Richard. n.d. "The Rise and Fall of Jim Crow, Jim Crow Stories, the Great Depression 1928 - 1939." *PBS.* www.pbs.org/wnet/jimcrow/stories.

Young, Brigadier Peter. 1981. *The World Almanac of World War II.* New York: Pharos Books.

Young, Gerri. n.d. "From 1980 publication The Fort Nelson Story by same author." *The Story of Fort Nelson.* Accessed July 2014. www.sd81.bc.ca/rla/fns/fnstoc.html.

TIMELINE

September 16, 1940
Selective Service Act passed

December 1940
93rd Engineering Battalion Camp
Livingston, Louisiana

August 15, 1941
Lt. Turner Timberlake reports for
active duty at Camp Lee, Virginia

December 7, 1941
Attack on Pearl Harbor

January 1942
Lt. Timberlake transferred to Camp
Livingston, Louisiana

February 2, 1942
Corps of Engineers ordered to
build the Alaska Highway

February 12, 1942
General William Hoge dispatched
to Canada

February 21, 1942
Hoge orders 35th Engineering
Regiment to Dawson Creek

March 9, 1942
35th arrives in Dawson Creek

April 2, 1942
Lt. Timberlake transferred to 93rd

April 7, 1942
18th arrives in Skagway

April 6, 1942
93rd Engineering Battalion becomes
93rd Engineering Regiment

April 12, 1942
93rd leaves Camp Livingston

April 14, 1942
93rd arrives in Skagway

April 24, 1942
Highway Command divided
between Hoge and O'Connor

April 22, 1942
340th arrives in Skagway

May 1, 1942
93rd arrives in Carcross

May 1, 1942
97th arrives at Valdez

May 1, 1942
341st arrives in Dawson Creek

May 14, 1942
Tragedy at Charlie Lake

May 22, 1942
2nd Battalion of 340th departs
Skagway for Whitehorse

May 30, 1942
95th arrives in Dawson Creek

June 1, 1942
93rd crosses Tagish River

June 4, 1942
Heavy equipment for the 93rd
arrives

June 6, 1942
1st Battalion of 340th arrives in
Carcross

June 16, 1942
1st Battalion of 340th and 93rd
arrives at Teslin River

June 17, 1942
340th at Morley Bay

July 11, 1942
93rd crosses Teslin River

July 15, 1942
General Hoge changes the route
and the plan for the 93rd and 340th

July 21, 1942
93rd arrives at Teslin Post

August 10, 1942
93rd completes road from Carcross
to Teslin Post

August 20, 1942
93rd crosses Nisutlin Bay

September 2, 1942
93rd completes road from Carcross
to Whitehorse

September 12, 1942
General Hoge is fired

September 24, 1942
340th & 35th meet at Contact Creek

October 8, 1942
93rd builds barracks for 18th

October 12, 1942
93rd completed their section of the
highway

October 25, 1942
97th and 18th meet at Beaver Creek

November 20, 1942
Dedication of the highway at
Soldier's Summit

January 3–February 18, 1943
93rd bivouacs at Chilkoot Barracks

MILITARY ORGANIZATION CHART

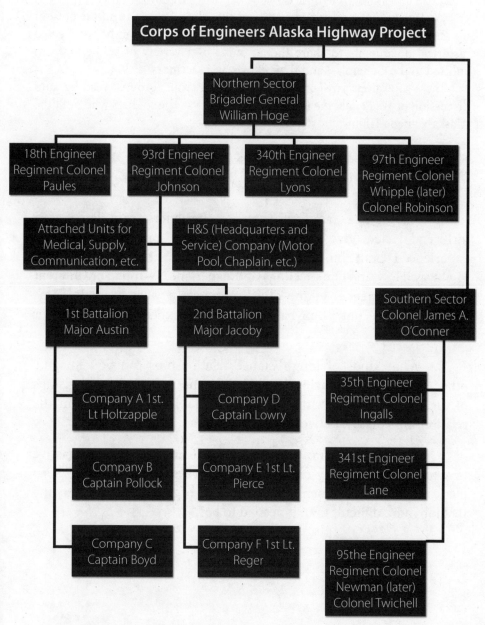

Corps of Engineers Alaska Highway Project

Northern Sector
Brigadier General
William Hoge

18th Engineer
Regiment Colonel
Paules

93rd Engineer
Regiment Colonel
Johnson

340th Engineer
Regiment Colonel
Lyons

97th Engineer
Regiment Colonel
Whipple (later)
Colonel Robinson

Attached Units for
Medical, Supply,
Communication, etc.

H&S (Headquarters and
Service) Company (Motor
Pool, Chaplain, etc.)

1st Battalion
Major Austin

2nd Battalion
Major Jacoby

Southern Sector
Colonel James A.
O'Conner

Company A 1st.
Lt Holtzapple

Company D
Captain Lowry

35th Engineer
Regiment Colonel
Ingalls

Company B
Captain Pollock

Company E 1st Lt.
Pierce

341st Engineer
Regiment Colonel
Lane

Company C
Captain Boyd

Company F 1st Lt.
Reger

95the Engineer
Regiment Colonel
Newman (later)
Colonel Twichell

READING GROUP DISCUSSION GUIDE

We Fought the Road tells the story of the Alcan Project from the bottom up, through the lens of the soldiers' eyes and feelings. The authors collected historical documents to share the accounts of a variety of soldiers—from enlisted to the Generals—and their efforts and sacrifices.

These questions are offered to enhance your group's reading and discussion of *We Fought the Road* and the history of the soldiers who built the Alaska-Canada Highway.

QUESTIONS AND TOPICS

1. The authors' family documents, the letters from Tim to his girlfriend Helen, give special insight into the journey the soldiers experienced both building and traveling on the Alaska-Canada Highway. How are Tim's feelings and experiences similar or different from the experiences of the other soldiers? In what ways do Tim's letters provide a contrasting background to the experiences of the other soldiers?

2. What kinds of long-distance relationships can you imagine other soldiers experiencing? How might the lives and relationships of the other soldiers, both black and white, have differed from the relationship you saw between Tim and Helen?

3. In 1942, the Army and the Corps of Engineers had a massive task to accomplish very quickly. In what ways did the need to keep black men and white men separated make organizing and managing that job more difficult than it needed to be?

4. The United States Government needed the highway to supply and transport men and material north to defend Alaska and especially the Aleutian Islands. Furthermore, the Japanese attack at Dutch Harbor drove home the potential threat of invasion. In the end, though, the course of the war took a very different direction. How important was the highway to America's ultimate victory in WWII? What role did the highway play in the larger scope of American history?

5. The book shares the accounts of senior officers in the army and how they felt about the integration of black soldiers into the ranks of the army. What kinds of changes came to the Army due to the introduction of black regiments who built the road? Black non-commissioned officers operated dead center in the efforts of all of the segregated regiments. In the Army, officers command but senior NCOs run things. In what ways did you see the clash of the NCOs and their white commanding officers, and in what ways did they "beat the odds"?

6. What examples of patriotism do you see in *We Fought the Road*? How did different soldiers express their desire to do his part in defeating America's enemies?

7. Thousands of soldiers descended, seemingly from out of nowhere, on British Columbia, Yukon Territory and Alaska. They brought illness in the form of germs, tons of equipment and supplies, and their own expectations for the region. They accomplished an epic task, but they were invaders. How did the people who lived there before the Army came react, and how do you think you would have reacted? Where could the Army have changed their approach to the Alaska-Highway to make their task easier, and where did they make things more difficult—either intentionally or unintentionally?

8. A central theme of *We Fought the Road* is that ordinary men, simply by standing up and doing their duty, can accomplish extraordinary things. What kinds of nearly-insurmountable obstacles did the soldiers face? How do you think you would have performed in those conditions? What would have driven you to continue?

ABOUT THE AUTHORS

Christine and Dennis McClure married in 1992. Christine was born in Annapolis, MD, and later served in the United States Army as a registered nurse at the end of the Vietnam Era. Dennis was born and raised in Northern Michigan and pursued a PhD on the pre-Civil War history of the Mountain South after serving with the United States Army. They live in Weaverville, NC.

Upon discovering her father's letters to her mother during World War II, Christine set out with Dennis on a journey to document the untold stories of the Alaska-Canada Highway.

Learn more about their journey at 93regimentalcan.com.